Capricorn Rising

❦

If anybody has been the scribe for the history and growth of the music known as Southern Rock, it's been Michael Buffalo Smith. His devoted and in depth writing has for decades kept the public abreast of the music, the players, the triumphs, and the tragedies. Smith's new book, *Capricorn Rising* gets to the heart of the matter with one-on-one conversations with the artists who have made this music part of American culture.

—Charlie Daniels, 2016 inductee into the Country Music Hall of Fame

Phil Walden and Frank Fenter gave all of us Southern kids who dreamed of having our own place in music a label full of artists who spoke to us. From The Allman Brothers Band and The Marshall Tucker Band to Captain Beyond and Wet Willie, those of us who were raised in the land where Rock and Roll was born finally had OUR bands. Who better to write about it than Michael Buffalo Smith, a man who lives, breathes, and respects that music and those times. Hats off to Phil and Alan Walden and Frank Fenter.

—Billy Bob Thornton, Oscar® and Golden Globe Awards® winning actor, director, writer, and musician

I've known Michael Buffalo Smith for several decades and have the utmost respect for him and his talents. In this book of interviews with various musicians, artists, and folks in the music business from the South, he brings forth great insight into the making and development of the Southern Rock sound. You get all sides of the story and the history unfolds as he leads the interview subjects with dexterity and great questions. This is a highly entertaining, interesting, and important read!

—Chuck Leavell, author and keyboardist with The Rolling Stones and former member of The Allman Brothers Band

In *Capricorn Rising*, Michael Buffalo Smith has put together a collection of personal interviews that take the reader through one of the most important periods in the long, wonderful history of Southern music. His care for and love of the genre and the musicians who added to it are present in each and every question. We should all thank him for his patience and ability to document the history—by presenting it from the inside view of those who were right in the middle of it all!

—Tommy Talton, recording artist and
member of the band Cowboy

Michael Buffalo Smith has a deep passion and knowledge of Southern music and Capricorn Records, the label most singularly associated for bringing the Southern Rock genre to the world. His journalistic chops go beyond the superficial writing that often skims the surface of Southern Rock by sharing the real story. *Capricorn Rising* is an on point oral history of Southern Rock where Smith interviews those who helped create the genre by always asking the right questions. If you are a serious student of Southern Rock, *Capricorn Rising* is a must read.

—Rob Duner-Fenter, son of Frank Fenter,
Capricorn Records co-founder and partner

Capricorn Rising

Conversations in Southern Rock

MERCER UNIVERSITY PRESS

Endowed by

TOM WATSON BROWN
and
THE WATSON-BROWN FOUNDATION, INC.

Capricorn Rising

Conversations in Southern Rock

MICHAEL BUFFALO SMITH

MERCER UNIVERSITY PRESS | MACON, GEORGIA

2016

MUP/ P534

© 2016 by Mercer University Press
Published by Mercer University Press
1501 Mercer University Drive
Macon, Georgia 31207
All rights reserved

9 8 7 6 5 4 3 2 1

Books published by Mercer University Press are printed on acid-free paper that meets the requirements of the American National Standard for Information Sciences—Permanence of Paper for Printed Library Materials.

Names: Smith, Michael Buffalo.
Title: Capricorn rising : conversations in southern rock / Michael Buffalo Smith.
Description: Macon, Georgia : Mercer University Press, 2016. | Includes index.
Identifiers: LCCN 2016014437 | ISBN 9780881465785 (pbk. : alk. paper)
Subjects: LCSH: Rock music--Southern States--History and criticism. | Rock musicians--Southern States--Interviews.
    Classification: LCC ML3534.3 .S573 2016 | DDC 781.660975--dc23

Dedicated to the Memories of

Phil Walden and Frank Fenter

The Southern Rock Prophets

Contents

Foreword	xi
Introduction	xiii

The Interviews

Dickey Betts (Allman Brothers Band)	1
Gregg Allman (Allman Brothers Band)	14
Butch Trucks (Allman Brothers Band)	19
Chuck Leavell (Allman Brothers Band)	24
Jimmy Nalls (Sea Level)	41
Tom Dowd (producer, Allman Brothers Band)	49
Galadrielle Allman (Allman Brothers Band)	76
Bonnie Bramlett (solo artist)	81
Johnny Sandlin (producer, Allman Brothers Band)	86
Paul Hornsby (producer, Marshall Tucker Band)	99
Alan Walden (co-founder of Capricorn Records)	114
Robin Duner-Fenter (son of label co-founder, Frank Fenter)	125
Jimmy Hall (Wet Willie)	132
Scott Boyer (Cowboy)	139
Tommy Talton (Cowboy)	147
Tom Wynn (Cowboy)	157
Pete Kowalke (Cowboy)	169
Randall Bramblett (Sea Level/Cowboy)	178
Dru Lombar (Grinderswitch)	184
Larry Howard (Grinderswitch)	190
Doug Gray (Marshall Tucker Band)	204
George McCorkle (Marshall Tucker Band)	211
Chuck McCorkle (brother of George McCorkle)	215
Charlie Daniels (Charlie Daniels Band)	219
Tommy Crain (Charlie Daniels Band)	224
Charlie Hayward (Charlie Daniels Band)	234
Taz DiGregorio (Charlie Daniels Band)	242
Elvin Bishop (solo artist)	251
Donnie Winters (Winters Brothers Band)	255
David Cantonwine (Eric Quincy Tate)	263
Appendix:	

Phil Walden Memorial   267
Remembering Capricorn's Frank Fenter:
    The Push to Get Him into the Georgia
    Music Hall of Fame.   270
Index   277

Acknowledgments

The author wishes to thank the following people for their contributions to this book: Colleen Knights and April Knights for proofreading; the late Jill McLane Smith for transcription of the original tapes; the staff at Mercer University Press, Robin Duner Fenter, Alan Walden, Willie Perkins, Bill Thames, Kirk West, Michael Mellendore, James Calsmine, Russell Hall, Greg Loescher, John Charles Griffin, the Allman Brothers Big House Museum, and the late George McCorkle, Mark Pucci, Mark Burrell, Peter Cross, and Bruce Wall for photos; along with all of the great artists who gave their time and memories for these interviews.

Many of these interviews have appeared previously in magazines including, *Goldmine, Discoveries, Mojo, Hittin' the Note, Relix, Sandlapper, Y'all, Gritz,* and *Kudzoo.*

Foreword

Willie Perkins

When I was hired as tour manager for The Allman Brothers Band in June 1970 the term "Southern Rock" had not yet been coined. Indeed, an early advertisement for the Allman's initial recording in the trade magazine *Billboard* referred to their music as "Swamp Rock." Thankfully, that term did not stick. I have heard Gregg Allman proclaim on stage that he only plays two kinds of music, "Rock" and "Roll."

The "Summer of Love" hit the South in 1969 about three years after it's West Coast debut. After the hugely attended second Atlanta Pop Festival in Byron, Georgia near Macon, the Love Valley Festival in North Carolina, and similar events, the hippies, college kids, and rednecks throughout the South came together and "ate a peach for peace." Soon all of America would be listening to The Allman Brothers Band, The Marshall Tucker Band, The Charlie Daniels Band, Wet Willie, Lynyrd Skynyrd, and many others. Although not universally loved by musicians from the South, the term "Southern Rock" has become generally accepted by the public, media, and critics.

If we agree that there exists a phenomenon known as "Southern Rock" then surely Michael Buffalo Smith must be "The Ambassador of Southern Rock." He has written books and countless articles and reviews on the subject as well as being a performing musician himself. Creator and publisher of the legendary *Gritz Magazine*, he currently publishes a similar online magazine called *Kudzoo*. (www.kudzoomag.com)

In this latest book, *Capricorn Rising*, he has published in-depth interviews from over the years with a veritable Who's Who of Southern music, including Gregg Allman, Dickey Betts, Butch Trucks, Chuck Leavell, Jimmy Hall, Charlie Daniels, Bonnie Bramlett, producers Tom Dowd, Johnny Sandlin, and Paul Hornsby plus many other performers of the genre. He also profiles Phil Walden and Frank Fenter, founding partners in the iconic independent Southern recording company, Capricorn Records.

I have had the honor of personally knowing or meeting almost every artist and producer in this book, and I personally worked for and with several of them and, of course, worked with Phil Walden and Frank Fenter on almost a daily basis. I found these interviews interesting and illuminating. I learned many fascinating and previously unknown aspects of the upbringing and careers of these great artists and pioneers. So, dig in and enjoy this encyclopedic and riveting collection.

—Willie Perkins
Macon, Georgia

Introduction

My introduction to Capricorn Records was also my introduction to what would become my most favorite music of all time. As a matter of fact, I have stated publicly that if I were told that I could listen to records that came out only on the Capricorn label for the rest of my life, it wouldn't be so bad. The event that altered my life so dramatically was a 1973 episode of the television show *Don Kirshner's Rock Concert* titled, "Saturday Night in Macon Georgia."

Being born in Spartanburg, South Carolina, I was already a huge fan of our "hometown heroes," the Marshall Tucker Band, and I had discovered the Allman Brothers Band in about 1972 when a friend at school turned me on to *At Fillmore East*. That was the day the earth stood still for me, so when I saw this concert on my black-and-white television—with rabbit ears pulling in the signal—featuring the Allmans, Marshall Tucker, Wet Willie, and comedian Martin Mull, I knew my life would never be the same.

Capricorn Records and their artists became the touchstone of my youth, and I quickly discovered the wide variety of sounds recorded in the sleepy little town of Macon, Georgia. I latched onto Jimmy Hall and Wet Willie, Cowboy, Grinderswitch, Bonnie Bramlett, Stillwater, the Charlie Daniels Band, Eric Quincy Tate, the Dixie Dreggs and so many more. The Walden connection also gave me a new appreciation for R&B artists, especially the mighty Otis Redding, as well as Sam & Dave, Percy Sledge, and more.

I used to read magazines such as *CREEM, Rolling Stone, Circus*, and *Crawdaddy!* during those pre-internet days when you really had to look for information on your favorite bands. I would read about the annual Capricorn Picnics and dream of being there, perhaps even meeting heroes such as Dickey Betts, Bonnie Bramlett, or Jimmy Hall. Through my many years of writing about all of these folks, I have been blessed to not only meet many of them, but to also call them friends, and even perform and record with them.

Collected in this volume are a little more than sixteen years of interviews, some published in magazines such as *Gritz, KUDZOO, Hittin' the Note, Goldmine, Discoveries, Y'all, Mojo*, and others, and some having never been published. I have had a blast interviewing these folks, as well as meeting them, writing about them, befriending many, and playing music with several. It is my hope that the following conversations will add to your education and appreciation of Southern music, and maybe make you smile or even laugh. These are many of the greatest stars of 1970s music, produced by the greatest Southern record label of all time, Capricorn Records.

—Michael Buffalo Smith
SPARTANBURG, SOUTH CAROLINA

Dickey Betts

November 2000

The words, "no introduction necessary" come to mind as I sit down to write a few words about my interview with one of rock and roll's true living legends, Dickey Betts. A founding member of the Allman Brothers Band, leader of Great Southern as well as several versions of his own solo band, and a true road warrior, this Florida guitar player has given the world a peach truck full of great music, including instrumentals such as "Jessica," "In Memory of Elizabeth Reed," "High Falls," and the newer "Rave On," as well as classic tunes such as "Blue Sky," "Ramblin' Man," "Back Where it All Begins," and "Seven Turns." Dickey has put out a fine country album (*Highway Call*), great solo albums (*Pattern Disruptive* with Warren Haynes, Matt Abts, and company), and his work with the Allman Brothers Band has earned permanent status in the lexicon of classic rock.

When I talked with Dickey in November, 2000, he spoke about his recent firing from the Allman Brothers Band, his time with the new Dickey Betts Band with Mark May on second guitar, his musical beginnings, his early days working the carnival sideshows, the movie *Almost Famous*, Bonnie Bramlett, and much more.

❧

Thanks for agreeing to speak with me, Dickey.
You are quite welcome, Michael. We really appreciate all the support you have given us.

Thanks man. I just got finished interviewing a friend of yours, Dangerous Dan Toler.
I tell you what, he's playing great these days. He was over at rehearsal when I was putting this new band together, and he of course sat in. He's developed a great style that's really his own voice, you know. He was always a great guitar player, but he would sound like this guy, or the other guy. You could tell his influences real clearly when you'd listen to him, at least a musician could. I was really impressed with him.

What does he sound like, or is it just totally original?
I'm not a big electronics guy. In fact I don't even use any outboard stuff except a wah pedal, and I don't hardly use that now that Mark May is in the band. I'm just kind of a straight amp kind of player, you know? But he has a little contraption about half the size of your hand, about half the size of a cigarette pack, I guess, on the back of his guitar. He said it was a MIDI. I have no idea what that is, but obviously it's some kind of computerized deal. But he's also playing a Stratocaster with a bar on it, and he incorporates that MIDI, it's like a real smooth distortion to sustain it, and he uses that bar, but he uses it differently than I've ever seen it used. He kind of presses it down and plays through while it's going down, and then plays his lick continuously while it's coming back up. It's just a real neat sound. Instead of just grabbing it and tuning the note down, he plays out of the sweep he does with that bar. It really is nice.

I'm thinking of putting together a thing, probably at the Beacon next year, and call it *Guitar Town*—and like try to get Derek Trucks and Jack Pearson, Warren Haynes and Les Dudek, and my boy Duane Betts, and Danny Toler. You know, all of the guitar players that I have been involved with in my career, and have them all sit in, and have my band as the "band," and have all these guys come out and play.

That would be great.
I think everybody would really enjoy coming out to hear all these guys play.

That reminds me of an album I had in the '70s called *The Guitars That Destroyed the World*. (Laughs)
I'd do my best to keep all of us from getting onstage at once.

It could cause a meltdown.
It would sound like a gymnasium full of hornets. But I mentioned it to a couple of promoters and they kind of liked the idea. Hell, we could fill the place up with guitar players in New York, you know?

Are you planning to record with your new band?
Yeah. We'll start recording this winter. In fact, I just wrote a real nice song. It's kind of in the style of "Revival," as far as the hallelujah kind of

song. It's called "Let's All Get Together." It's brand new. I haven't even played it with anybody yet.

Got a gospel feel?
Yeah, a real hand-clapping kind of song you know. And of course I've got "Rave On," and I've got the bebop tune that I've been calling "JJ's Alley." That's at least the working title, I don't know what I'll end up calling it. It's according to how it sounds when these guys get through with it. Then I went back and got the very first words I wrote to "Tombstone Eyes." I don't know why I rewrote that song so many times, because the original one is really good. (Laughs) I do know why I rewrote it. Because it was a sad song, and playing with Gregg, Gregg does a lot of melancholy stuff, so I always tried to get upbeat things to kind of blend with his more melancholy stuff. But now that I'm with a new bunch musicians I think that it'll work. I can hear Mark May singing it too.

Mark has a good voice.
He does. It's kind of Freddie King-sounding. My keyboard player Matt Zeiner has a great voice, too.

I don't want to dwell on the subject, but could you shed some light on what happened between you and the Allman Brothers Band?
I can tell you pretty much what is happening, and it's becoming more obvious if you've read any of Butch's quotes on the internet. Butch [Trucks] has kind of taken over the band, in my opinion. The way I see it, and I was there when all this shit went down, and I really didn't realize how much pent up resentment and damn near hatred, I guess, Butch has for me. And a lot of it has to do with the fact that he kind of blames me for the Allman Brothers not getting involved in his business things. To put it simply, Butch has finally taken over the band. And the first thing he does is get rid of me because he feels I was keeping the other guys from going along with his business ideas. I'm not sure Gregg was going along with them either. We had meetings and voted on it and all, and Gregg and I and Jaimoe [Johanson] would all vote against these things because we felt like it was a conflict to mix Allman Brothers business with Butch Trucks business. But I just saw on the internet that the Allman Brothers had gotten out of the deal with Sony and were signing with what they call the ABB Record Company, which, I have an idea will be the Flying Frog Records. So really I think that's

what is the problem in the band. But if that's what they want to do it's fine with me. I certainly don't want to be involved with it if that's what they are going to do anyway.

I was deeply saddened when I first heard you were out of the band.

Well it surely saddened me. It broke my heart as a matter of fact. And to think that Butch Trucks would get in there and mess things up the way it seems he has done. That's kind of pitiful. I was kind of hoping that the Allman Brothers Band would all say "Let's do a farewell tour," and everybody go do your own thing, and leave the thing in a more graceful or dignified way. But it turns out we end like all of the other bands end, with differences that just can't be dealt with.

The thing is, they kind of trumped up these things on me, when that's not the problem at all. It wasn't my playing, or any kind of substance abuse. About the playing, there was one absolute train wreck on those tapes, and Derek and I laughed about it when it was over. Derek started the wrong song. We started "Black Hearted Woman," and he was so positive he had the right song that he came in playing real loud, and it threw the whole band off. We almost had to stop playing before we could figure out what the hell was going on. Because "Black Hearted Woman" starts in a 7/8 time, and Derek came in with a 4/4 time thing, and everybody was second guessing what song we were playing. That was the only thing I heard on the tapes that was outstandingly out of whack.

I wanted to ask you about a couple of things that have been running through the internet's rumor mill. The first one concerns you playing with Willie Nelson. Is this true?

Yeah. That's kind of an idea that Willie and I cooked up, and it took some of the promoters to go for it. They don't like to mix a quote "country act," with a rock and roll act. At first glance, it's kind of an unlikely thing until you start listening to the music. And Willie is damn near a jazz player. He's so subtle you don't realize what a great guitar player he is. But we're talking about, not just opening the show and then the next band plays and everybody goes home. We're talking about doing it as I open, or he opens, or we flip it around each night. Both bands play, and then at the end the key players from both bands come out together and have a big jam.

Those are the moments I live for. I love the jams.
Yeah! Make an evening out of it. Willie and I have known each other for thirty years, so I'd probably sing some of his stuff and he'd sing some of mine. Actually, we're trying to add Bob Dylan in the mix as well. His management people have been in Ireland, so I've got to return their calls. So we're trying to get the three of us together.

Well, as for Willie being country and you being rock, I don't agree with that. Willie's done rock and blues, and you've done straight up country, blues, rock...
We're not really that far apart. It's just the way I present my music, there's a lot harder of an edge to it, and it's more in a rock and roll style. But melody is really what it all comes down to. Willie's really a melodic kind of player.

Another rumor finds you touring with Les Dudek.
Well, what's really happened is Les and I have been playing a lot of golf together. He's been coming down and we play golf a couple of times a month or so. So we started talking about his band playing with my band, or either just a mixing of the two just to do some dates this winter. Just some long weekend kinds of tours. Just go out and play about three days and come home. We are talking about doing some stuff, but right now we're just throwing it around with the business people, the people that pay us. We've got to get them into it before we can go out there you know. (Laughs)

When did you first become interested in playing music, and who were some of your early influences?
(Laughs) I was actually playing music before I was in the first grade. My dad brought home a ukulele for me. My dad could play just about any stringed instrument, but he was a fiddle player, which was his main instrument. He was really a fine bluegrass player. Back then we called it "string music." Bill Monroe kind of coined that phrase "bluegrass," because he called his band the Bluegrass Boys. So, my uncles all played, and my dad played, so when I was about four years old, I started playing little tunes on the ukulele, and started playing in the jam sessions when we'd get together on weekends a couple of times a month.

So I went from that to a mandolin, and I started playing banjo for a while, and after that I went to guitar. I didn't start playing guitar until I was sixteen. I had started getting interested in rock and roll and hot cars and girls, things like that. But as soon as I started playing guitar I studied everything that Chuck Berry did. And back then Chuck Berry was what Jimi Hendrix would be to the late sixties, that real different guitar sound. If you think about it, nobody bent strings and made sounds like Chuck Berry did back during the fifties.

Definitely one of the true guitar innovators.

Yeah, I mean, he had that loose tuning, and nobody knew what loose tuning was back then. I mean everybody sounded like Duane Eddy or the Ventures. (Laughs) Anyway, then I met a guitar player from Boston that could get that Chuck Berry sound, and I looked at his guitar and he had an unwound third [string] on there, which, everybody does that now, but then, it was a wound third string, and you couldn't get that Chuck Berry sound with that. That was my early influence and introduction, Chuck Berry. And then I started playing a lot of the Ventures stuff along with that, and started studying B.B. King and Freddie King. I loved Freddie King when he came out with "Hideaway." It knocked me out. I had everything Freddie King did, and played a lot of his tunes. By then I had my own bands together. When I was seventeen I went on the road for the first time with a circus show. We had a tent on the midway, like at the state fair, and it was called "Teen Beat." (Laughs) And we were the band! And the barker, you know, he'd come out and tell all of these outrageous lies about how the band had just been on *The Ed Sullivan Show*. (Laughs) You might have missed 'em, but they were there! It was like a sideshow on the midway. We did about twenty shows a day, these little thirty-minute shows. And we'd jump off of the top of the amps and do splits. And I could do the Chuck Berry duck walk. It was kind of a little quick show. It was called *The World of Mirth* shows. And I learned how to talk carny talk, which was like, if I was going to say "Michael" I would say "Me-a-zee-a-zikle." They put "z's" and "a's" all in the middle of words and you can't understand 'em. It was quite an education.

After that I came home and forged my birth certificate and started playing nightclubs. I got more into a lot of the real old blues stuff. I had a friend here in town that was kind of an oddball. He already knew who Lightnin' Hopkins was, and Muddy Waters, and all of these people. He said, "Hey man, Chuck Berry is like pop. You've got to listen to some of the real stuff!" Then he showed me all of these real old players, he had all of these 78s and stuff. I got educated that way. I just met a lot of good people along the way. And then Lonnie Mack came along. He was like a ray of sunshine. There was just so much Beach Boys and that big sound from Philadelphia, (sings) "da do ron ron ron, da do ron ron." (Laughs) Then Lonnie Mack came out, and I played every damn thing he put out, you know. I don't play anything like him now, but back then I studied him. And I kind of got my shake from B.B. [King]. Learning how to get that tremolo the way he does. And I never really studied Django Reinhardt, but I think every guitar player listens to and gets influenced by him. And I love Charlie Parker. I put my Charlie Parker stuff on and just listen to it. I don't try to learn any licks or nothing, I just put it on and enjoy it. Of course, when you're younger, you just put it on and learn it lick by lick.

How well I know. One of the first records I did that with was "Jessica."
There you go! And I still do it with Robert Johnson. He was such a genius. You can't just pick up a guitar and start playing his stuff.

One of my all time favorite albums was *Highway Call*.
That album was done strictly for fun. We were making a lot of money with the Allman Brothers Band, and we had some time off, and I think Gregg was working on one of his records, and I just wanted to do a fun record. Get a bunch of guys I know and have some fun. The original idea for that was I was going to do more of a country jazz kind of thing with Stéphane Grappelli, but he will not fly. He would only go by steamship, and hell, he wasn't going to be over here for six months. I was going to have to go to Paris if I wanted to record with him. During that same period of time I ran into Vassar Clements at a bluegrass festival. I just got a bunch of unusual people that you wouldn't expect, like the Rambos, to play on it. And Conway Twitty's steel player. The thing on there, "Let Nature Sing," that was from my old Navajo friend, he's passed away now about six months ago, but he was a Navajo priest out in Arizona. And one of his things was "let nature sing." When your mind is troubled and everything, just sit and let nature sing. The guys that played on that had never been in a recording studio before. They owned a feed store down here in Manatee. They had big shows they would do on Saturday—they were professionals. They would charge people to come in and everything. They were real good players, but they had never been in a recording studio or anything. So next time you spin that you might kind of get a kick out of it. They were like a bunch of guys

who had just been to the city for the first time. (Laughs. Does backwoods accent) HEY MAN! This mic here is real sensitive, ain't it?!

Out of the body of work you've created, what would you say are some of the things you are most proud of?
We all get asked that question a lot, and I just don't know how to answer it. I like all of 'em. It would be easy for me to say the one that I don't like. (Laughs)

Okay, which one is that?
The one that none of us in the band liked at all was *Brothers of the Road*, because Clive Davis [Arista Records] kind of ran a producer in on us. And they mixed out all of the guitar harmonies, and tried to really disco-pop it up, and we really were trying to do some kind of hit single jingle kind of stuff on there. (Sings) "Straight from the heart, baby my love." You know, some of that shit. So even when we tried to make the best out of having to do some of those tunes, the guy mixed out some of the hardest work we did on it, and even simplified it from that. So none of us really liked that record. That's when we said hey, we're just going to split the Allman Brothers up until the disco period gets behind us. We went to playing clubs, you know, Gregg took his band one way and I went the other. But I love the *Brothers and Sisters* album of course, and I like *At Fillmore East* a lot. You know, *Shades of Two Worlds* is a good record, and so is *Seven Turns*. It's just different periods of time. I can't really say that I like the music we were playing back in the seventies any more than I like the *Seven Turns* record. In fact, the stuff I'm writing right now will probably be one of my favorites when we get it done, you know?

In the new movie *Almost Famous*, the central character Russell looks an awful lot like you in the early days. Was any of that actually reflective of your life?
Cameron Crowe says that the band in the story is a compilation of the Allman Brothers, Led Zeppelin, and some of the Eagles. And the actor that does the part of the guitar player says that he based his character a lot on me. It was kind of unsettling. (Laughs) He looked like me about twenty years ago—that's what they say. And you know how you hear people in a certain business, whether they are a cop or a mafia guy, say. "That movie was the closest to the way it really is." As far as rock and roll movies go, I felt that

one was the closest anybody has come to depicting how it really was. But the thing with Cameron Crowe and I really did happen like that. He was real young, and everybody was kind of brushing him off, and I defended him. A lot of that stuff really happened. Gregg got his tapes, and wouldn't give his tapes back to him because he got paranoid, and I ended up going and getting his tapes from Gregg and telling Gregg he was alright, and giving Cameron his tapes back. But what Cameron did was he took some of that and mixed it with some of his experiences with Led Zeppelin.

I read where Robert Plant said he was the one who yelled, "I am a golden god," and jumped from the top of the house into the pool. (Laughs)
Yeah. It wasn't me! I thought it was a real good movie. In fact, my son Duane just came in from California, and he and my wife are gone to see it right now. Yeah, I thought it was good, and a lot of that stuff reminded me of situations that really happened. I always liked Cameron. He was so young that no one took him seriously. But I found him to be a real good interviewer. He was really knowledgeable about what he was talking about.

He seemed to really care about it too.
Yeah. And yeah, he was a little young, but so what.

We recently ran an interview with Bonnie Bramlett, and she said some nice things about you.
Oh, I love Bonnie. That's the singing-est son of a bitch. (Laughs) She taught me how to sing. I'd be a great singer if I had a voice, you know? (Laughs) 'Cause I can really sing, I just don't have a voice! But what little I have I got from her. She told me, "You can't try to control it. You just got to open up and let it go!"

She told us there are two Dickey's. The cowboy and the Indian. She loves the Indian, but she doesn't much like the cowboy.
(Laughs) She tells me that all the time. She says you make a better Indian than you do a cowboy. I'm not very good at the honky-tonk hero thing. I always get in trouble.

Another person I was speaking to recently about you was Bobby Whitlock.

Oh, yeah! Bobby is a great player and a great singer. We're road buddies. I used to run into him on the road. Music is what usually brings Bobby and I together. I haven't seen him in a while. I'd like to see him again.

He just put out a great new album.

I tell you what I'm going to do with ours, if I can get out from under the iron hand of the Sony conglomerate. I'm going to just do it myself and sell it on the internet—and the Allman Brothers website, of course. We each have our own forum page. If I see a running commentary on something that I feel needs an answer, I'll get involved and try to answer. But I really don't think that thing should be a commentary between the players and the fans so much as for the fans. Then if somebody from the Allmans, or my band, or Gregg's band, sees a question on there that nobody can answer, you put a comment on there, you know. It makes it interesting for everybody.

One thing I wanted to ask you is for your insight on a couple of your old friends and brothers, Duane Allman and Berry Oakley.

Well, there are so many feelings, I could tell you a damn book. Well, Oakley and I were closer than Duane and I. Oakley and I were both young adults when we met, and we were both still searching for our style of playing. He had so much insight and vision. I was playing nightclubs, and I was making what would be the equivalent now of about $3,000 a week. Back then it was about $600 a week, which was real good money in the sixties. Oakley would come around and he's say, "You gotta get out of these clubs, and do your original stuff!" I'd say, "But Oakley, we'll starve to death. I'm married, and I've got to pay rent." But he kept telling me we had to break out of it and kind of starve for a couple of years. I used to kid him, I'd say, "you're like my big brother, but you're younger than I am." (Laughs) He was the real visionary in the band.

He and I got together, and we started doing about half cover stuff and half original stuff. The band was called the Blues Messengers. A guy from Jacksonville came down to this club we were playing at called Dino's in Tampa. It was a real big blues club. The guy had a club in Jacksonville that had all this Plexiglass® that lights came through, psychedelic lighting, an electric dance floor. Jacksonville didn't have anybody in that town that wasn't playing soul music. They were kind of behind the times. He came down and saw our band and said, "Man, I want to bring you guys to Jacksonville. But I've got to change the name of the band to the Second Coming." He thought Berry looked just like Jesus Christ. Oakley hated that! (Laughs) So we went to that club, and we were the only people in that great big city that had long hair and were playing that kind of music.

So Oakley said, "We've got to get out and get our people together." I said, "Oakley, we don't have any people. He said, "Yeah we do, they just don't have anywhere to go." So we got out, and some of our hippie friends built us a stage on this lot that some people let us use. They had electricity on it. They had about twenty acres there, and they told us we could play there on Sunday afternoons. So we got one guy to build the stage and another guy to get the electric lines run, and we set up our stuff and just did free shows. And in about two months we had like three thousand people coming there, and everybody's hair kept getting longer and longer.

But Oakley was the visionary. Kind of the guy who could see how to get people together and make things work. And that's kind of what he brought to the Allman Brothers Band. When the Allman's started out, it was supposed to be Jaimoe and Duane and Berry. They were going to be a power trio like a Hendrix or a Cream. But the more Duane played with our band to get used to playing with Berry, the more we realized that Duane and I played great together. So then it was two guitar players, and Butch started coming around, and we saw it sounded great with two drummers. So we rehearsed that way for about two months. Duane and Gregg were in a big fight at this time. They weren't speaking. We kept telling Duane, "You've got to call your brother, man, because nobody in this band can sing good enough for the kind of band we've got. So we finally got Duane to call, and Gregg showed up and that was the Allman Brothers. But when it started out, it was supposed to be a trio. And of course Phil Walden was going nuts. He was ready for a trio, and all of the sudden he had a six-piece band, and we had to have all this new equipment and stuff. He said, "I've got all kinds of bands, and they have their own stuff." He had been dealing with Percy Sledge and Otis Redding. But a rhythm and blues band didn't have to have all that stuff like a modern band needed.

But Duane, the thing he had, Duane and I were just musical brothers. We would sit up late at night and get us a bottle of Ripple you know, and talk about how the thing that breaks up every band is jealousy, and fighting over women. So we had the women thing figured out. Nobody messes with anybody else's girl. But we talked all the time about how easy it was for he and I to get jealous of each other. It was just a human nature thing. It was just something we dealt with straight ahead and talked about it in private. I'd say, "Sometimes when you play, I either get jealous or it makes me want to play harder." But Duane was just so assured and straight ahead. When he wanted to get something done, he would just go straight ahead, and nothing would stop him. And that's what he offered to the band. That confidence and the "we can do it!" Not a cheerleader, but keeping everyone's morale up. And of course his playing was incredible. (Laughs) We know about his playing! But when Duane got his mind set, he was straight ahead. And he would inspire people around him. So it was kind of an interesting mix. Berry was kind of the guru of the band, and Duane was the real fire-breathing, straight-ahead, nothing-can-stop-me guy. It was really a good mix.

What's next on your agenda? As far as touring and recording?

Of course I am planning on the album. We've got tons of material. Mark May has got so much material. Besides what he and I are writing, he's got three CDs that are really new material. Because not that many people have heard it. I don't mean that to sound derogatory, it's just that he's not yet that well known, so not everybody has heard his stuff. So we can take some of the really special things from his albums and re-do them with this band and it'll be like new material. Plus, he's writing all the time. And our keyboard player Matt Zeiner is a good writer too. Matt is interesting. He's from Hartford, Connecticut, and his dad had a band back in the early sixties called Wild Weeds. His dad was a B3 [organ] player too, and he sang. And as time went along, they changed the name of the band to N.R.B.Q.

You're kidding? What a great band.

That was his dad. And Matt is just a chip off of his daddy's butt. He plays B3 and sings and writes. He comes from a musical family and just falls right in.

Is your band going to tour again soon?

We're not going to tour until March. Mark is out with his band, Mark May and the Agitators. They have a great little Texas blues band. We're going to get together between Thanksgiving and Christmas and do some writing, Mark and Matt and myself. Then in January we're going to start recording down here. I'm going to get [producer] Bud Snyder to do it, and kind of do it almost live, but have the instruments baffled enough so that if anybody makes a mistake we can go back and repair it. But I'm not even going to go in a recording studio, I'm going to use a rehearsal hall. The only reason you need a recording studio is if you get a thunderstorm or something, it'll get all over the tape. Hell, if you're doing it and you've got enough time, if there's a thunderstorm you can just cancel the session.

And then you're not paying those ridiculous prices for studio time.
$400 an hour for studio time!? That's crazy. We can get this garage over here for $1,000 a month! And if we get a thunderstorm we'll just take the night off. Actually in the wintertime we don't get any thunderstorms, and there's no big heavy traffic over there. But that's what we're up to. And I'm going this weekend to Tom Dowd's birthday, and Tom Petty, it's his birthday. And they're honoring a bunch of us Florida musicians at the museum in Tallahassee. So we're going up there for that. It'll be a blow out. Great. It'll be fun. Stephen Stills is from here, and Bo Diddley.

Any last comments on the Allman Brothers Band?
All I can say is I had thirty-two years with one of the greatest bands in the world, so all good things have to come to end, so if this is the way it's got to end, I guess I'm gonna have to accept that. But I tell you, I'm having a hell of a good time with my guys. These guys are great and they're enthusiastic. It's a lot of fun.

Well I certainly do appreciate the interview. I think I've taken enough of your time.
Well, I've enjoyed it. I'm in no hurry. Like I said, Donna and Duane are gone to the movies, and I'm just sitting around having a glass of wine and talking. I very much enjoyed it myself.

After turning off the recorder, I got myself a cold beverage and sat and talked for another hour with Dickey, just chatting about the music we both love. It was one of the best nights I can remember. About two years later, Dickey found himself re-forming Great Southern with former band mate Dan Toler. (This following the departure of Mark May, who chose to work on his own solo career.) Toler left a few years later and was replaced by Dickey's son, Duane Betts. Danny Toler would pass away a few years later.

Gregg Allman

Spring 1999

In 1999, just after Warren Haynes and Allen Woody had left the Allman Brothers Band to pursue Gov't Mule full time, and Jack Pearson came on as guitarist, along with Oteil Burbridge on bass, I sat down with Gregg Allman to discuss his recently released solo album, *Searching for Simplicity*, and how the Brothers were continuing to sell out their shows at the Beacon in New York, the Fox in Atlanta, and nationwide.

❦

You have so many classic songs that you have been singing for twenty-five or years. Do you ever tire of singing the same songs? Also, what's your favorite song to sing?

Well, when you do them night after night, you try to do them different each night. You couldn't do them verbatim night after night, you'd go crazy. You'd probably run off howling into the night. (Laughs) With the band, it's just a natural thing. It's not like we're trying any great experiments onstage. But there's definitely some of that. When one guy starts going off in a certain direction, the rest of us will follow. As for my favorite song, I just finished a solo album, well, it's been out for about a year now. It's called *Searching for Simplicity*. I did a song on there for my brother. We cut "Dark End of the Street." Duane had recorded it with Clarence Carter when he was working on the staff down there in Muscle Shoals [Alabama]. He was always on me to do that song, and my voice just wasn't that thick. I mean, James Carr first did it. It takes a big, fat "Moon River" type voice. (Laughs) I didn't have the voice for it at the time he wanted me to cut it.

Besides that one, what are your favorite tracks on the album? I know that's like asking you which is your favorite child.

(Laughs) Yeah. I like the new version of "Whipping Post." "Silence Ain't Golden Anymore," that's a good ol' Scott Boyer song. It's like you said, it's hard for me to name specific favorites.

I like the country one, "Memphis in the Meantime." John Hiatt is a great songwriter too, isn't he?
He is, and a helluva guy too.

Out of all the songs you've written, what is your favorite?
I guess it's probably "Queen of Hearts."

Your favorite album?
Probably *Idlewild South*. Lots of good songs on that one.

There's a massive tape trading community happening these days. What are your feelings on the taping of shows for trade and the effect on record sales?
Well, at first we were kind of concerned about it. Then we did like a survey. It doesn't hurt our record sales at all, and I think it's really a great thing. I really do. It's kind of like—hell, it's better than baseball cards, because you can listen to 'em. (Laughs) Some of them are really great, and if you ran them through a compressor, you could probably release them. But the way people are going about it, just having them for there own listening use, I think it's as cool as it can be.

I really believe it helps record sales in a way. It certainly helps build on the legend of the band.
Right. I agree.

With almost thirty years of gigging behind you, are there any shows that really stand out in your mind?
Yeah. A couple of 'em stand out. Certainly the closing of the Fillmore [East, in New York] stands out. I once took out a twenty-eight-piece orchestra and cut what became my second solo record. It was called *Gregg Allman Tour '74*. It was recorded at Carnegie Hall. And you put a Fender bass in Carnegie Hall [because] the place is built for the spoken word. You put an electric bass in there, you've got a problem, man. We used one 12-inch speaker cabinet for the bass. It was like a Vibrasonic. And one 8-inch speaker for the lead guitar. We had six horns, six violas, seven violins, seven cellos. We had the orchestra leader and everything. I want to do that again, now that I'm old enough to do it. I'd like to do it right. (Laughs) It didn't make any money, but it was ballsy. (Laughs) They said, what's Gregg doin', is he

out of his mind? (Laughs) But we had a helluva lot of fun doing that record. It did pretty good.

With the two (relatively) new guys, Jack and Oteil, is the sound different on stage? How are they working out?
They are an enhancement. They enhance anything they touch, really. Both of the guys are terrific.

By now, everybody knows that Warren Haynes and Allen Woody left the Brothers to do their Mule gig full time. Would you comment on Gov't Mule?
They are a terrific band. A killer band. Just the best.

How about the Derek Trucks Band?
Also killer. And Derek has got some incredible, incredible musicians in his band. That drummer [Yonricco Scott] is awesome.

We just saw them here in Greenville. He put on a killer show.
Isn't he great? Oh! God, if I could play with any drummer in the world [Yonrico Scott], it would be him. You can print that. Someday, maybe.

The way the brotherhood is, it seems like you all end up jamming together at some point along the way anyhow.
Right. And all is fair too. (Laughs)

As a singer, who are your favorite vocalists?
I guess my favorite one was Little Milton Campbell. I don't know. It's between him and Bobby Bland and Ray Charles. I mean, there's a lot of good singers, and it's hard to say one is better than the other. You can't say Hendrix is better than Clapton. Both of 'em are number one.
And the great thing about it is, we don't have to choose. We can have it all. That's right.

Any comment on your guest spot on Toy Caldwell's 1992 solo album?
Oh yeah. Toy Caldwell was a good ol' guy. I played on his last record, and I never got to see him after that. I really enjoyed it. "Midnight Promises." We recorded down at Mud Island in Memphis in that old firehouse

they made into a studio. They had a B3 set up and hell, I was out of there in two hours. I was in the *moooood*!

We've heard great reports on the Gregg Allman and Friends tour. I spoke with Jimmy Hall [Wet Willie] the other day, and he said it had been lots of fun. How have you enjoyed the tour, and how does that band compare to playing with the Brothers?
There's not even a cross word in this band. They're wonderful people. I ran into the Alameda All Stars. Tommy Miller, the bass player; Tommy Thompson, the keyboard player; Preston Thrall, the drummer; and Mark McGee, he plays slide and lead guitar. Those four I've been playing with off and on for about seven years I guess. I started jamming with 'em, and then I added Floyd Miles, who I had grown up with on percussion and vocals. He pretty much turned me on to rhythm and blues and black music and Motown. And Jimmy Hall, and last but not least, Danny Chauncey from .38 Special. It really is one hell of a band. It's an eight-piece, and it smokes. We just finished our tour in Chicago of all places. We stayed at the House of Blues Hotel and played at the House of Blues. If you're ever in Chicago, stay there, man. It's decorated just like the clubs are.

At this point, Gregg is "attacked" by his dogs. He has an English Springer Spaniel and a Miniature Poodle, "without the weird hair cut," he says. One of the pooches is named Delta Blue.

How would you describe your long-term relationship with Dickey Betts?
Off and on, just like anybody else. We have our ups and our downs.

Well, thirty years is a long time for anybody to be together.
Yes, it is. We all have our demons, and we all have to deal with them in our own ways. I think he's great, and always wish him the very best.

I know you are mostly associated with the B3 organ, but I've seen you play some pretty hot guitars over the years. What have been some of your favorite guitars?
Washburn makes a Gregg Allman signature model acoustic now. Each one is numbered and signed. They're on sale now, but they made one before that. It was called the Melissa model. I don't know if they still make that one

or not. It's a black one, they had a twelve- and a six-string. It had Melissa written up the fretboard. It was really pretty. These new ones have a mushroom on the head. They are really nice. They're nice and simple. They have an Equis II [pre-amp] in them, for the electronics, which is almost like a Fishman. That's what I play. I have a J-200 that I play. Gibson acoustics are about the only other acoustics that I can tell you about. I have another good one. It's a Taylor. Those are incredible guitars. They're making new ones each day that are great. They've really got it down. They surgically took a Martin apart, and put it back together, but using lighter wood. I mean, if you dropped it, it'd break like an eggshell, but it is something else, I'll tell you.

What about electrics?
Probably just a [Fender Stratocaster]. The one with the least amount of knobs on it. (Laughs) A Strat or a Telecaster. They have two knobs and a toggle switch. That's about all I can handle.

What would you say is the most important lesson that you learned from your brother Duane?
I think it would be to stick to your guns, and not to let anybody weasel you into their pattern, you know? Like trying to get you to play some other kind of music, or sign something by hook or crook, you know? I learned a lot of things from my brother, and I think I can safely say, vice-versa. But that's one that really sticks out. Stick to how you really feel about things. Keep your own mind about things.

The Allman Brothers Band retired from the road in 2014, but Gregg kept touring, carrying the music even further down the road.

Butch Trucks

March 2009

There was major excitement in the air surrounding the Allman Brothers Band camp in March 2009. Their annual run at the Beacon Theatre in New York City was about to begin, this time celebrating forty years as a band and twenty years of Beacon appearances. The band had also chosen this particular year as the perfect time to pay tribute to the group's founding father: the late Duane Allman.

The 2009 Beacon run went on to be the biggest ever, with a massive list of special guests, including Eric Clapton, Bonnie Bramlett, Levon Helm, Boz Scaggs, and many more great surprises. What made it even more exciting was the fact that anyone who owned a computer was able to view every single night, every single song, every single guest star, as the event unfolded, streaming live via Moogis, the brainchild of drummer Butch Trucks. I spoke with Trucks about Moogis, the Beacon and a little Allman Brothers Band history.

☙

I'd like to start with a few questions about the beginning of The Allman Brothers Band, if you don't mind. We have written in many interviews and articles over the years about the history of the band. Please tell us from the drum riser, so to speak, how you came to be a member of the Allman Brothers Band.

Duane, Gregg, and I had played in a band together in '67 and '68. When that band fell apart Duane went to Muscle Shoals and did the session work that included Wilson Pickett's *Hey Jude*. After about six months of the studio, he got really bored, and about that time Phil Walden signed him to management and recording contracts and sent Jaimoe to Muscle Shoals where they hit it off, and Duane and Jaimoe eventually headed to Jacksonville to find more players for the new band that Duane was going to form.

At first he thought it might just be a trio so he took Jaimoe and Berry Oakley back to Muscle Shoals and recorded a few songs. After hearing himself singing on those recordings they all headed back to Jacksonville to grab some more players. We spent about a month or so getting together as often as possible and jamming. Finally after going through many combinations, we were at the Second Coming's—Dickey and Berry's band house—and six of us got into a jam that lasted about two to three hours. It was incredible. When we finished Duane walked to the door and said, "Anyone in here not gonna play in my band is gonna have to fight his way outta here."

The group was Duane, Dickey, Berry, Jaimoe, me and Reese Wynans—he went on to play with Double Trouble. Duane knew that we had to have a singer and he knew who that needed to be so he called his brother, Gregg, who was struggling in L.A. and told him to get his butt to Jacksonville. Two days later we had our first rehearsal and learned "Trouble No More," "Don't Want You Know More," and "Dreams." The rest, as they say, is history.

Duane has truly become a legend. Tell me a little about Duane as a musician and a friend.

Duane is the most powerful human I have ever known. If not for him I would be a math teacher at some high school. He was the kind of person that, when he entered a room every one would stop and look—he had that kind of presence. He was a self-taught intellectual. Few people know this, but his line about "every time I go south I eat a peach for peace" was [inspired by] T.S. Eliot's "Love Song of J. Alfred Prufrock." The metaphor has to do with when you eat a peach you make a mess just like when you live a life full of experience.

He reminded me of Goethe's *Faust*, he wanted to experience everything life had to offer, good and bad. The great thing about him was when the bad experiences began to adversely affect his life, he would stop them. Duane experimented with just about any drug there was. As soon as he realized that they were affecting his music he would stop and never use that drug again.

As for me, I was riddled with self-doubt about my playing. Although I was a very good drummer, I lacked that confidence. Jaimoe had been telling Duane that I was the second drummer for the band. I think Duane knew on one level that was true, but there was no way that he could have me in the band with my lack of confidence. I think he reached a point where he decided that I was his man but not with the lack of confidence I had. One day we were jamming and things weren't really going anywhere. I did my usual, "Oh, shit everybody's looking at me" thing, and Duane whipped around locked eyes with me and play a screaming riff with a "come on you s.o.b." look. My first reaction was to back off even more. After about the third time he did this I got pissed and started hitting my drums like they were Duane's head. Needless to say the jam just took off with all of the energy I was pouring into it and Duane backed off, looked at me and smiled and said, "There ya go." I swear it was like he reached inside of me and flicked a switch. It was an epiphany. I have played from that moment to this with all off the power at my disposal. No more nervousness.

What are your memories of the concerts that made up everyone's favorite record, *At Fillmore East*.
Those were the high points of that part of the band. We were really gelling as a group, and Tom Dowd was able to catch it all. After every show we would head to the studio and listen to what we did and say, "We got that one; we'd better do that one again." We knew we were onto something very special.

What are your happiest memories from the original band with Berry and Duane?
There is no way I could give you one or two moments from that two years and a half. I'll tell you that I still can't believe that we did all of that living in that short time. I swear I lived more in that short time than all of the rest of my years combined. It was just a nonstop living at full speed experience. Duane would not allow anything less.

I remember hearing a tape of the band BHLT. What do you remember about that band?
That was a very good band. I had a lot of fun playing with those guys. Not a lot of stories because it was so short lived. Me and Dickey, Chuck Leavell, and Jimmy Hall.

What was the real story behind Dickey leaving the ABB, and would you guys ever reunite with him?
All I'll say is that we reached a point to where we couldn't [deal with Dickey] anymore...so I called Gregg and Jaimoe and told them "no more." They agreed, and we decided to do the summer tour without him.... We were going to do the summer tour with another guitar player, and in the fall we would get back with [Dickey] and discuss continuing the journey that we had been on for all of these years.... Dickey hired a lawyer and sued us. As Jaimoe said, "Dickey quit" that day.

I have been watching your nephew Derek Trucks play since he was 12. Give me your thoughts on this young man.

Derek blows me away. After all of the years we have been playing together I still have no idea what to expect from him. He continues to take us all into realms that we have never visited. And he's only 29.

Same question, Warren Haynes.

Warren is one of the greatest guitar players alive today. He is also a great singer and song writer. He brings all of these elements to the band and a solid presence that gives us a real focal point when we play. He does take charge of the music when we play and I doubt if we could play the way we do if he didn't. He does it in such a way that he pulls everyone together without stepping on anyone's toes. It is a very tough thing to do and he does it very well.

You show up in lists all the time for greatest drummers. Who were your personal influences or favorite drummers?

I'd have to say Elvin Jones, Joe Morello, Dave Weckl, Steve Gadd, and Billy Cobham.

I am a friend of Paul T. Riddle of Marshall Tucker Band fame. Please share your thoughts on our hometown boy.

Paul is one of my best buds. We've been touring together for decades and Paul has been one of the solid, feet on the ground, guys when all of the rest of us were losing touch with reality. I am proud to call him my friend.

What have been some of your high points from the band's recent years, 2004 onward?

That's really an easy and obvious answer. The Beacon shows. There isn't any venue that comes close. The tour last year was fun, but we missed the best part of the year, which is the Beacon.

What have been some of the most fun memories from past Beacon runs?

Once again, there have been far too many to try and grab one or two. It's the main reason we love playing there as much as we do. There are always surprises. We either have very special guests show up to play with us—this year is gonna be through the roof—or we just have one of those nights where you just play in the moment all night long. It's as close to a religious experience as I have.

The Beacon run is off and running and you guys are sounding great. This is quite a special year. The fortieth anniversary of the ABB, and rumors are raging. What can you tell us about the run this year, special guests, songs? Is there anything that we can print?

We have many very special guests coming. As of today there is only one night that won't include at least one guest and that is the 26th. March 26, 1969, was the day we started this journey so we have decided that we would do the night of the fortieth anniversary without guests. As far as who is coming and when? It's a surprise. We have invited Dickey but no word yet.

And there is the excitement surrounding your new project, Moogis. One can now subscribe and watch the entire run on their computer. How cool is that? Tell us all about Moogis.

The best thing to do is go to the Moogis site and take a look. All of the info is there. We are web casting all fifteen shows from the Beacon run. It is Thursday the twelfth, and we have already done two shows. They look and sound fantastic but don't take my word for it look at the forum section on the Moogis social site (it's free) or go to www.allmanbrothersband.com and check the guest book from Tuesday and get a lot of praise about what we are doing with Moogis. The real upside is that we are going to leave all fifteen of the shows plus about fifteen other shows going back to 2001 with full video as well as about forty audio only shows from the past few years all on Moogis for six months after we finish the run (September 30). $125 gets you all fifteen shows live and on demand as much as you like for another six months. Check it out. We're having a ball here.

What are the immediate and future plans for the band?

We will do an extended tour this summer and next year we will begin pulling back. We'll play in the range of eighty shows this year, and next year we will do the Beacon and no more than twelve to fifteen special shows after that. How many more years we will continue doing this is anybody's guess.

Well, I for one hope it's many more years. Thanks Butch.
Thanks Buffalo.

Chuck Leavell

June 2000

Chuck Leavell is, and continues to be, one of the most sought-after keyboard players in rock and roll. In addition to his classic work with the Allman Brothers Band—remember "Jessica?"—and starting his own band, Sea Level, Leavell has performed on tour with the the Rolling Stones, Eric Clapton, and George Harrison. On his albums and during his live appearances with everyone from the Black Crowes and Blues Traveler to Gov't Mule, Leavell has maintained a reputation as one of the very best musicians. Dividing his time between his music and his homestead, Charlane Plantation, Chuck is truly "the hardest working man in show business" (besides Warren Haynes, of course!) In this exclusive interview, Leavell talks about forestry, President Carter, Mick and Keith, the Allmans, and more.

֍

Chuck, where are you from originally?
I was born in Birmingham, Alabama, in 1952. My dad was an insurance salesman and worked for Protective Life there at the time. We moved to the country outside of Montgomery around '56 for a few years. I went to first and second grades there…then back to Birmingham for a couple of years, then finally when I was in the sixth grade we moved to Tuscaloosa, and we stayed there. So there was some moving around, but we finally settled in T-Town, and that's what I consider the hometown of my youth. And you know, there were so many good players that came from Tuscaloosa. Some of which unfortunately aren't with us any more. Like Lou Mullinax, a great drummer that worked with us early on. And Tippi Armstrong, one of the best guitar players ever. There are guys that are still around from Tuscaloosa that are still playing that many people don't know much about. Bill Connell was a top-notch drummer. He played with the Allman Joys and others, and probably is still playing some. My old pal Glen Butts still plays around Birmingham, and my good friend Dr. Jim Coleman has at least three really good records out. Tuscaloosa was a hotspot there for a few years, for sure.

Tell us about where you live now. It's a bed and breakfast, tree farm, animal farm, all in one, right?

Well, not exactly a bed and breakfast or an animal farm, although we do have some horses and lots of pointing dogs. It's a plantation. A plantation is technically a farm or parcel of land that is devoted to one central agricultural commodity, such as in a sugarcane plantation, a cotton plantation, and so on. Ours is a pine plantation. It started when my wife inherited 1,200 acres from her grandmother back in '81. We had to overcome some problems, like high estate taxes, and the fact that the place had somewhat run down due to Miss Julia's (Rose Lane's grandmother) bad health the last ten years of her life. When she was running it, it was more like a farm, but had some timber on it as well. We managed to get through the hard stuff, and over the last ten years we've added about another 1,000 acres to the inheritance, so we have about 2,200 acres now. In addition to being a pine plantation, we manage intensely for wildlife and have a commercial hunting preserve. We offer guided deer, quail, turkey, and duck hunting with lodging and meals. From time to time we also book conferences and other events, but mainly the accommodations are for the hunters. We are also very involved in using Charlane [Plantation] for educational purposes, and occasionally sponsor tours to that end for young and old. Our website tells a lot about what we do; it's www.charlane.com.

I noticed you have Jack Russell terriers. We have two, Taz and Tessa. Tell us about your doggies.

We *love* our Jacks! We unfortunately only have one now, a female named Lilly. We've had three litters out of her, and kept one female out of the last one before we had her spayed—named her Bama—but she's gone now, hit by a car. So sad. She was really special. We do have a close friend that has one of Lilly's pups, another female, and we plan on breeding her to get another female for us to carry on the line. I'll always have a JRT, for sure.

You recently "retired" from the road life with the Rolling Stones, at least that's what I heard. What caused this decision, and how long did you perform with the band?

Wrong, wrong, *wrong*!! Where in the world did you hear that? No, I have no plans to stop rockin' and rollin', dude! We did what turned out to be almost a two-year tour with the Stones, and we finished last June, almost a year ago now. I think all of us wanted to get off the road for at least a year after that tour. It was an enormously successful run, and we had a blast, but it was long, and we needed a long break. I've taken the last ten months to work on Charlane Plantation, and do some other projects. Rose Lane and I were named the National Outstanding Tree Farmers for 1999 by the American Tree Farm System, and we've been very active in the forestry community this past year. We sit on the operating committee of the American Forest Foundation, sponsor a scholarship at the University of Georgia's Forestry School, and I'm writing a book on forestry now. I'm about halfway through it at the moment, and hope to have it out before the end of 2000. I serve as a spokesperson for the Georgia Forestry Association (GFA), and give speeches to groups from time to time.

I went to Yale University within the past year and had a great experience there. I will be the keynote speaker for the PERC organization (Political Economic Research Center) in Montana later this year, and will keynote the GFA annual meeting in Savannah in July. Also did the Leadership Georgia keynote several months ago (a special organization within the Chamber of Commerce here in Georgia), several Rotary Clubs, and the Southern Forest Products Association. I'm also working on a solo piano CD that I hope to have out at the same time as the book. I'm on the new Richard Ashcroft (formerly of the Verve) CD that is out now, and have played a few isolated shows in various settings since the Stones tour ended. As far as the Stones future plans are concerned, of course that is up to the four main guys. And they don't share their decisions with the rest of us until after they meet and decide what path to take. I have no idea at the moment what the plans are, but I hope they aren't done. I think they have a lot of music left in them, and my best guess is that the Stones will be back before too long. So we're pretty busy over here, and no "retirement" in sight.

Sum up for us the real Mick Jagger and Keith Richards?
Oh, man. Why does everybody ask that? Well, I'm afraid that you can't "sum up" Mick and Keith. It's too complicated. Hey, they are rock icons! They are legends, but they are also people, human beings just like you and me. I really don't want to go into their private lives. They are both intensely interesting individuals, as we know. They are extremely good songwriters/performers, as we know. They have a strong handle on who they are and how they want their career to go. They both (as well as Ronnie and Charlie) have an incredible work ethic.

The Stones have over fifty albums now, and God knows how many tours under their belt. Close to forty year's worth now. That takes an enormous amount of energy, planning, writing, rehearsing, performing, promotion, and everything else that goes along with it. It take a strong will and a lot of work to accomplish a track record like they have. And like all of us, they have private lives to live with families and such. Mick's mother just passed away this month (May, 2000). I know it was a blow to him. So remember that these guys go through all the stuff that the rest of us do. In my opinion, Mick and Keith handle fame better than most. It's a tough thing to be so public...to be so recognizable, and still try to maintain some sort of "normalcy" in your life. I feel very fortunate there. I wouldn't want that much recognition myself. It's nice to be known and for people to tell you that they listen to your music, and perhaps that you've made some difference in their lives, but it's quite another thing to be hounded all the time like they are. Like I said, they handle it very well.

What are some of your most cherished musical "moments" and memories?

So many, but here's a few: recording *Brothers and Sisters* with the Allman Brothers Band, and Johnny Sandlin producing. Playing [the Summer Jam at] Watkins Glen with the Allmans, the Band, and the Grateful Dead—600,000 people there; Sea Level shows with Jan Hammer on the bill; my audition with the Stones; playing Prague with them in '90 on the *Steel Wheels* tour just after the Czech's gained their independence—102,000 at that show; club dates with the Stones; Moscow with the Stones; touring with the Fabulous Thunderbirds; Eric Clapton sitting in with the Stones at Shea Stadium doing "Little Red Rooster" on the American *Steel Wheels* tour; *24 Nights* at the Royal Albert Hall in London with Eric Clapton; *Unplugged* with Eric, especially playing "Old Love"; touring Japan with George Harrison, playing all those great tunes, like "While My Guitar Gently Weeps"; doing the Chuck Berry movie, *Hail, Hail Rock and Roll*; playing with Ray Charles, Little Richard, B.B. King, Jerry Lee Lewis and others in Italy for a live TV show; playing with Rod Stewart, Steve Winwood, Seal, Robert Palmer, Chaka Kahn, Mary J Blidge, Toni Braxton, and more at Wembley Stadium in London for a live broadcast just three years ago. There are many, many other fantastic memories, but those stand out at the moment.

I just interviewed Jimmy Nalls today. What a great player and a great guy as well. Your thoughts on Jimmy, and then on his new recording, which you play on?

Jimmy is a special person in my life. We recruited him way back when some of us Alabama boys were playing with Alex Taylor. Jimmy was the right guy, and we were grateful to get him. He not only fit in, but added a spice that we needed. After my stint with the Allmans, '72-'76, we got him for Sea Level, and he was perfect for that band as well. We used to have the best times together. We roomed a lot on the road, and of course spent lots of time traveling with those bands, so we became very close friends. He's having a hard time of it now with Parkinson's, but I think he is maintaining a strong positive attitude, and that says a lot. I'm proud to be on his solo CD, and enjoyed the grooves I played on. I hope he can do other ones in the future, and will be glad to contribute if he asks. He's got a wonderful family, too, and I miss him since he moved to Nashville.

Let's touch on the Allman Brothers Band. Probably my all-time favorite group. "Jessica" has become such a classic. How many takes, or how long did it take to get that incredible piano part down?

Well, thanks. And thanks to Dickey Betts for writing that piece. It's been berry, berry good to me! As I recall, Dickey first played it to us on acoustic guitar. We sort of toyed with it at first, just getting comfortable with the changes and getting the harmony parts between the guitar, piano, and organ. Then we ran through it like, once a night for a few nights in a row until we felt confident about all the twists and turns, and slowly developing some of the transitions that occurred. I don't know how many takes it was, but not many after we really learned the song. I'd guess three or four.

There may be an edit in there between takes, I can't really remember, but Johnny Sandlin could probably answer that. As far as the piano part, it just came. I tried not to think about it, not to "organize" a part, other than to learn the harmony and the other necessary parts. I was just trying to keep up with those guys, and the notes I played on the solo just fell off my fingers. The solo just sort of played itself. It felt very natural, and I was just thrilled to have a song like that with a strong role for my instrument.

What was it like for you during those Allman days?

How much space do you have for this interview?! To give you a feel for where I was coming from, I had just turned twenty years old. I had what I think was pretty good experience and maturity for that age, and really wanted to be in a good band. I mean a really good band. I wanted a gig with a band like that sooo bad, guys that could really play, and that had something different and special. But it came totally out of left field to be asked to come into the Allmans. As you know, they had gone out as a five-piece band for a while after Duane's tragic accident. I was with Alex Taylor, and shortly after that, Dr. John at the time, and both bands opened up for them quite a bit.

We were all so impressed that they went out as a five-piece. That took a lot of guts. Well, they had finished *Eat A Peach* and had done some dates, and I think they were trying to sort out their future. Gregg was to do a solo album, and Johnny Sandlin called me in to play on it. As it turned out, the rest of the Allmans came down to the studio, hanging out, and we just started jamming. We had lots of these fun jams between Gregg's solo sessions, and things just felt really good. After a couple of weeks of this, sometimes doing Gregg's music, and sometimes jamming with the Allmans, I get a call to have a meeting with the band and Phil Walden at his office. I didn't know what was up, but when they asked me to join the band I nearly fell over! I was trying so hard to be cool about it, but I'm sure it was obvious that I was surprised. I couldn't believe my good fortune, doing the new ABB record and Gregg's first solo record at the same time! It was a huge boost for me, and I was over the moon to be alive and playing with these great musicians! There's not enough space to tell you about the years that were to come, but I can just say that during my whole tenure with the band I was proud to be there. There were tough times, as we all know, and I wish so much that things had not come in the way of the music, but eventually they did. So I was heartbroken when the band broke up. But Jaimoe, Lamar, and I decided to carry on and formed Sea Level, and that led to a whole other story.

Yes, we're still friends. But I don't really stay in close touch with them. I talk to Jaimoe more than anyone else. However, recently at Joe Dan Petty's memorial service at the Grand Opera House in Macon, we all played together again. It was the first time in twenty-five years that I've played in public with the ABB, and it was a thrill. It felt really good to do those songs again, and it made me have this melancholy feeling, plus losing Joe Dan— such a fine man he was. It was all very emotional and uplifting at the same time. I could just see JD smiling at having all those players on the stage. In addition to the Allmans, there was Bonnie Bramlett, the Grinderswitch guys, Lee Roy Parnell, and others. Quite an experience. Dickey said to me later, at the Big House, the "communal" house that the band occupied back in the late '60s and early '70s, and now is Kirk West's house: "Chuck, it was so good to hear that piano in 'Jessica' again. You know, it's just not 'Jessica' without it" I had to hold back the tears. Now, just today, I read in the *Macon Telegraph* that the Allmans have at least temporarily "suspended" Dickey from the band. Wow, that's strong. I hate to hear that. I just hope that things work out for everyone. There has always been the element of turmoil with the Allmans. It was there when I was in the band, and I know it was there before, and it's been there since. It's a shame that the music can't take control and somehow make them all realize that that's what it's all about. You can rise above the rest if you maintain that focus. The Stones have learned to do it. They've had all the turmoil, and have realized that the whole is greater than the sum of its parts. You have to respect each other, though, and I guess for the principal members of the ABB, it's come down to that. I love 'em all, and can only wish them all the best.

What are your most vivid recollections of the band Sea Level?

Well, as I mentioned before, we had some great shows playing theaters, with Jan Hammer being the opening act, and then he would sit in with us. Sea Level was a great band. We had a hard time with the record company and the retail stores, because we were so hard to tag. We did instrumentals, but we sang, and we played rock 'n' roll, but we played R&B, and we had tinges of jazz. I felt for the label and the stores, because they couldn't figure out where to put us. Rock? Instrumental? Jazz? But we didn't really care. We just played and had fun. As you know, the personnel changed a good bit. Jaimoe left, and we had George Weaver on drums for a while. Jaimoe had suggested him to us. He played in Otis Redding's band for a while, then later Joe English. We added Randall Bramblett and Davis Causey to the lineup. And very late in the game we had a guy named Paul Brodeur on bass—great player, but he died of cancer, a tragic thing. Also had Matt Greeley playing percussion and singing for a couple of years, who also died of cancer, but much later, years after the band had broken up. I loved playing with Sea Level. We had wonderful times in the studio, and on the road. Stewart Levine (producer on three of the records) is still a very good friend, and I learned a lot from him during those years. I guess the theaters were the most fun for me to play with that band. It just seemed to work better than clubs or big dates. I somehow think that Sea Level never really reached it's potential, and that's a shame. But I don't like looking back over my shoulder, and really all I can say is that I'm grateful for the experience, and think I'm a better musician for it.

I have a bootleg tape somewhere of you jamming with the Marshall Tucker Band. Reflect on that group, if you would, especially the Caldwell brothers.

Toy and Tommy were the greatest. I suggested Stu Levine as a producer for them after Paul Hornsby stopped working with them, and played on a few tracks on a couple of albums with them. I would always sit in with them if they asked. They were all good guys, and I had wonderful times playing and just hanging out with those boys. Toy was so funny. He could crack me up. They were both good joke tellers. Toy definitely had the fastest thumb in the world as far as guitar players go, and was a great songwriter. Tommy was a little more serious, sort of the bandleader, as far as I could tell. It's so sad how it all happened, Tommy's accident, and after that Toy was never really the same. Then Toy's death, and their other brother died as well. I know that had to be tough on their parents. So sad. But I'll always remember them fondly, with a big smile on my face.

I have recently begun talking with Bobby Whitlock. Do you have any stories concerning Bobby you could share?

Well, not that I can tell here! Oh, Bobby and I were, and are, good pals. We lived not too far from each other in Macon, and hung out a lot. Our wives were friends, and our kids played together. What a voice he has, and a versatile musician. I'm glad he's got the new CD out, and think it's really good. I know he was on Jools Holland's BBC television show recently with Eric [Clapton] playing. I didn't see it, but I'll bet that was great. Bobby and I have a lot in common—mainly that we live in the country and love it—and he's one of my good pals, for sure. But he could be pretty wild in those Macon days. We all were, to some degree. I was proud to play on the record he did for Capricorn way back when, and am glad to know he's back in action. We've been communicating lately, and it looks like there is a possibility that we may do some show over in London this summer. We'll see.

I really enjoyed the Eric Clapton tour of, I believe it was 1992. He did the Cream and Dominos tunes, and you sang a lot. How was it working with Clapton? What's he like?

Eric is a champ. What a talent! What an honor to play with him, and it was certainly a highlight of my career. I just hope to get to do it again someday. But it wasn't just Eric, you see. It was that band. Nathan East on bass, Steve Ferrone on drums, Andy Fairweather-Low on guitar, Ray Cooper on percussion, Katy Kissoon and Tessa Niles singing, and when I first came into the band, Greg Phillinganes was there as first keyboardist, and I was sort of the "second." All of those people are just extraordinary players and singers, and I couldn't believe I was playing in this band! Then when we did the tour of Japan with George Harrison, Greg resigned. He had been there a long time, and wanted to get off the road and do other things, like produce. So Eric came to me and said, "Well, Greg is leaving, and I want to do some dates after this tour with George. Do you want to handle the keyboards on your own, or do you think we should get someone else in?" I said, "Eric, let me sleep on that." The next day I went to him and said, "You know, I think I'd be happy to try this myself. It would give me some room to stretch out and contribute more." So he agreed, and the next thing we did was the *Unplugged* project. That was like letting the tiger out of the cage, man. I had loved what I'd done with Eric up to that point, but it was really a rather minor role.

When we did *Unplugged*, I just couldn't wait to play. You must understand that it was a whole different set of music, as well. We had been doing the regular set, and when we rehearsed for *Unplugged*, we only had, I think, three days of rehearsals to do something like fourteen or fifteen totally different tunes, or different arrangements, like the treatment of "Layla," for instance. We had rehearsed "Old Love," but Eric decided he didn't want it in the set. But when we did the show, we played all the tunes we had rehearsed, it had gone just great, and the crowd still wanted more. I don't know why he turned to me, but he did, and said, "What can we do now?" I said "do 'Old Love.'" So he agreed, and called the tune. Man, I was just laying for that solo at the end, all wound up like a spring, and when it came, it was the huge release I'd been waiting for, and I cut loose. It felt soooooo good to get that out, I just can't tell you.

I'll give one more *Unplugged* story. As you may know, after the song "Alberta, Alberta," he calls out my name, in his English accent, "Chaulk LaVelle!" Now, I have this friend that works in the forestry industry, and she tells me, "My little boy, who is about six years old just loves that part where he calls out your name, because he thinks Eric is saying 'chocolate milk!'" I just love that! Anyway, after that we had a couple of days off, then went back and rehearsed the regular set, and I had to adapt a lot of what I had done before with him, as Greg had done most of the major stuff before. But I did my homework, and pulled it together for the tour. Along the way, Eric said, "So who's gonna sing those parts that Greg sang?" I said, "Well, I'd like to give it a go." He put me right on the spot then and there, and said, "Okay, let's hear it." So I sang the part in "White Room" that Jack Bruce originally did for him, and he said, "You've got the gig!" That made me feel really good, as I hadn't really had a chance to sing much since the Sea Level days. Eric was good to me, and good for me. And again, it was such an honor to be on stage with all those players. What a team it was! I miss all of them a lot.

Tell us a little about your recent Christmas album. What compelled you to dip into the holiday cheer?

It's called *What's In That Bag?*, and it started as a Christmas card. I had decided to record a few tunes just for fun, and have 1,000 CDs and 500 cassettes made up to send out to friends and family. I had wanted to do it for years and finally made myself do it. David Clark had a little studio in Cochran, Georgia, which is just about fifteen miles from our place, and I had my little studio at home, so between the two we recorded maybe seven or so songs in about a week, using local guys, and of course some of it was solo piano. We finished it up, and David did the cover, as he was good with computer graphics. I called it *A Homemade Christmas*. It was a really fun project, and I had tons of people I had sent it to call me up to comment on it and thank me. My manger, Buck Williams, had sent a bunch around to industry people, and Phil Walden of Capricorn Records called me up to say how much he enjoyed it, and would I be interested in putting it out to the public?

Well, it was such a quickie recording that we had done, and I said, "Okay, but only if you let me rework some of it, and add some more to round it out." I recruited my old pal Johnny Sandlin to assemble the musicians, and we did the additional recording at his home studio in Huntsville, Alabama. I was lucky to get some fine players, like Bill Stewart and Rodger Hawkins on drums, David Hood on bass, Kelvin Holly on guitar, Scott Boyer on guitar and vocals, and others. We had a blast, and we did it on a couple of short visits, on my breaks from the Stones tour in '97. I'm really happy with it, and the only problem is that for some reason Capricorn seems unable to get it into the retail stores it needs to be in. So I tell everybody that it's available on the net at Amazon.com—all those dotcom places that sell CDs. No problem getting it there.

Who were some of your major musical influences through the years? Jimmy Nalls said you studied some serious Dr. John.

Well, yeah, of course. Playing with Mac was like going to the University of Funkology. I learned so much from him, and still do just by listening to his latest releases. I mean, he is the man as far as I'm concerned. But my influences started way before that. My mother was my first influence. She played for the family. She wasn't a professional or anything, just played for enjoyment. But she definitely influenced me, mainly by teaching me to think in terms of feelings and emotions rather than just notes. Later, I listened to a lot of gospel music on the radio, both black and white. Then still later, artists like Ray Charles, Little Richard, Jerry Lee Lewis, Nicky Hopkins, Leon Russell, Elton John, Billy Preston, Otis Span, Pinetop Perkins, and still later, I started listening to some of the jazz guys, like Earl Hines, Monk, Oscar Peterson, Art Tatum. And Keith Jarrett is one of my favorites of all times. I'll never be in their league, but listening to them is still being influenced by them to some degree. Ian Stewart taught me about the boogie-woogie greats, like Albert Ammons, Meade Lux Lewis, Montana Taylor, Pete Johnson, all those guys. Boogie-woogie is a real art form, and it's not easy to play, especially when those left-hand figures get complicated. I love that stuff!

I think I mentioned the last time I interviewed you [1991] that a friend of mine is Rudy "Blue Shoes" Wyatt. He just put out a pretty killer CD a few months ago. Any thoughts on Rudy, or stories?

Rudy is a pal, and a great player. He does the best version of "Route 66" that I think I've ever heard. I try to copy that, but I'll never do it like he can. He is pretty well known around the Carolinas, but should be known beyond that. I think that is beginning to happen a little bit for him, and that's a good thing.

Who do you listen to these days?

Well, I still listen to all the guys I mentioned above when you asked about influences, but as far as contemporary stuff, not much to be honest. I have a hard time finding something on the radio dial that I can deal with these days. So I usually listen to talk radio, and especially NPR. Mostly for the in-depth coverage of mainstream issues, but also for the great music that comes on from time to time on their various programs. At home on my five-disc CD player, at the moment I've got Santana's new record, Bruce Hornsby's *Spirit Trail*, Miles Davis's *Kind Of Blue*, an Ella Fitzgerald CD, and Keith Jarrett's *Standards, Volume 2*. I love the blues, and will always listen to guys like Little Walter, Muddy, Memphis Slim, Otis Span, all of that. I've been listening lately to Gov't Mule's new one, *Life Before Insanity*. Really good, Warren and gang. Bernie Worrell played really well on that.

My old pal Randall Bramblett has an absolutely fantastic yet unreleased CD that I just love. I don't think it's got a title yet, but it is so great. I still stop the radio dial on some of the old rock or R&B stuff, say, like Sam and Dave, Aretha, Otis, or Steve Winwood, a Beatles tune, Dylan tune, even the Stones. I still enjoy listening to something like "Honky Tonk Women" or "Jumpin' Jack Flash." I also enjoy classical music sometimes, even though I'm not well versed in it. The same with jazz. I've never really been into the hard stuff like Nirvana, Megadeath, Ozzy, anything like that. It just don't talk to me, ya know? And I don't like formula pop stuff, it's just so predictable, like most of country music. I do like the good ones in country, Clint Black, Lee Roy Parnell, Travis Tritt. Randy Scruggs is very cool and I had the pleasure of playing on his record with Roseanne Cash as the featured artist and Mark Knopfler on guitar. And of course I love the classic country artists, Hank Williams, Johnny Cash, Willie, Waylon, all of that, and Reba, Winnona, Trisha Yearwood. But most of what I hear in country these days, like pop, is just as I said, predictable.

The new black music, rap, hip-hop, well, some of it speaks to me, but honestly not much. I do like some of the inventive rhythms that come out of it, and some, like Arrested Development, or Lauryn Hill have some social commentary that I think has merit, but for the most part all of that stuff seems so negative to me. There are no stories, and the lyric content is either violent or stupid sex gibberish. I mean, is that really interesting? Is that enduring? Not to me. Not like "Respect," or "Try A Little Tenderness," or "Young, Gifted and Black." And so much vocal acrobatics in some of it—really overdone as far as I'm concerned. The vocal phrasing just goes over the top for me on a lot of what I hear on the radio. I mean, why try to sing every phrase you know in one song? It's like shooting all of your guns off at once. Hey, save some of your ammunition!

Well, enough bitchin' from me on all of that. I do like some of the contemporary artists out there now, like Faith Hill, Sarah McLaughlin—Macy

Gray is pretty cool. I don't mean to say that I don't like anything on the radio these days, I do, but I think we're in sort of a gray era for rock/pop music right now. I don't think most of what is out there at the moment is anything that we'll all care a hoot about ten years from now.

I believe I recall you playing for President Carter. How was that? Seems like that would be a kick. Toy Caldwell told me once that it was a big thrill.

It was an honor to play for Jimmy Carter. And I'll tell you about a fantastic experience I had earlier this year. I went quail hunting in Plains with President Carter, former Attorney General Griffin Bell, and two of my friends in forestry. One manages Carter's forestland, and the other has a consulting forestry and investment firm in Atlanta. So it was the five of us hunting together all day. Wonderful! Carter is 75 years young, and Bell is 82 years young. I tell you, they were like kids. They are both in excellent shape, and both are inspirations to me. Such energy! Carter has done so much for humanity. As far as I'm concerned, he's way up there with people like Nelson Mandela, Martin Luther King, Jr., John and Robert Kennedy, that league. He's an American treasure...and a darn good shot, too!

I am hoping to get him to do the forward to my forestry book. [Editor's note: President Carter did indeed write Chuck's foreword.] As I mentioned, he has forestland down in Plains, and manages it well. He knows about the concerns of folks like me that own and manage their land, trying to do the right thing for the big picture. If he agrees to do the foreword, I think I could just go on to heaven. We all had a great time hunting together, and we talked about those dates way back with the Allmans, and about when, as Governor of Georgia, he came down to Capricorn studios when we were recording Dickey Betts's *Highway Call* record. He asked good questions back then about music, the recording process, the business, and the personalities that make music, and on our hunt, he asked about the state of the music industry today—the problems, the successes, the failures, the changes in the last thirty years—and he even asked what Mick is like!

Give me your thoughts on Gov't Mule. Your work on the *Live with a Little Help from Our Friends* box/book set is fabulous.

Warren has been a friend for a long time. You probably know that I produced his first solo CD, *Tales Of Ordinary Madness*. That was a wonderful experience, and I'm very proud of the outcome. Too bad that it sort of got lost in the shuffle. Maybe one day it will get the attention it deserves. Matt Abts is a helluva drummer. I worked with him on a Betts tour ages ago. He's one of those guys that had to be born with a pair of sticks in his hand. I was very glad that Woody and Warren got him for that spot. It's been a groove to see them mature. As I stated earlier in this interview, the new CD is the shit—it's Mule to the next level. There is no doubt in my mind that if they keep at it, they will be huge. Maybe even on this one. As for the New Year's Eve gig. What fun! Warren was a champ to ask all those players to come: Randall Bramblett, Bernie Worrell, Derek [Trucks], everybody. He's like that, though, always finding a situation to invite interesting musicians to play together. I love that tune on the new CD, "Bad Little Doggie." Just great! Mule rules!

What about the Black Crowes?
Yeah, a great opportunity for me way back then. I got a call when I was in L.A. working on a Dave Edmunds record in, like '89? It's been a while now, and I forget exactly the year. Anyway, this guy calls me out of the blue and tells me that he's producing an Atlanta band called Mr. Crowe's Garden, and they wanted me to play on it. That was George Dracoulius. So he says can we get together for lunch and he'll play me a tape. I tell him, sure. So he shows up at the hotel in an old Cadillac convertible…this big guy with hair down to his knees, almost, and I'm thinking, "What have you gotten yourself into here?" We go to lunch, and in the car he plays me this really raw. I mean *really* raw tape made at a rehearsal with these guys. It was hard to hear anything on that tape, except the main thing came shining through was the energy there—the energy just jumped off the tape. I could tell they had something going, and agreed to do the session.

It was quite a while after that that we actually did the recording back in Atlanta. I was just about to go on tour with the Stones and only had a day to do it. At first, they only wanted me on like two or three tracks. This was all overdubs, by the way. So I start playing, and it's rockin'-good songs, lots of energy on the tracks, and it was easy for me to do my thing on it. After a couple of tracks, George says, "Well, how about adding some organ on this one?" So I did that, then, "Ah, there's this one more,"…and I did that. Then, "Ooooh, this other one might work." So the bottom line was that I worked my ass off all day, and came back the next day to do even more. I can't remember how many tracks I wound up on, but it was a lot, maybe seven or eight. I really, really enjoyed that session. When it's that easy to contribute something, you know it's working.

Then after the CD came out, they were going to do a video, and asked me to do that. I agreed. It was "She Talks To Angels." A day or so before that, I get a call from Eddie Harish, whom I had met when I was touring with the Fabulous Thunderbirds. Eddie was playing with Albert Collins, and we did some shows together. I first heard Eddie at a sound check. He was playing by himself, getting a sound for his keyboards. I heard this fantastic playing and went up to him to introduce myself. We became friends straight away. So Eddie calls me and says, "What about these Crowes boys?" And I said, "Well, yeah…I'm doing a video, and they are going on the road soon. They need a keyboard player. I can't do it because of the Stones tour, and you should come down and check it out." He did, and got the gig the next day. So I put myself out of work!! Eddie has done a superb job with them. They have survived a great deal in the last ten-plus years, and that says a lot. It takes a survivor instinct, and a lot of "stick- to-it" to overcome the difficulties that they have had—and they have done it. I haven't bought the latest thing they did with [Jimmy] Page, but have heard some of it on the radio, and I will be ordering it, for sure!

I just heard that you may be involved in the project coming this fall reuniting Whitlock and Clapton, Derek Trucks, etcetera. Could be a new Dominos! Any thoughts on that gig?

That's the thing I referred to before. But I don't like talking about stuff prematurely. Bobby has asked me if I'd be available if it comes together, and I told him that if he assembles all these guys, you darn tootin' I'll be there! But I think it has a lot of clearance to go before it's for sure…so keep your fingers crossed!

If you could go back in time and change one thing about your life or career, what would it be?

No way, dude! Nada. Zilch. Zero. There have been times when I thought I should have studied music a little more before I turned pro…. Maybe I could have learned to read music, learned more about orchestral music and been able to write charts for orchestra and the like, but then I would have sacrificed something to do that, and would have missed some of the wonderful times that I had in those early years touring and recording. And I wouldn't have developed my particular style, and, therefore might not have done myself any favors...so really, no regrets, I do what I do, and I am the most grateful person in the world for my life. I have a wonderful family, I've played with some great artists, I've been able to make some contribution in the realm of forestry, and I'm able to continue all of the above. The way I have it figured, I'm going to live to be about 120, so there is lots out there that I still have to do!

You've played with everybody! Is there anyone, living or dead, you wish you could/had perform(ed) with?

Well, not everybody, my friend! Yeah, there are a lot of artists I want to play with. I love Sting's music, and he needs me in his band! I like what he does, but sometimes I want to hear some "edge" in there and I think I could give an artist like that something to rough it up a bit. I've had a call recently that may turn into a session with the Proclaimers from Scotland. I hope that turns into reality. I'm a big fan of Joni Mitchell, have been for years and years, and would walk to L.A. from Georgia to play with her. I like the calls from the up-and-coming, like I got from the Crowes and from Blues Traveler, so I hope there are bands that I've never heard of that I'll wind up playing with. I would have loved to play with some more of the blues greats. I have played with or jammed with Albert Collins, Buddy Guy, Johnny Johnson, B.B. King, Muddy Waters, Stevie Ray, and a lot of others, but would have loved to play with Albert King, Little Walter, Robert Johnson. God, I could go on and on....

What's next for you musically? Otherwise?

There is the forestry book to finish, and the solo piano CD to do. That is the immediate focus. And I truly hope the Stones want to do it again, and that I'll get the call again. I don't think it's over for them.... Mick and Keith still write great songs as far as I'm concerned, and I was sorely disappointed not to have played on the Babylon CD. Of course I did the tour, but when they were recording in L.A., they chose to use local boys—that's okay—Billy Preston was on there, as was Benmont Tench, and they did fine,...but I would have done better. That's what Mick and Keith need to know. So we'll see.

I still have tons of things I want to do at Charlane Plantation—expanding our accommodations—and would love the opportunity to add to the acreage here. And there are a lot of things that concern those of us within the forestry community that I'd like to make a difference on. As a matter of fact, today, Rose Lane and I fly to Washington, D.C., to meet with our congressmen and senators, as well as some CEOs of major timber companies to discuss several issues concerning forestry. We have an important election coming up in November, and I want all of the candidates to fully understand the important issues facing forest landowners and the forestry community in general. It's very important, and the future depends on their understanding of what's going on, so wish me luck!

One final question. Do you like to eat grits, and if so, how do you like 'em cooked?

Do I eat grits? Is a mule stubborn? Does a bear shit in the woods? *Of course*, I eat grits. Several ways: cheese grits with catfish; grits with breakfast; with fried quail; with red eye gravy and county ham; fried grits from the pot you left in the refrigerator the day before—I could write a whole book. I'll share with you one recipe, and I hate to admit that it came from a Yankee, but it did. It's good for variety, not exactly a purist's version, but it does work, and I shouldn't even tell you, but here goes:

You prepare the boiling water as usual, but instead of grits only (not the instant type, of course) you do half and half grits and cream of wheat—and that needs to be mixed up pretty well before you pour it in. Then you add a scrambled egg and some parmesan cheese about five minutes before it's ready. Mix it in, and stir it a bit while the mixture is still sort of soupy; then let it finish to the proper consistency, and add butter, of course! Salt and pepper to taste. Mmmm!

Jimmy Nalls

Fall 2000

(Original introduction, 2000) Jimmy Nalls is one tough guitar player. For six years, he has battled the menacing effects of Parkinson's disease and will soon undergo brain surgery in an attempt to regain the ability to tour. In this inspirational interview, Nalls talks about his heady days with Sea Level, playing with Dr. John and Alex Taylor, his friends Chuck Leavell and Bobby Whitlock, recording his new solo album, and life in general. In rock and roll, as in the wild, wild west, you have both good guys and bad guys. This is a conversation with one of the good guys. Jimmy Nalls.

∂

Your new album is really great. It's one of the best CDs I have heard lately, and that's no lie.
Well, God bless you, Michael. That's awfully nice.

Let me start out by asking you who some of your musical influences were early on?
Well, Michael, I'll have to say that my first influence as far as guitar had to have been my father. When I was a little kid he used to get together with my grandfather and my uncle at my grandparents' house, and they'd play and sing and drink beer and smoke cigarettes. I just thought that was the coolest thing. Guitars and cool music. Outside of the family and people who came from my home state in Virginia, like Link Wray, I guess B.B. King and Albert King, Duane Eddy, even bands like the Ventures. Lonnie Mack, everybody who could play guitar back then was an influence on us kids. We had a pile of us back in our neighborhood that played. We'd all get together and sit down and play our acoustic guitars, and try to figure out riffs like "Rebel Rouser."

And of course, later on, with the British invasion, Jeff Beck, Eric Clapton, guys like that. They were hitting us with our own stuff in terms of reinventing black American blues, you know? But there are a whole lot of influences. Everybody I listened to. When I met Lonnie Mack about ten years ago, I took "Memphis" and "Wham," those two 45s with me and got him to sign them. When I was with T. Graham Brown, we played with him up at the Bottom Line in New York. I had my picture taken with him, it was just big fun. I had my picture taken with Duane Eddy a couple of years ago. That was cool.

Some of my friends rag me about having my picture made with different people I meet or interview, but I love it.
Especially if he turns out to be a nice guy. It's bad when you say, "Here's my chance to meet him," and he turns out to be a big jerk.

And you walk away with a Charlie Brown head hanging.
(Laughs) Right. Feeling like you're about eight years old.

Tell us a little about your new album *Ain't No Stranger*, the events surrounding that, and let's touch on your Parkinson's disease. A lot of people may not know about the battle you are fighting with that.
We've got to go back to the executive producer whose name is Rick Moore. He was working on a project a couple of years ago that he wanted me to co-produce. When I came down with Parkinson's disease, I kind of took myself out of the musical arena for a few years to regroup. That was a big shock. But I had suspected that I had it for about a year. My mother has it, and I had some classic symptoms. But I had met Rick Moore sort of socially here in Nashville and we started hanging around together a little bit and writing songs. He told me that he was doing a little project and said that he would like for me to co-produce it. I said, man, "I really don't think I have it in me right now." And he said, "No man, it'll be easy." It turned out to be a pretty cool project. So, he said, "You've got a lot of fans out there. A lot of folks who love you, and you've been off the bus, as it were, for a few years now. People are probably wondering what in the world happened to you." He said you ought to think about doing a solo project. I thought about it, and I had a batch of songs I had been demoing here at the house—I put a sixteen-track workstation-slash-studio here in my house—and I had been writing and had more than enough material. We talked, and he kind of talked me into going ahead with it.

With this Parkinson's thing, Michael, I kind of don't know how I'm going to be from year to year. I figured now, while I still had the goods, obviously not like I used to have—I'm not the gun slinger I once was—but I still had the goods so, we decided to go ahead with the project. He said,

"Man, you got *carte blanche*. Anybody you want to use on it. just let me know who it is and we'll make it happen." Of course I got Chuck Leavell on it, and Lee Roy Parnell, and T. Graham Brown, and Steve Mackey, and all the heavyweights I could find here in town that were good friends that I thought would have a good time and lend a helping hand. It was rough at times, but we pulled it off. I think the project speaks for itself. It's a classy project and I think it came off pretty well.

Well, as far as your playing goes, you sound just as good as ever. I play guitar myself, and I aspire to play like you. I never tried to play 'too many notes," instead trying to put feeling and emotion into the notes I do play. That's one thing I learned from you.
God bless you, Michael. I appreciate that. I've always said, it's what you don't play that makes what you do play make sense. I like to leave a lot of breathing space in my solos. Even when I was a hotshot, standing on the edge of the stage—which I am bound and determined to get back to the point, and I'll tell you why in a second—I still like some breathing space. You can admire all that fancy stuff for what it is but when it comes right down to it, for me it gets old quick. After about a song or two you go, alright, enough already.

There is obviously a lot of New Orleans influence cropping up on this record. Weren't you heavily influenced by Dr. John?
The influence was the direct result of a playing experience I had in a band we had with James Taylor's brother, Alex Taylor. Chuck Leavell, me, Charlie Hayward, who is now the bass player for Charlie Daniels and has been for years, and Paul Hornsby, who is a big producer. He produced a lot of Marshall Tucker. He still lives in Macon. We had a huge band, man. We had two drummers, two keyboard players. Well, Alex freaked out and decided to get off of the road. It just so happened that Phil Walden had signed Dr. John to some kind of recording situation or something. This was back in 1972, so the details are starting to get a little sketchy. We knew that Mac [Dr. John] was moving to Macon and he needed a band. Phil said, well, look, you guys are looking for a lead singer. So we became Dr. John's band. We actually played with him on one album, an Ann Arbor Jazz and Blues Festival album. I tell you man, I was a twenty-year-old kid, and he scared the hell out of me.

CAPRICORN RISING

We practiced every day for about two weeks trying to learn to play that New Orleans thing, that second-line feel. And all the grooves he had on the *Night Tripper* album. Man, we thought we had it down cold. We were in tall cotton. We said, "We got this." And Mac arrived in town, and he came to the little rehearsal space where we were playing. He said, "Y'all sound pretty good, but I'm gonna have to show y'all how to play some second line." Talk about busting your bubble. The thing about Mac is he could go to each guy and show them what to play. He could play all the instruments. He's a helluva guitar player. He's a great drummer, he's a good bass player. So he went around to each man, and if he was having trouble with a chord or a feel he could show you first-hand what to do. But he was kind of a scary guy back then to us kids. But I've seen him since and he's not so scary any more. I guess it's because I'm older or whatever. That was like going to college. You couldn't have gotten that education in college or off of records. That was learning at the knee of the dude that invented a lot of that stuff. Of course, he influenced Chuck's playing tremendously. Chuck is an incredible piano player. All of that Professor Longhair stuff that Mac does kind of rubbed off on Chuck.

Chuck has one of the best résumés in the business, doesn't he? He's played with everybody.

It's a shame he can't keep a job. (Laughs)

While we're on the subject, tell us about Chuck Leavell.

When I first met Chuck he was seventeen years old and he was already Alex's bandleader. He was so focused for such a young man. See, I left Virginia and moved to New York City and started getting session work when I was nineteen. I was real lucky. And through Peter, Paul, and Mary I met Paul Stookey up there and played on his first solo album—and he knew Tommy Talton from Cowboy. I heard that Alex was looking for a guitar player because Joe Rudd was quitting, so that's how I got the gig and met all those guys. When I met them, they were rehearsing up on Martha's Vineyard 'cause that's where Alex and all the Taylors lived. But when I met Chuck, he was such a mature, focused, schooled, streetwise player at such a young age, it was incredible. We became fast friends very quickly. In fact, we became roommates. He was a vegetarian, and he talked me into being a vegetarian. They used to call us "the Omelet Brothers." Because that's all we'd order. Cheese omelets.

So anyway, Chuck has just grown into one of the most sought after, respected players in the business. You can hear his influence everywhere. All the playing he did with the Allmans, and of course with Sea Level. He's just a phenomenal player. And what a human being. He's got a heart as big as Georgia. He's a genuinely nice guy. Like we talked about earlier, meeting people that you admire, I think he's one of the ones who doesn't disappoint somebody when they meet him, if they like his playing and have been following his career. When he speaks to you, he is genuinely interested in what you have to say. He's been a real friend through this Parkinson's thing. Somebody that I could talk to. Shoot man, I just can't say enough good things about him.

Going back to the song, "Hey Brother," how did that come to be?

The album had already gone into production when the co-producer, Phil Dillon, saw that I was really struggling to complete the project, as one does struggle when one has Parkinson's, especially if one is a guitar player. Phil got together with a songwriting buddy of his name Bill Edwards and wrote "Hey Brother" about my struggle with Parkinson's. He demoed the song at his home studio. He played it for me and I said, "I think it's a great song, and I know where you're headed with this." He said, "Yeah, I think it ought to be on your record, and I think we ought to get a couple of guest singers to do it. Either Delbert McClinton or Lee Roy Parnell or Brown. I said, "I think it's a great song, but I don't want it on the record. It's not a pity party." He said okay, but he kept badgering me until I said, "Okay, I love the song. Let's cut a track and see how it sounds. You do the rough vocal and we'll see what happens." So, we did it. It just turned out super. So I called Lee Roy and T. Graham, and they both said they'd love to be involved in the project. As a matter of fact, when Lee Roy first heard the track, he came out to where I was talking to Brown, and said, "I heard you didn't want this track on your record. You s.o.b." He said, "If I have anything to do with it this song is going on that record. It's a great piece of work and it really says what needs to be said." So, they did the vocal. It took them all afternoon. They had never sung together, which was a little piece of history. They were in the vocal booth singing together, which was very cool, having a great time. And then Le Roy said, "You want some slide? I brought my slide guitar." I said, "Man, let's do it." So, he spent four or five more hours, nose-to-nose with me, recording the guitar part. He said, "Man, I want to just be an extension of you here." He said just sit right here beside me. We were getting cosmic. (laughs) It was fun. We'd play for an hour and then we'd shoot the bull. Then he'd play another hour and we'd b.s. another hour. This went on until I guess midnight. We just had a great time. I think it shows on the track. The performance of Lee Roy and T. just singing and playing so well.

Would you reflect a little on your old band, Sea Level?
Gosh, it was quite a ride. We had a great band. I think we cut a lot of new ground. I think maybe the band was a little ahead of its time. A lot of it is, unfortunately, a blur. We just sort of jumped on the old horse and rode it 'til it stopped. That again was sort of like going to college for me. It was just a great situation to get involved in. When all that happened with Alex Taylor and the band broke up, I was living back home in Virginia, but I kept an apartment in Macon because I was getting a lot of session work down there. The Allman Brothers were playing in Largo, Maryland. Chuck called and told me they were gonna be in town and did I want to go. I said shoot yeah! He said, "I'll go you one better. Jaimoe and Lamar and myself and possibly Butch will be doing a soundcheck that afternoon, and Gregg and Dickey won't be there. So you can do the soundcheck and plug into Dickey's rig." So, I went over and met 'em. So it was Butch, Jaimoe, Lamar, Chuck and myself playing to an empty stadium for about three hours. When it was over, we kind of looked at each other and said, "Damn, I think we've got something here!"

At that time, things were rocky between the three of them and the rest of the band. So they made a move about six months later, in June of '76. They quit the band. Chuck called and said, "Hey man, we've quit the band and we're going to start another group called Sea Level. Do you want to be involved?" It all went back to the soundcheck we did that day. I said, "Sure, I'd love to." So that's how the first Sea Level album got started. That was before Randall and Davis; it was just the four of us. There was a fire on that first album. Not taking anything away from the other albums because as a body of work I think they all hold up, but I think my favorite one was the first one. We had to overplay to fill up a lot of spaces because it was just a four-piece band. We just played it for everything it was worth.

Butch was in on the first jam session. Why was he not in the band?
Butch was in on it for about the first two weeks. The first thing we did was a live radio broadcast in Athens, Georgia, and he was part of that. I

think in the eleventh hour he decided he was just going to take some time off and not go out on the road. I don't think it was anything malicious. He just decided to take some time off.

In one of your interviews, you mentioned Bobby Whitlock's Capricorn album, *Rock Your Socks Off*...
Oh man, what an album! Have you heard that?

Oh yeah. I have all of his records.
That one needs to be out on CD. Spread the word, Michael. I have tried to get Capricorn to do it. That Whitlock album is some of the best guitar playing I ever did. I was just a kid. Must have been twenty-one years old. But that lead on "Why Does Love Got to Be So Sad," the vamp out...it still just tears my heart out to hear that. It's so emotional. You know, they originally cut that song on the Dominos record almost double time. Really fast. The groove that we have on Bobby's *Rock Your Socks Off* is that half time.

Tell us a bit about Bobby Whitlock.
We see each other occasionally. He lives over in Mississippi. It's been several years since we've seen one another. I think the last time was at a Rolling Stones show over in Memphis. That was six or seven years ago. Whitlock, what a hard worker. And again, he's one of those you hear about through the years and you finally meet up with him and he's just a super nice guy. When I met Bobby he had me over to his house eating supper with him. He's just a regular guy.

What are your immediate and future plans?
Well, I really miss the stage, Michael. And I've taken myself off the stage for a reason. It was just time to regroup and sort of flow with this Parkinson's thing and learn all I can about it. The immediate future is I have a neurologist in Atlanta at Emory University, and there are several brain surgeries that are available to patients with Parkinson's. Unfortunately, with Parkinson's disease, no two patients have the same symptoms. But it looks like I am going to have what is called the deep-brain stimulator surgery. I go back for the second half of the screening in July, or what I like to call "the audition." (Laughs) I passed the first audition last month. I've had it for six years, and it's affecting my life. It's starting to kick my ass on some days, to

be blunt. So in July I'll have an MRI scan done, and speak with three other doctors. But it looks like it's a shoo-in. And hopefully, I'll be the first bionic blues player on the planet. I really miss the road. I'm in my late 40s, and I should be just coming into my stride. I really want to go back on the road. You know what it's like, man. You're a player. For that hour and a half you're onstage you are bulletproof. I don't feel like I'm done yet.

Tom Dowd

Summer 2002

We know that Tom Dowd has produced some of the greatest records in the history of rock and roll, from the Allman Brothers Band's *Fillmore* album to "Layla" by Derek and the Dominos and *One More from the Road* by Lynyrd Skynyrd. But did you know that Dowd has produced records for Charlie Parker, Aretha Franklin, and Otis Redding? He is, without doubt, one of the most prolific record producers in music history, a man whose contributions to rock and roll are countless. (The invention of 8-track recording, for instance.) In this exclusive interview, Dowd shares some of the gems from a goldmine of a career.

❧

I have read that you were trained as a classical musician and as a physicist. Do you feel that training helped you with your career in music?

Absolutely. Understand I have a premise that I operate on. One, when I am working with people, and if I find out that they are multilingual, I know that I have a person that has a more open mind than a person that only speaks one language. Now, I know that is hard to take, but that is the truth. Now that is one. When I say multilingual, there are some people who can only converse in one language, whatever that language is, but when I say multilingual, I mean they are sensitive to mathematics, they are sensitive to geography, they are sensitive to different cultural backgrounds and historical occurrences. They are multilingual, do you understand what I am saying?

Yes, exactly.

When you find people that are multilingual it is a whole different demeanor for communication and for getting things done quickly or for finding ways to get things done quicker. So, when you asked the question, there are lots of groups that I have had to work with over the years where it takes me a day or two, or maybe a month to find out what is the best way to communicate with that person or different members of a group. I might say something to one of them and I have to be guarded because I might offend another because they are not sensitive to where we are coming from. See, it is a game. The musical background helped me to develop my ears, helped me recognize chords. The physics background just put me in touch with reality and numbers, and it does not matter what the hay we are talking about because it all gets down to numbers. That is a way of looking at it.

Right. What would you say was your first big break in the music industry?

None of my doing, but by accident. A musician's strike in 1948. People do not know, and again this is history, and don't take the time to do research on it but it happened. In 1947, the head of the American Federation of Musicians was James C. Petrillo out of Chicago. Because of the war, there had not been any renegotiated or updated musicians' contract since before World War II. He was nobody's fool. He saw the advent of television and he wanted to get as many musicians working and continuing to work more and more as he could. He announced in 1947 that if the networks did not come to terms (because all of the contracts had expired and they were all working on licks and spit) that he would have a general musicians' strike. There was no FM [radio] and there was no TV, but they were around the corner, and he saw it coming.

[Petrillo] insisted, and one of his demands was that when NBC went to have FM and television shows, he wanted to have separate contracts for separate musicians for separate house bands for those shows. That did not go well, if you know what I mean. There were only three major networks NBC, CBS and there was Dumont, and that was the whole thing. He wanted all of these people who were blossoming FM stations and TV stations, and wanted separate house bands for each of these stations. Instead of them hiring a pool of musicians and have them do the Arthur Godfrey show in the morning and you do this show in the afternoon and do this show at night...No, he wanted three separate bands. So that, strangely enough, made an explosion in recording for the last like three months or four months of 1947. I had been in the recording business maybe thirty or forty days, and I was recording bands and I thought "what am I doing here," I don't belong here, but it happened, you know what I am saying?

Yeah, right.

Then out of the clear blue sky, I was making the coolest records you could ever think of! I was doing a lot of Leslie Young, and Charlie Parker. These are people, by being a music buff, I used to love to go to 52nd Street [in New York City] and see. Well, I wasn't going to 52nd Street and seeing what the hell was going on anymore, I was recording these guys! It was like I could not believe what I was doing here. But I managed to sneak in here and that was a major contributing factor. The other thing that fit with that was that I had also worked on the Manhattan Project from June 1942 until 10 December 1946.

I had applied for school credits for some of the things that I had done during that time. I took a summer job to see just what I was going to go back to school for and what I was going to do. At that time I found out that I could not get any credit for anything that I had done during [the Manhattan Project] for national security reasons. Which did not make me a happy camper. The truth of the matter was that if I had gone back to [Columbia University], they would have still been teaching physics classes under the premise of the way things existed in 1938, '39, '40. I have whole ways of substantiating that, and it is very simple. The national security back then—security of atomic bombs and every other fool thing. Back in 1943, a man named Wen P. Seborg out of the University of California, Berkeley, rewrote the Periodic Table, which was major, major, major. If you went to school from 1940 to 1953, they were still teaching the old Periodic Table. The paper he had written in 1943 could not be published for national security reasons, okay, and that is kind of devastating if you think about it. They were still teaching things that they knew were wrong from ten years before for national security reasons.

I don't object to what they were doing because they had good reasons for doing it, don't misunderstand, but what am I doing going back to school for four more years, when I know what they are teaching me is a waste of time, and if I do not show up for class I get failed? So when all of these things came to light, I thought what the hell am I doing here, and I just decided to keep doing the music business. That is the evolution. Very simple. (Laughs) There are so many important aspects to recording like clarity, pitch, that type of thing.

What do you think are the most important things as a producer to concentrate on in order to get a good record?

The most important thing is that you must have a good song. You must have a good song. You have got to have a song that is so good that if the kid delivering coffee walked into the door, he could sing the song and you would have a hit. That's how strong the song has to be. It's as simple as that. Now if you have a song that is that strong, you are half way home. That comes from the monetary, from the recording point of view that if you have a hit song that is all you need. A hit song and get out of my way, I am home free. You have to have your hand on the pulse of the audience. You must know what they like, what they are sensitive to, and what they are ready for. Unfortunately in the last six to ten years, we have gone through such wacky permutations in the industry. This is a time where TV is selling records based on what people see rather than what they hear.

Right. The video revolution.

Exactly. People are buying what they see, not what they hear. "Oh, look at that guy, he looks great," and they run to the store, or "Look at that chick," and they go to the store and pay anywhere from $10 to $20 for a damned CD, and that has an hour's worth of music on it, and the two minutes of the song that they saw on video does not sound as good on the CD. That has affected record sales. We also have got to go through the social changes that have taken place because when I started in the business, we did not have tape machines and we went direct to disc, and that meant that you had to have much better musicianship than you have today. You were recording anywhere from four to thirty or forty people collectively in one shot. They all had to play well, and they had to play what was written, and they had to know what they were doing. You could not hide or duck.

Today, it is a different game, but back in the forties, anybody playing a blues or gospel song and making it sound pop-ish, it was a ticket to get them out of the world that they were stuck in, particularly if they lived in the South or in the ghetto. Everyone was trying to get out and learn how to do this or that and take a shortcut to get out of whatever stress that they were suffering. Today, I look around, and I have grandchildren at this point, but I look at kids and what effect the parents are having on the kid's future. The kid comes home from school, and the parent puts him or her onto a damn tennis court for three hours because that is going to make them money and get them out of whatever the hell well they are in. The escape route is now sports, not creative or artistic. The kids on the street corner shooting baskets and not going to school have a better chance of getting into a college and a higher education than a kid with a 5.0 average. These are social changes. It's ridiculous!

You were talking about songs, and talking about the power of a good song. You have done so many it is hard to say, but can you name like five or six songs off the top of your head that you knew upon hearing them that they would be a hit?

There are two or three old songs that I knew that never had hit status, but when I did them, I knew ultimately one of them would be a hit, I just knew it. "Mack the Knife." Stephen Stills song, "For What It's Worth." That was a classic bit of writing, a classic lyric, and a classic delivery. Everything that you would want, there it is in one lump. Enjoy it. I thought, wow, where did this come from? It was like he took a picture in his mind and he painted the picture perfectly.

And it kind of reflects the feel of the '60s in that one song.

Exactly. There is the evolution. Protest songs are not new. If you go back to the '40s, and '50s, King Cole, [sings] "they tried to tell us that we were too young," that is a protest song, but a polite protest song. There is a whole pile of things of that nature. On the other hand, that is one species of song. When I heard and recorded "What I Say," I knew I had a hit.

Ray Charles?

Yeah, I knew I had a hit because, one, it was Ray Charles; two, it was danceable; and three, it was just an outstanding performance, well organized, and put together. Everything fell into place, and all the chips are still there. I knew it, I knew "What I Say" would tear everybody's head off.

And it still does…as does the Stephen Still song. The good songs just endure don't they?

Yes. Now, there is another masterwork that I hear all the time, and I want to cry because people do not know what it is. Charlie Parker, "Yardbird Suite," they do not know that "Hucklebuck" is from there and "Ragmop" is from there, and there are a dozen songs that come out of "Yardbird Suite," and they do not know what "Yardbird Suite" is. I know what I heard, and I thought, that is forever. There is no way you can get rid of it, or hide it. It is there now and forever. That is another world. The other one that I knew was a hit, and it was the second time I had recorded the song, and I never thought it was going to be a white hit, I knew it was R&B, and a black hit, was "Respect." They did the original record with Otis [Redding], who wrote the song, and then a couple of years later I did it with Aretha [Franklin], and when I heard Aretha's version I just sat and I thought, "Otis, I am sorry, but you lose." (Laughs)

The lady could sing, and man she laid it down, didn't she?
(Laughs) Yeah, she put it there, no question about it!

I love that song, and I love Aretha. I want to ask you several questions because our magazine focuses on music that comes out of the South, and I want to ask you about a few friends and people that you have worked with and just get some of your insight. One is a friend of mine, Jimmy Johnson.
Oh, Jimmy from Muscle Shoals, he is a beautiful, quiet, soft-spoken guy. Always kept to himself, and he never got the claim to fame that he deserves. A sweetheart of a person, a good person, and a nice human being. Give him a hug and kiss when you see him again.

What was it like working with Cream.
(Laughs) That's funny. The first time with Cream, because of the political and social climate of the time, the United States and Great Britain were not in love with each other exchanging musicians. There were strict rules that you had to go by; you could not do this or you could not do that. Visas were necessary for the bands to play. It was tacky, it was sticky, and it was stinky. The English were in distress. When I say that they were in distress, they did not have that much national product going for them. So they had their hands full just trying to stay even, and the greatest export that they had was the Beatles. This led to a very strange situation where, if a five-man English group came over here, they had a twenty- to twenty-eight-day visa, and they would work so many days, but only if America could send a five-man group over to England to work for the same amount of time.

Okay, somewhere along the line Ahmet Ertegun was in England and heard Eric Clapton playing in a club where Wilson Pickett was playing, and he said that he had to get that guitar player and so forth and so on, and it turned out that it was Eric Clapton, and he was signed to Robert Stigwood, and Ahmet then grabbed Stigwood and made some kind of deal with him that when that group came to the United States, Atlantic would try and record them. That is it in a nutshell. Then I was sitting in my studio one day on 60th Street and remixing something for them. Ahmet called me on a Wednesday night and said that there was a group coming in here tomorrow and they have to be on a plane back to England by Monday—and see if you can get anything out of them. I did not know the group from squat. They had made an album in England called Fresh Cream, and they were over here as one of those reciprocity deals promoting their English album.

When I went into the studio at ten in the morning and there were some roadies setting up double stacks of Marshalls, I was thinking, what the hell am I walking into? So, I say, okay, I had to put earphones on to protect my ears when I walked into the studio, they were loud and ferocious. I went in and moved a couple of mikes and talked to them, and we did this and that, and it was a long day, and they came back on Friday, and we did some more songs, and I said that we should do this one again, and I think that we could do it better. Generally, we made acquaintances and became friendly, and then on Saturday we changed some solos and horsed around with that, and I am trying to think what else we did. We overdubbed some vocals and changed some vocals. Then, the next afternoon on Sunday, we came in to listen to what we had done and redo some stuff, and then at about 5 P.M., a chauffeur came into the control room and said he was there to pick up three guys to take to the airport, and they looked at each other and said, "Oh, that's us." They just got up and said their goodbyes and went out to the airport. They left me with all the tape. The following week I mixed it down and sent a copy of the tape to England, and like one week later the album was out on the street and was tearing everyone's head off. We did the whole album in about three and a half days. That was *Disraeli Gears*.

Oh, the best one!

Yeah, in about three and a half days we did it. I am still reeling from it, if you know what I am saying. (Laughs) I didn't know the songs; I did not know what they were playing. They walked out and never said another word, got on the plane. When I sent the rough mixes, they said that was great, and let's put it out. They had never been exposed to 8-track recording before. In England, even in those days, they were still recording on 3-4 tracks. I had been recording on eight tracks since 1958, and I had like eight or nine years of head start on them recording wise, so all I was doing was restoring information. Then, when we were listening back, I was thinking that I could change that or move this, so I was thinking ahead of where they were before they did it. We just got along famously, and when that album hit, and it came time to record again they never said, "Oh, we don't like this or that." They never argued with me or said anything to me. We got along famously, and it was a love affair.

What did you think about Jack Bruce's singing?
Oh, great. The band was a magnificent band. Personally, they did not like each other. They did not get along with each other in the studio, and there were all kinds of strange things going on all the time. At the end of the day, I would ask them what time they wanted to start tomorrow, and they would say about 1 P.M., and I would say "just be there," and they would show up clean as a whistle. When they were done, they might have been fractured six ways from Friday. When they showed up and counted off, they were all starting together and clear-eyed; we were in business. There were times they would sit in the control room and listen but not converse with each other. Then there were times when they would converse for half an hour and banter around a whole evolution of change taking place. I learned to know the group in a hurry during those exercises. It was unusual.

It goes back to what you were saying earlier, you just watch and study whoever you are working with and learn how to communicate with them. I guess you had three different kinds of communication going there.
Oh, yeah, that was an entirely different world. That gets down to the same thing, that when I was doing either Lynryd Skynryd or the Allman Brothers, I did not know who could read or write music. All I knew was Duane because I had used him as a side man down in Muscle Shoals. I had to be careful if I would say, "Let's go to the F-chord" and somebody would look at me and say, "What's an F-chord." You know what I mean?

Here, watch me and play this?
Yeah, give them a lyric, and they know where they are. So you must find different ways of communicating with people, so you can get the best work done. Another thing that I learned in time was that if I was having a problem with a part and did not feel comfortable or well enough to communicate properly with the guy that was giving me the heartburn, I would then intentionally change a part on somebody that I had good communication with that was playing an exclusive part. I would change that part dramatically, the worst way it could be changed and that was to get other people to do different things. Because when I changed one part, then the other parts would change and all of a sudden the guy I can't communicate with is doing something great and I tell him to keep it up and don't forget that.

Then I go back to the original guy and change it back to where we started and tell him to do what we were originally doing.

A little psychology goes a long way...
Yeah, because if I gave the miscommunicating guy a part, he might not learn it, or take offense. If I let him invent something and fall in love with it...you get things to play better and you are not the bad guy.

You produced what have always been my two favorite albums. *Layla* **and** *At Fillmore East.*
Oh, yeah, the *Fillmore* album. I had been in Africa for a month doing a show called *Soul to Soul*, doing a film and a recording. I got home on the weekend, and I did not expect to be home by the time I got home, because I ran into inclement weather coming out of Africa. I came all the way back to New York. I called in and said I was back in New York and that I was going to take a day and then go home. Jerry Wexler said, "I sure am glad you are here because the Allman Brothers are recording on Monday down at the the Fillmore." I thought, that's interesting, and he set up an exquisite recording space. I went down because I had experience with the two drums and the bass and the two guitars and this and that and more or less told them how to lay out the tracks and they put up the microphones.

It was good crew. I was just being a catalyst about things. As things were going I was sitting in the truck, and the Brothers didn't even know I was there. I was sitting in there, and I was saying, "Alright, there is going to be a guitar solo, we are going onto multi-track, and I am just alerting the engineer as to what to look for." About four or five numbers into the show, the second comes up and taps me on the shoulder and says, "You didn't tell me where to put the horns." I said, "What horns?" I'm thinking that he is being a smart-ass and being funny or something. But no, there are two horns and a harp coming onto the stage. I am thinking, where am I going to put them? Stick them on one of the vocal tracks—I really don't give a damn! Then when I heard what the horns were playing, I bee-lined it out of the truck and went backstage, and as Duane came off the stage, I said, "You son of a bitch. If you ever do that to me again you're gone, and if those horns walk onstage one more time I am pulling the recording." He just looked at me because I had never spoken to Duane like that. Duane and I were hand holders. I had never accosted him like that.

They did another show that night and I said, "Now, I want you guys to come up to the studio, and I am taking the tapes with me, and I am going to play you tonight's show." We argued in between shows, and I told them they could put the harp player back in, but don't ever let those horns onstage again or I am pulling the pin. So that night we went back to the Atlantic Studio, and I played them the entire show, and I let them hear what the horns were doing, and Duane said, "Okay, the horns are fired; they are gone." So then we made it a practice, after every show, 2 A.M. we were in a taxicab and going back up to Atlantic—grabbing hamburgers, hot dogs, Chinese, whatever the hell—and we would sit down and listen to the entire show, both sets. By so doing after the second night, four shows, we would say, well we don't have to do "Elizabeth Reed" again, or this song again, and so let's put this song in and this song in and change the next day's shows, saying we don't have to do this song, we have it already.

So after four nights, the album was all together and we knew what was going to be the top priority or pick of songs that were going onto the album. Because everybody in the band had come up to the studio every night after the show and listened to every song, and we had all agreed on what we wanted to do, with who and so forth. In listening to the various takes, Dickey Betts wanted to use a solo from one version of "Elizabeth Reed," and the band said, "Whatever he wants, we love this take," so I wired Dickey's solo from one take into another take—they were that close in tempo, you never knew. I used "Hot 'lanta," but I could not use the best version because I could not get rid of the damn horns! Remember, we were going onto 12-inch discs so that we only had seventeen to nineteen minutes on each side, so we were limited as to what we could employ. In going through the "Whipping Posts," because that song closed every show, there was one show where some guy in the audience yelled out and the band cracked up when they heard this. So when it came time to mix the album down, the band was back on the road, I had already decided what seven or eight cuts we were going to use, and I had come up with the correct "Whipping Post," but as tongue-in-cheek so that when they heard it they would crack up, I threw in an overdub of this guy in the back of the audience yelling onto the tape we were using. (Laughs)

So when I am asked twenty-five years later to remix the damn thing for CD, we transferred everything that was ever recorded, and it took three or four days and I sat there and listened attentively to everything. I had the band's blessings, and I put "Elizabeth Reed" back together the way it was, and Dickey did not object. I used my favorite version of "Hot 'lanta" because going to digital I could find ways to hide the horns that I could not find in the old analog days. So I switched the take on "Hot 'lanta," and I used the echo version of "Whipping Post," but I did not add in the idiot that screams, "Play 'Whipping Post!'" You know, I am still getting mail that I used the wrong tape, can you believe it?! That's how much people know, you gotta crack up laughing. (Laughs)

That album taught me something, and it worked years later with Skynryd when we did the *One More From the Road*, and the first night I thought the band was going to stay in some community outside of Atlanta in a house, and instead they got into trouble and got into some fights, and the next day when we went down to rehearse in the afternoon for that night's show, I told them that they didn't have to do this song or that song again, and they were like what do you mean? I told them they had done it well the night before and that we should insert this song or that song. So I was doing the same thing for the Skynryd band that I had done to the Allman Brothers and not repeating the same show every night. So this made them change their set list and we would rehearse in the afternoon so that when they did it that evening it would come close to good, if not excellent, and after the first night, the second night I had a case of bourbon, a case of champagne, and five cases of beer, and all the floozies you could find in a suite in a hotel room. And we sat there and listened to the first night's show and we listened to the second night's show, and tomorrow night we should do "T For Texas," because we have not done it, and we haven't played this song in three years, and we had better rehearse. Well, we go back in at 2 P.M. in the afternoon and rehearse for three hours, and when they did the show that night, they killed three more songs. And that is the way that album transpired, but I was doing it to keep them out of clubs where they would go get arrested. The last thing I needed was two of them in jail, and then I wouldn't have a show, do you know what I'm saying?

Right.
So that's *The Road*. Now, as for *Layla*, after I did the three albums with Cream, which were *Disraeli Gears*, *Wheels of Fire*, and the studio portion of *Farewell*, I did not hear from Eric for about two years. I could not reach him. He was having a love affair going on and was completely out of it. Then out of the clear blue sky I was working on *Idlewild South*, or *Eat A Peach*—I guess it had to be *Idlewild South*— but in the middle of it I got a

phone call. Now, the only phone calls that I would take during a session were from my wife, my kids, or Ahmet Ertegun or Jerry Wexler, because it would be something urgent. This was Robert Stigwood, and I thought, "Oh, boy, what does he want?" I figured I had better accept the call. So while I am taking his call, the Brothers are recording, and they finish recording and they walk into the control room, and here I am with the monitors turned off, and I had no idea what the hell they had played, and I am talking to England, and when the call was done I said, "You guys will have to excuse me, that was Eric Clapton's manager, and he is talking to me. Then Duane says, "Eric Clapton," and he starts playing me Cream licks, and says, "that guy?" And I say, "Yeah." He asks me if I am going to record him, and I explained that they were coming here in a couple of weeks, and they wanted to find out what my schedule is like. He says that he wants to be there when Clapton comes, and I have to tell him when. "Fine," I say, "so in the meantime, let's get back to what we were doing."

Sure enough, in about three weeks to one month later, Clapton and Raddle, Gordon and Whitlock show up. I know Bobby Whitlock from Memphis—the other two I had never met before—and Eric I know from the Cream days. I said, "What are we going to do?" and they say, "Oh, this and that." I had warned the studio that the last time I had recorded this guitar player he had double stacks of Marshalls and was going at 120 decibels and this and that. Well, when we walk into the studio, here he is, and he has a little Champ and Princeton [amplifiers] with him. Literally, he has a Champ and a Princeton. I am thinking to myself, "What the hell is this about?" They start running songs and I am saying, "What's the name of this?" They tell me that they don't have any names of anything yet, that they are still just working on songs. So I get my engineer, I have two or three of them, and I say just keep the two track rolling on whatever the hell they are doing, and we will index it and be able to play it back to them so that I can say, okay, this series of chords should be the bridge for this song, or if you are going to do this song, you need to start on this section.

So we are talking this way, and they are running endless jams by me, and during one of these jams who calls but Duane. He says that he will be playing there tomorrow night with the band, and he wants to come by the studio. While I am talking to him, I shut everything down, and Eric walks in and he looks at me, and I told him that it was Duane Allman on the phone. Then Eric looks up at me and gives me the Duane Allman solo on the back of Wilson Pickett's "Hey Jude," he plays it note-for-note. I told him that Duane wanted to meet him, and that his band was playing in an open-air concert at Miami Beach tomorrow at 7 P.M. and he says, "We'll be there!" So I got a limousine and threw the band in, and I take them down, and the Allman Brothers are already on stage. I sneak them in from backstage, and we are sitting in the barrier that protects the band from the audience. Nobody knows that we are there because we are behind the security line, and have crawled in on all fours. Duane is doing a solo and he opens his eyes and here is Eric staring at him, and he just stops dead in his tracks. Then, Dickey is like, looking sideways at Duane, and he figures that either his amp is broken or his string is broken off and Dickey starts soloing. You know what I'm saying (Laughs). Then when that show is over, we all go backstage and everyone is hugging and talking and playing licks, and then by about 11 P.M. at night we all go back to the studio.

I had all the engineers, and told them whatever the hell, roll 16 tracks, don't let anything go unrecorded. We recorded everything that was going on. We had Gregg Allman playing organ, Whitlock on piano, Jaimoe on drums for his song, and Jim Gordon was playing percussion, and here Eric and Duane were playing licks to each other, and all of a sudden Duane would say, "Oh, no, that's not how I do it, I do it this way," because he would recognize what Eric copied. Then Eric would recognize something that Duane copied and correct him, and here they are switching guitars, switching fingerings, it was like a marriage made in heaven. None of this, "I can play better than you" crap. It was a marriage made in heaven. They proceeded to jam until three or four in the afternoon. Everyone was exhausted. They talked about when could we get back together to record. They had formulas for two or three different songs. In a couple of days Duane came back, and we did the whole album in ten days. If you look at the sheets of the reissued version, we did it in ten days.

It's amazing; I've seen it. You always seem to get things done quickly.

Well, when you're hot, you're hot. And I just don't want to run up a studio bill. The difference is this. I have had this argument with prosperous artists, although it doesn't really affect them. I look at the recording studio like an emergency room in the hospital. When you show up in the recording studio, you are supposed to be a professional, and you should know what you are going to do and let's do it. Do you understand what I am saying?

Boy, do I.
As opposed to groups in later years, and it goes on today. Three days to get a drum sound. Nobody buys the damn record for the drum sound! You are paying $400 an hour for three days—$10,000—so when we mix, you are going to say that it's too loud. What the hell are we doing? Then they say, "What's the intro?" They argue for three days about the intro, and then you end up with $7,000 recording budget. I am saying give me a rehearsal hall, and lets beat the crud out of the rehearsal hall and have all the fights and arguments there for $25 to $40 an hour, and when we have the song down to anywhere from three to ten minutes, let's go into the studio and do and then be done with it! We do it in a day. That way, your budget is like a quarter or a third of what people normally spend.

It seems like a lot of it has to do with how much of a prima donna someone is; some of these people just get spoiled and think they can do anything that they want to do.

I did not teach it to them. This is something that the Stax crew used to do because before they became nationally prominent, they all had day jobs and they would show up in the studio after the day job, 7 or 8 P.M., and each would be carrying a doggie bag from what they grabbed on their way over from whatever the hell their day job was, and again Al Jackson was pumping gas at the family station and Steve Cropper was working behind the counter at Stax Record shop. Each one of them had input from each segment of society that they had been exposed to on a daily basis. They would be jamming on things, and they would say, "Hey man, you know that lick we were talking about before, that would be great right there, and they would be composing and arranging things on the fly, and this is how they put some of their stuff together. Then when an artist came in and sang them a song, they would say, "Hey man, you know that thing we were doing the other day that belongs there?" and from constant playing and recall they would conjure up an arrangement that would make you go, "Wow." That's how tight they were. They knew what they were doing.

This next question I would like to do is a word association with names. Just to call out a few of the people that I have admired over the years and give me a brief description, like what you did earlier.

Duane Allman.

A pussycat, an absolute humble, soft spoken, brilliant leader. He never provoked anyone in the band. He was never demonstrative, but he was in charge, and he got everyone to go the right way whether he did it by playing them something or saying something to them.

Eric Clapton.

A basically insecure person for a very, very long time. In his heart a good human being and a kind human being, and ultimately through the years he decided that he had been making mistakes for a long time and accepted the responsibility and has since become a very sober, very serious still good person. Like Eric in the '60s and '70s would never get out of bed before three or four in the afternoon, and you never knew what was going to climb out of bed. When we were recording in Nassau in Compass Point, I am an early riser and would be up at 6 A.M., and I would look out the door of the cottage I was in, and there was Eric walking down the beach in a bathing suit with an acoustic guitar walking ankle deep playing and singing. Hello? Now if Eric is in a community and you go look for him and want to interview him, is he out on a binge again? Hell no, and it does not matter what community he is in, he is in an AA or drug rehab clinic, and he is now available in the hotel at 2 P.M. and able to talk with you. He is in a clinic somewhere out there every day and telling people that he did this and that and he was wrong and that this is better. That is devotion and obligation; that is the nature of the man.

Bobby Whitlock.

I like Bobby, but he does exaggerate once in a while. I have challenged him once or twice and told him that he has bad recall. Because Bobby Whitlock would tell you if you asked him that drugs were rampant and all over the floor during the *Layla* sessions, and it was here and there all over the place. Not true.

I did read in an article last night when I was doing some research that he had said that, and then read something where you said that during the *Layla* sessions it was not that way.

Yes, that's right, and what I will say is that I have never taken an artist to task about what he does with his time or his life; it is his, he's entitled. About the *Layla* sessions, and the same with the Allman Brothers, they were just a step above trouble, if I said 2 P.M. tomorrow we record, whether it was the Allman Brothers or Whitlock, Derek and company, I would have five guys in front of me, clear-eyed, with their hair combed, and with their instruments in tune, ready to play. They were ready, because I said be here at 2 P.M., and they would be there, ready and asking what we were doing today. Now at 6 P.M., or if it was a bad day, I would say, "What I am doing for the rest of the day is overdubbing, and the rest of you can go home." I couldn't tell you if they broke out the door or started doing lines on the floor because I could really give a damn. Because they would say, "Oh, we're done?" and all hell would break loose. That would be the respect that they were showing for my saying to be here at so and so, and they would show up clean as a whistle and ready to play. Four hours later, they would be standing there drooling to get into whatever they were into, understand, but... [T]hey were not going to break ranks until I said I am done with you and go home. I was not going to argue with them. On the other hand, I never had a problem when I charged members of those groups with responsibility; they met the obligation and were ready to meet it. Now, there might have been drugs ongoing one or two hours after the session was over, but I really did not give a damn. That is the way it was.

I went for a long time assuming that it was Whitlock that played the coda on *Layla*, but it wasn't was it?
No, that was Jim Gordon, the drummer.

That part of the song for me really makes the song. Not taking anything away from Bobby or the rest of the band, of course.
Well, that was thrown in like two weeks later. I mixed the entire album of *Layla* and sent it to them in England. I got a call that they were coming back into the United States to do a tour, and they wanted to part and mix the sound. It took longer to do that than it took to do the whole damn album.

Yeah, you had a lot of tracks on the song "Layla," with guitars going everywhere.
Oh yeah, we only had sixteen tracks and didn't have computers, and I was just stacking things to store them. Later, I could look at them and say how can I use this, where do I put it, and we were playing checkerboard squares.

Layla has always been my all time favorite album because the summer at Myrtle Beach when I first became exposed to the record, I had never heard anything like that. When you hear all that Duane Allman stuff riding over the top of Clapton, it is just amazing. I still turn that up on the radio and it is still so good.

Thank you. (Laughs)

Back to the names. I had a couple more to ask you about.

Dickey Betts.
We get along famously, and I have to look at him sometimes, and only because of that common 1940's background do I realize where Dickey is coming from sometimes. Now, Dickey is the first to say that we used to sit on the back porch with my grandpa, and that's how we learned and so forth. Dickey was extremely sensitive to Django Reinhardt and Stephane Grappelli, and he did not know who they were. He was sensitive to Grappelli particularly, if you listen on *Beginnings* and *Idlewild South*, some of his solos start like the Grappelli violin solos, and they start on row strings and go up; now all of a sudden he is a blues, jazz, rock guitar player. He never just jumped on it like that. He set a foundation and then slid into it. I recognized that right away from my jazz sensitivity days, and I could not say that to him for fear that I would upset him, so I choose to leave him alone because what he is doing is beautiful. I would admire him and tell him that the way he started that solo is magnificent, and that what you are doing is great don't change it; try and start everyone like that. I would tell him to try and do every lick with that touch you have right now because I never wanted to criticize him because I would send him off on a tangent that would take him a week to recover; but, on the other hand, if you just stroked him, oh, he would come up with some exquisite playing.

Yeah, when we interviewed Dickey for this magazine he mentioned Reinhardt and Grappelli as influences.
Really? Well, that is the God's honest truth, we have talked about it. At the time I don't think that he knew them, and that is not a criticism, it's just that he never put a brand on it. It's just classic, and he is an exquisite musician.

He writes some of the most beautiful instrumentals too.

Now, there is something that you have to know about Dickey, and it took me a long time to figure out how to handle this with the band. Dickey in his intuitive plane has a clock that does not run by the number system. It could be a 4/4 bar, 5/4 bar, or 6/8 bar, and he just invents these melodies that are incongruously in keeping 4/4, and when the band starts playing with him, it's like, let's go over that section again a few times to figure out how to handle the 7/8 bar or the extra this or half that. At the time, when I was working with the Brothers, I didn't know who I could speak to in the band that I would relate to musically. I knew I could talk with Duane, but if I said something, was Berry Oakley going to change his part or would it make Gregg react? So I had problems finding out who I could communicate with like looking and seeking that if I had a problem with one how could I get to the others? It was perpetual and a heartbreaker and would drive me up a damn wall!

Gregg has a touch on the piano as light as a feather and is an exquisite pianist. Of course, when we got Warren in the band that was another world; now I could talk music, chords, and so forth, but if I did that, and I did it too quickly I'd lose Dickey, you follow me? Because I would say, "Okay, you know when Dickey goes to the 5/4 on the A-flat chord?" Dickey would not know what I meant because he doesn't relate that way to it. But you don't want to affect him so that he changes; you leave him the hell alone. If you affect him, you can destroy his creative abilities.

How did you like working with our Carolina boy, Warren Haynes?

Oh, fine. That's funny because there was a golf pro down here, and I used to play a lot of golf, and I was out one morning, and he said, "You really get out early, what kind of business do you do?" I told him I was in the music business, and he said that he used to have a Little League team, and there is a kid who used to be his best player and he is a guitar player now. It was Warren Haynes. So Warren used to be on a Little League team in Carolina, and he played for this guy and was the best player on the team. Then, a couple of nights after that when I saw Warren, I mentioned to him that I didn't know he had been a sports player. Warren just laughed. Warren is brilliant. I have scolded Warren about this once or twice. I have gone and seen the old Gov't Mule and said to him afterwards that I wished I had recorded the live set. He would say, well I would have changed this or that, and I told him no, I wished I had recorded it before you put your hands on it.

He goes back in with his brilliant concepts and his facility to be able to adapt to equipment and takes the most spontaneous, lucid, greatest feeling and flying stuff and time corrects it and screws it up. I want to kill him. I told him that.

My wife and I have been fans of Gov't. Mule from the time we first heard them, and I have in my collection a lot of the shows that were recorded live, and they are incredible.

When you look at what comes out of the studio, it's the same damn recording, changed this, moved that around and substitutes this, and basically sterilizes them. They should have been recorded and released as played. Nobody should ever touch a Gov't Mule recording, or try to correct it. I have told Warren that time and time again.

The last name on my name list is someone that has become kind of a legend in our Southern Rock genre. What can you say about Ronnie Van Zant?

Ronnie was a gem. Ronnie was a brilliant writer. We spent most of our time together traveling on the road for a day or two at a time, or if I had them for a day or two in the rehearsal hall in Jacksonville and in the studio. But we very seldom socialized until the very last album when I was rehearsing them up in Jacksonville and Ronnie said that I should stay out at his house instead of a motel. I stayed for about four days there, and that was about as close as we got. I can say that Ronnie was a true consummate professional.

There are two artists when we were recording that would look at me and say, "I want to sing tomorrow," or, "Let's sing a week from Thursday." I would agree, and we would set up a schedule for them to come in and sing. There would be songs set up ready for them to sing. Ronnie was one of those, so was Rod Stewart. They would walk into the studio and say, "Play me this song," and I would play the song they were looking for, and then they would sing. Now, we were not in the studio thirty or forty minutes and they would sing maybe one verse, stop the tape, and come into the studio and sit down and listen. Then they would say that they were not ready today. Let's do it tomorrow, and just get up and walk out the door. They knew where their instrument was and would not sit there and sing for six or seven hours and not hit the note.

On the other hand, with Ronnie we would be making a track, and I would be working on the band, and he would always have a bottle of Jack in his hand, and he would put it down on the end of the console and he would say that at 2 P.M. tomorrow he would be ready to record the song. Then he would walk out the door. The fact that he put the Jack down on the console meant that he was going home and have something to eat and have some tea, and he would come back in the next day. And if it was one of those days when he said, "No, not today," then the Jack would stay on the end of the console again. On the other hand, if he heard himself sounding good, then he would go through it in half an hour, and then he would be feeling really good and know that this was the day and do two or three songs in about two hours. He knew when he was ready to deliver and knew when he was wasting his time and running up the bill. He would just walk out the door. I was talking about how the other musicians were coming in at 2 P.M. clear-eyed. I never had to say anything to him because if he was going to try to sing tomorrow, whatever the hell he was doing, he would stop when he walked out that door, until the next day or two days later. Just a dead stop, because he knew he was not ready, and that was the kind of person he was.

Now Ronnie had two or three things going on in his mind. He had been asking me during the year between the live album and *Street Survivors* if I would help or teach him how to produce because he was working with two groups. One was Molly Hatchet, and the other was .38 Special. He used to say, "Donnie is a better writer than I am, and Johnny is a better singer than I am." Now, this is Ronnie talking about his brothers, and that's the way he felt about it. It just killed me when, after his demise, that Donnie is trying to sing and Johnny is trying to write because if he was alive, he would have punched them both out if you know what I mean! (Laughs). Because he said Donnie is the better writer and Johnny the better singer, but they switched hats and he is ready to kill them. That is not his game at all, or how he saw their careers.

Ronnie was an avid fisherman, and he used to love to get with Gary and Allen, and they all had bass boats on the St. John's River. Ronnie had said to me while we were doing the *Survivors* album that his next album was not going to be a Skynyrd album. He and Waylon Jennings, and Merle Haggard were going to make an album together. He asked me if I was interested and would I help him do it. I told him it would be my pleasure. That was the next endeavor. I could just imagine these three guys with their wry wisdom writing "Okie from Muskogee," or whatever. I could just imagine the three of them and what it would have been like, and I looked forward to doing that. It never materialized, but I thought, what an album that would be!

In the meantime, he was working with .38 and Molly Hatchet trying to get albums out of them. Ronnie was intelligent. He was belligerent or whatever you want—I don't care, I never had a problem with him. He and I would dispute on something, but we'd discuss it. One night at a band meeting, he said, "There are two people in this world that if I had an argument with, I won't hit!" And I knew who they were: Lacy and me. Other people giving him the same static he would have punched them out on the floor.

I wanted to ask you about the Marshall Tucker Band, I grew up in Spartanburg, South Carolina, around them, and I knew that you had worked with them at one point.

I worked with three of them on the *Dedicated* record, after Tommy Caldwell died. The only one that I worked with really was Toy because the other two were so far off the world that their feet never touched the floor. With Toy, I had good memory, contact, and communication.

What do you mean that their feet never touched the ground?

There was no way to communicate with them.

But you enjoyed working with Toy?

Oh, yes. Toy had a wicked sense of humor. Oh, God, he was so funny. I only had short contact with him for about one or two months, but he would say and do things, and then when I went back to the room to reflect on the day, I would realize what he was doing and think, "That son of a gun, now I just realized what he was saying or doing!" He was hilarious.

What ever happened to Thom Doucette?

Oh, he is still in the Sarasota [Florida] area and shows up once in awhile at Allman Brothers Shows and will play harp on "One Way Out," or "Southbound," or something like that. He is the one that I allowed onstage during the Fillmore recording, otherwise I would throw the rest of those guys out. Doucette went through a self-destruct problem and then went through recovery and has been a very conscientious, contributor, member of the society. He does blues jams and fundraisers and everything else in the

Sarasota area. He is a good guy and still there and very lucid, talks about it but would never go there again.

Is there anyone that you would personally like to see voted into the Rock and Roll Hall of Fame, and why would you name them?

Alright, this is the conversation that I had with someone the other day. Jessie Stone, and Jessie Stone is a name that nobody knows. He had another name Charles Calhoun. Last November would have been his 100th birthday. Jessie Stone was part black and part Indian. He had a touring band in the '20s and going through the West, Midwest, Northwest. He did big-band type things, a cross between Dixieland and big band. One of the songs that you hear a big band play and was popular during the '30s was "Idaho." That's a Jessie Stone composition. It was his theme song, and his wife was in his band—used to be one of the singers in his band. Evelyn is still alive, and she is about 86 or 87 years old and she still sings like a bird. She threw the 100th birthday party for their anniversary, and in her speech she said, "Jessie, you can tell by the audience and the fun we are having that I am not wasting your money!" It was a humbling thing. Jessie was the man who from 1949 or '50, until about 1955, did all the Atlantic Records with the Clovers, Ruth Brown, Laverne Baker, the Drifters, the Cardinals. With any of those artists it was a Jessie Stone arrangement and a Jessie Stone session. Let's see, "Momma, He Treats Your Daughter Mean," by Ruth Brown, that is a Jessie Stone chart and a Jessie Stone session. "Shake, Rattle, and Roll," was a Jessie Stone, but he wrote and put it under the name Charles Calhoun so he could switch it from [music licensing organizations] ASCAP to BMI. Jessie Stone is the history of American music before people knew about Benny Goodman or Andie Kurk and the Clouds of Joy; twenty years before them was Jessie Stone. You follow what I am saying? There has never been a flag lifted; nobody knows who's Jessie Stone and who's Charles Calhoun. If you knew what he contributed to American music, you would not ask.

Now, I'll give you the other one and you will gag on this one. They never voted me into it. This is the first time in seventeen years that they inducted people into the Hall of Fame that I did not have at least one that I worked with. Every other year they have inducted someone in that I either did the arrangements for, produced the session, or wrote one of the songs. I make jokes about it, and Ahmet and I were at the Grammys together back in February, and we giggled about it. I thought, if they do it posthumously then they are not going to like what my kids are going to tell them to do with the award. (Laughs)

(Laughs) That's ridiculous. You are the most prolific producer out there, and you have not been put in? That's just weird.
No, it's not weird. I can tell you, I told Jann Wenner off one day, and he blackballed me ever since. That is his pleasure, and if that makes him feel better, I really don't give a damn.

What did you do to make him mad?
I made him look like an asshole. He said, "We will put the Hall of Fame in Cleveland." At that time in 1989, 1990, I was on the advisory council for the Department of Commerce in the state of Florida. They did have then a Department of Commerce. I had called Ahmet up, and I said, "Hey, Ahmet, I have a good deal for you; we can put the Hall of Fame in Orlando in between Disney and Universal so on rainy days people will have a place to go." In Cleveland, they are talking about raising a 40 million dollars bond. I said, Ahmet, remember the comedian W.C. Fields? He had a joke about Philadelphia. He was from Philadelphia. He would say, "Alright, we are going to have a contest tonight and the first prize is one week in Philadelphia, and the second prize is two weeks in Philadelphia." (Laughs). I said to Ahmet, "You are not going to get anyone to go to Cleveland from Columbus Day to the Fourth of July because the weather is insane there." I said, if you give me thirty to sixty days, I will get Universal, Disney, and the state of Florida to put it up down here and you will make more money on a rainy day than you will in Cleveland for one year. Jann Wenner said, "Allan Freed started in Cleveland, and Florida has nothing to do with rock and roll!" I told him he was a jackass, and had his head up his ass. That's it.

Florida would have made sense to me.
Jann is a good businessman, and that has nothing to do with intelligence.

And it doesn't have anything to do with rock and roll either.
No, nothing. I am pretty sure every time my name comes up that guy is shooting me down. I really don't care.

Well, you are in the GRITZ Hall of Fame, if that is any consolation. You were one of the first ones voted in!

I appreciate it, and it is quite flattering. Hey, you have got a friend of mine living up in that neck of the woods named Bill Simpson. I know he records out of a studio in North Carolina, but I feel like he is still living in South Carolina. He only did Bob Seger for about four or five albums and then *Hotel California*, what else do you want?

I bet Jimmy Johnson can tell me where he lives. Jimmy worked on all those Seger albums.

Bill Simpson was there. He is a good guy and has a wild sense of humor but very straight ahead.

I'll check into all that. Will you comment on the loudness of the music the way the kids play it today. I did not know what you would say about it, but what really gets on my nerves is the music today is played so loud that is rattles the windows in their cars. How do you feel about it? I have talked to so many people from the '60s and '70s that have had hearing loss, can you say anything to us about that?

I do lectures in the high schools, colleges, and engineering schools down here. I have started a campaign with the hearing foundation. The thing is that you are born with five senses. You learn hot from cold whether you put your hand on a hot stove or an ice cube, or you get burned, you learn the hot from cold. You are born with a sense of taste and you know salt from pepper and ice cream from whatever, you cultivate taste. Then you learn odors and how to detect something that is burning or dangerous that is this or that. Then in preschool, the teacher gives you crayons and tells you to color the Easter egg orange and you pick up the blue crayon and she says, "No, this is the orange crayon." So you learn hand to eye coordination. Everybody is talking to you, and they presume that your ears are working. No one has ever taught anybody how to employ their ears or how to protect them. The people that you can best learn from on this are the handicapped people, and these are the people that we don't pay any attention to. People like Ray Charles and Stevie Wonder see with their ears. They literally see with their ears. If we stood for two hours a day with our eyes closed listening to what was going on around us, then we might better understand how to use and appreciate our ears. People do not know how to employ their ears. They have no idea. They do not realize that as they listen at those high levels they are doing permanent damage. Eyes, you can get glasses for, laser surgery, or cataract surgery, all those things that can restore your eyes or get them closer to what they were when you were younger, but there is nothing that will help the ears. Once you have injured that nerve and established tinnitus, your hearing starts to go down. People don't know, and they don't realize it, that the rest of their life is at stake. They just cut themselves off.

Give me your thoughts of the state of rock and roll in the twenty-first century.
Well, I will give you an example. I was at a magnet school lunching with the children that aspire to do art of all kinds. They called me up and asked me to give a talk on Muddy Waters and blues artists, and I said, "Oh, that's right down my alley." So we had records to listen to with Leadbelly or Muddy Waters, and then I played them a couple of things. People today think that all blues are twelve bars, but if you listen to Muddy, some were thirteen and some were fifteen because he had a story to tell, and he didn't want to change the melody until he finished the sentence. I wanted to relate to them grammatically and poetically and why all Muddy Waters's songs are not 4/4 or 2/4. Then we took a break. Then we watched some videos that showed white people picking cotton and black people picking cotton and songs that the white people sang and songs that the black people sang. Here's the Methodist church and the Baptist church, the black church. Then I fielded a couple of dumb questions and this and that, and all of a sudden I had a kid about sixteen years old stand up, a boy, and he looked at me and said, "I thoroughly enjoyed it, and now I finally understand where some of those things come from." Then he asked, "What blues do we have to write about today?"

I looked at the kid and he stopped me right in my tracks. This kid probably rode to school in a BMW and has a cell phone, and he is asking me what blues does he have to write about, think about it, society has changed so much. There are still people suffering and being hurt, but they are finding other ways to express themselves besides that standard 8/12 church form that we know, but it is not a concerted effort that everybody accepts everywhere in the world. More and more the dancers are taking over the music business. I can not think of a rap record that will be remembered ten years from now, but they will dance to it. There is a social change, and words do not mean as much as they did thirty or forty years ago.

I had an interesting conversation with Kid Rock at the Grammys. I am not a fan of the way he is being merchandised or some of his music, but when I had a conversation with him, I realized that there was a lot of depth to him.

He loves a lot of good music.
Oh, I can not tell you how deep that man is intellectually, conversationally, and observationally. He knows what the hell he is talking about. The way they are selling him is something else, just trash.

I don't think that is really him. Just image.
Yeah, but there is depth to that young man. I am just thinking, I wonder if he survives the pressure they have put him under, how will he mature? What is he going to come off with next? He is a deep thinker and writer, and I never thought of it, but when I sat with him at Atlantic Records table, he ran things by me that made me think. Wow, he's no dummy!

I hear he is a die-hard fan of Skynyrd, Allman Brothers, etcetera, and all the things you have done, R&B and everything. He can sing, and write, and sing a ballad.
Yeah, listening to a record you think, get that damn stuff off. Having a cross-table conversation with him, I realize that I am biased and wrong and must reassess this situation. This guy has something going. I gained a great deal of respect for him.

I would like to see him do a good rock album and leave all that hip-hop behind for a minute, but I know that is what is selling for him.
Yeah, that's paying his rent and car.

Do you have a favorite album that you worked on?
People always ask me what's your favorite album, who are your favorite artists? I just look at them and say let's go by decades. I can't go through the '50s and omit Ray Charles, Joe Turner, the Modern Jazz Quartet, or John Coltrane. So argue with me. What do I do with Bobby Darrin? What do I do with the Drifters, Aretha, or Cream? And you go by decades, so ask me what's your favorite album? I just had a little angel on my shoulder wherever the hell I went, that's what it amounts to.

Thanks so much for this interview and answering all of our questions. I appreciate your honesty.

Something I learned when I was a physicist, and it was by accident: Don't ever be afraid to be wrong. Even if you make a mistake someone learns from it. Even if I say something wrong, somebody has to take me to task on it. If we all agreed, there would never be any progress. Difference is what causes progress. I am not afraid to put it out there, and if someone differs, fine, I am willing to learn.

Tom Dowd passed away on 27 October 2002, one week after his 77th birthday. He will never be forgotten.

Galadrielle Allman

June 2013

Talk about a labor of love. Duane Allman's daughter Galadrielle has gotten together with famed reissue producer Bill Levinson to create *Skydog: The Duane Allman Retrospective*, the finest tribute ever to her dad's music. Of course, it took her twenty years to see the dream come to fruition, but as the old adage goes, "it was worth the wait." The seven-disc set features the very finest, and often rarest, recordings of the Allman Brothers Band founder.

I spoke with Galadrielle about her dad, his music, and the new boxed set in this exclusive telephone interview.

❦

I know you were really young when Duane died. Were you old enough to have any memories of him?

I was two, so I really don't have any memories of him, which is sad. That's one of the reasons the music has been so important to me. You know I'm working on a book about him, and I've spent the last few years talking to his friends and talking to the family about him. You know his mother is still alive, and talking with Gregory, I have been trying to piece together the story for myself.

Speaking of, how is Mama A. doing?

She's doing great. She's going to be 96 in July, and she is as sharp as ever. She has no major medical issues, which is like a miracle.

Are you close to your Uncle Gregg?

Yeah, I am, actually. We've gotten closer and closer since I've gotten older. We try to spend as much time together as we can. I go to see the shows at the Beacon every year, and that's kind of a big hang time. And we try to get together for Thanksgiving, and it's been a couple of years since I made Christmas, but I try to do that too.

Your cousin Devon is really doing well these days. Any thoughts on Devon Allman? He's really burning it up these days.

He really is! I sent him a boxed set, and I'm waiting for him to send me *Turquoise*. (Laughs) I haven't heard it yet, but I've heard really great things about it. I was talking to Gregory about it when I was in New York in March, and he is so proud of him. Devon has been playing and woodshedding [going off to practice] for years, and it really does look like he's had that breakthrough moment. He's a fine, fine player, and he's got a great voice. I'm so proud of Devon, and he's a sweetheart of a man, which is almost as important in this industry.

Let's talk about the *Skydog* boxed set. Seven CDs. What drove you guys to create this massive set?

Well, it's a tribute to Duane. The amount of music he played and the variety of projects he did really deserved to be looked through. Many fans don't know much about him beyond the Allman Brothers and Derek and the Dominos, but it goes so much deeper than that. And I wanted to have the space to tell the story properly. From his early bands, playing Yardbirds songs with Gregg, going out there and playing club dates right out of high school—it was that drive and focus that Duane had that caused him to amass such a large number of sessions. That kind of humbled me. And it's just so great to have it all in one place and to show how hard he worked. It's very powerful to listen to it all together. It's almost like each disc is a different genre of American music.

We started this project, Bill Levinson and I, probably twenty years ago. I was just out of college. It got shelved for a variety of reasons, most of them logistical. While it was on the shelf going through all the processes, the market really changed, and box sets fell out of favor, and it really just got left behind. Then at the fortieth anniversary shows at the Beacon, which were dedicated to my dad, I talked to Bill, and I told him I was writing, and there was just a sense that the time was right. The Brothers label wasn't interested, so we took it to Rounder, and they got behind us right away.

How was it for you, working on this project from a father-daughter aspect?

It's emotional for sure, and it's humbling. In one way I'm really driven to find out as much about my dad as possible, and I am really aware of the need to pursue it actively. It's not going to just fall into your lap. I want to hear all of it; I want to read everything I can about him; I want to talk to all his friends—all of that has been a huge growing experience for me. It has been bittersweet, because you see him getting better and better every year, and then it ends. You know? The story only ever ends one way, and it's a heartbreaker. But his music really does hold so much of him, his talent and emotion. In that way, I feel like he isn't lost. And it's good to have it out there because he inspires so many people. A lot of these songs were on 45s and vinyl, and there was no other way to find them, so it's great that the music can be out there for people who have never heard it. It's what he dedicated his life to. That's the lesson for me; he was a really down-to-earth American character. He was a self-made person, and really excelled remarkably early on.

What was it like working with producer Bill Levinson?
Bill is a pleasure. He really carried a lot of the weight. He was absolutely the hero and the champion of this whole project. I helped a lot with the booklet and the photographs, and helped choose the songs, but for the most part, Bill did all the heavy lifting. He is a purist and a historian, and he has such a respect for my father, he was willing to take the time and do it right.

There are so many treasures here. I was especially blown away by the Delaney & Bonnie material, with the live banter between Duane and Delaney.
I live for that. I love it.

I think Delaney was like Duane. Those guys were the conduit that connected all the other musicians together.
I agree. I don't think Delaney & Bonnie get near the credit they deserve.

I signed a petition to get them into the Rock and Roll Hall of Fame.
Absolutely.

Do you have any particular tracks that stand out as your favorites?
There's a lot of them. I love the Delaney & Bonnie things. I loved hearing "Sugar Magnolia" with him. And the old stuff, it's amazing how that music holds up. And I love "Please Be with Me," the Cowboy song.

Oh, yeah. One of my own all-time favorite songs.

It really is so beautiful, and I love hearing him play that way. It's pretty hard to find a track that isn't moving and special in some way. I think he had a really unique way of interacting with the strong singers, so his recordings with all of those R&B singers are just amazing. And "Loan Me a Dime" will always stand as one of the greatest guitar solos ever. I love all the Johnny Jenkins stuff, that New Orleans groove. So, yeah, there a lot of moments to be proud of. He covered a lot of ground. But I'm like you. I think the Delaney and Bonnie stuff is the cornerstone of the whole thing because he loved both of them and loved playing with them. They were coming from a similar place of playing because they had a passion for it like he did.

Yeah. And they had so many great musicians come through their ranks, everybody wanted to play with them.
And most people don't realize that the Dominos were Delaney & Bonnie's band. Eric credits Delaney with teaching him how to sing. They were at the crossroads of so much great American music. And it's interesting, today, Derek Trucks and Susan Tedeschi cite them as the inspiration for their band.

I really like the choices in packaging. What compelled you to put his guitar case on the cover?
I think Rounder was originally considering doing a road case, like the ones on the *At Fillmore East* album cover, but I had seen that done before a lot, even with the Brothers, they had packaged things like that a few times. The guitar case belongs to the guitar in the Rock and Roll Hall of Fame, the cherry sunburst. I just thought it would be different, and they did such a great job following through with it. I mean, you open it up and there's a picture of the guitar in it. It's lined in red velvet like the guitar case, and there's a replica of Duane's guitar pick. And the CDs are housed in guitar string packets. I just know Duane would love it, because that's what he loved, that guitar. That's where his focus was. He wasn't about images or pictures of himself or being a show boat. That was his tool, you know? I just love it, and I think it's got a good vibe. The case is so beat up, it kind of tells you what his life was like—a lot of travel-wear. And the guitar itself is so gorgeous. I really do think that he had one of the most beautiful Les Paul's I have ever seen.

I have heard that there's a very limited run on the boxed set. Will there be more coming?

I am actually going to L.A. next month to talk to them about that. They know that there are a lot of people who wanted it but didn't get it. But we need to do something different because this was a limited edition collector's set, and we don't want to punish the people who bought it right away because they thought they were getting a collector's item, but there's got to be some way to make it slightly different, or do something else. I just don't think we had any idea what to expect when we put it out.

Have you received any feedback from members of the Allman Brothers Band?

They have been so supportive and so moved by it. I think I finally got a seat at the big kids' table. (Laughs) Because I really am still a kid to them in some ways, so they were like, "Oh, you did good." Gregg had actually seen some of the design stuff back before it came out, and he was just blown away by it. I went to see him do his solo show in Napa, and he was really excited about it.

After helping put together the excellent tribute to her father's music, Galadrielle published her first book, Please Be With Me: A Song for My Father, *to critical acclaim. (It's a must-read for any fan of the Brothers or music history in general.)*

Bonnie Bramlett

Spring 2008

Bonnie Bramlett is the true Queen of Southern Rock. An honest to goodness soul singer if ever there was one, Bonnie has performed and recorded with the best of the best, not the least of which was her former husband and singing partner Delaney Bramlett, along with Duane Allman, Gram Parsons, George Harrison, John Lennon and Yoko Ono, Little Feat, the Allman Brothers Band, Dave Mason, Charlie Daniels, Eric Clapton, Joe Cocker—and that's just the tip of the iceberg. She has recorded a stack of truly great albums with Delaney as well as solo, and has lent her voice to hundreds of albums, including one by yours truly.

This year, Bonnie has released what may be her best album ever. Now I realize that's a tall order, but just have a listen and then we'll talk. The CD is called *Beautiful*, and it is.

We caught up with Bonnie to talk about her new release, working with Johnny Sandlin again and acting with Kevin Costner.

☙

You guys couldn't have picked a better title for your new album than *Beautiful*. I mean, it is just that, and you are too.

Oh, thank you honey. That means so much to me. I really got to embrace the songwriters on this one, Buff. There are none of my songs on there. They are all just incredible songwriters.

How was it working with Johnny Sandlin again?

Well, I worked with him through the years on other people's stuff, like Walter, Jr., and stuff. Of course we were wanting to do a project, but it just didn't come up. Then it came into the universe, and it all just fell together. And Johnny and I work absolutely great together. I mean, I believe in him as a producer like I believe in God. He can do anything. (Laughs) I mean, those horn lines prove it don't they?

Who picked the musicians that played on the record?

Well, Johnny did. We got together, and he said, wouldn't it be good if we could get David Hood and Spooner Oldham and all those, and I said, "Yeah, get all the boys!" And they all just flocked it. I mean they came a-runnin' honey. They were ready to play. And we just whipped that CD out, truthfully. I was in the session three times, two to cut tracks and one to do master vocals. And then he overdubbed the background vocals with Bekka and with Scott Boyer, and then he did the horns, and the slide guitar and all. You know, he's a producer and I'm a singer. I let him do his job and he lets me do mine, and we do real good together that way. (Laughs) You know what I mean?

For sure. He's the best. How did you choose which songs to cut?
Well, for instance, "Some of My Best Friends," that song I've been trying to cut for ten years. When I first came to Nashville, I was in a meeting with the songwriter Gary Cotton, and I said play me your baby. Play me the one nearest to your heart that probably won't ever get cut. So he played me "Some of My Best Friends," and I went to the ground. I said, I want to cut this so bad. And nobody would touch it with a ten-foot pole. So when me and Johnny got together, I said, hey John, do you want to take a risk? He said, well I will if you will. So we decided to do it, and Johnny suggested "For What it's Worth." So we had those two. And then "Beautiful" was just in a stack. I didn't know the writer before, but Johnny submitted a file with his songs and "Beautiful" was on it, and I went, oh God, I can eat this one alive! (Laughing) This is like raw meat to me. That and "It's Gonna Rain All Night." I was in Heaven."

When I first heard "Some of My Best Friends" I thought you had written it.
Well, I must be doing my job because if I can make you think I wrote it then it must be coming from my gut and soul. That's great.

It sounds like your philosophy.
It is! When I first heard it my heart embraced it. I thought, I couldn't have said that better myself. I feel that from the marrow of my bones. When I sang it at [South by Southwest Music Festival] in Austin, it just came out, Buffalo, I swear it, I sang, "Some of my best friends are gone, I'm thinkin' about Stevie Ray Vaughan." I brought the house down. I swear to God it was not planned. It was totally channeled.

Do you have any personal favorites on the album?
Well, I loved "Witness for Love" because I got to sing with Randall Bramblett, and doesn't he have a sexy voice? It's hot. And of course I like "My Strongest Weakness," my kid and Gary Nicholson wrote that. And I like "Shake Something Loose," that's another Randall Bramblett song. Those are the up-tempo songs. But really I'm going with "I Do Believe," that one makes me cry. And "Some of My Best Friends." And I love "Bless 'Em All, Y'all." But I'm glad I ended with the Dan Penn song, "He'll Take Care of You," because it's a spiritual. It's a different kind of spiritual. My spirituality comes from a Christian basis because that's what I was taught, but I believe in many different spiritual beliefs. So my expression is a little different than the average. (Laughs)

It don't matter which road you take as long as you arrive at the right place.
That's right! Bless 'em all, y'all.

I love your rendition of the Stephen Stills song ["For What It's Worth"]. Do you feel it's a good time to revive that one? I sure do.
It's perfect. Look what's going on it the world. Stop, children, what's that sound? It's the same thing as in the Sixties, except our young ones are not as willing to step up like we were. Of course, we had better drugs than they do. Their drugs are killing them right away. Before they can do anything. I'm sorry. That sounds awful, but it's true.

I was looking at your résumé online. You've sung on so many great albums from Joe Cocker, to Eric Clapton, Little Feat—I have to admit it was a rush to see my name in the credits.
(Laughing loudly) Oh, yeah! I love it. I love what we did. That was great fun, and the duet was great. ["I Don't Want to Say Goodbye," *Southern Lights*, Michael Buffalo Smith]

Well, thank you. It was sure an honor for me. You sure sang on a ton of records.
I always say I'm like cow shit in Texas, you can dang near find me anywhere.

How did you feel about working with your daughter Bekka again on this album?

Oh, honey, I just love working with her. She's so good. It's not just because she's my kid. She's just amazing. But I didn't give birth to no princess, honey, I had another queen.

I saw several albums on there I didn't know you sang on, like John Lennon's *Some Time in New York City*.

We were on "War is Over if You Want it" with John and Yoko.

And one album I loved back in the '80s was Hank Williams, Jr's, *Born to Boogie*.

Oh, yeah! Let me tell you something cool. I sang "Honky Tonk Women" with Hank on that album, and later on Bekka sang the same song with Travis Tritt. How cool is that? They should be back-to-back somewhere.

And you sang on a Public Image Limited album with Johnny [Rotten] Lydon?

I just went crazy on that one. It was fun. And I just recorded on the new John Oates [Hall and Oates] album with Bekka. It's coming out, and it's going to be great. And I really enjoyed working with Shooter Jennings on his album.

I haven't had a chance to talk to you much since *The Guardian*. How was that, working with Kevin Costner and Ashton Kutcher?

I love the acting. I love the whole process. The dialog I had, I meant it from the bottom of my heart. I was the perfect vehicle for that character. And I learned so much from Costner. He was always showing me things like how to not let somebody get in my light. But I don't go out reading for parts. People call me up and say "will you do it." Because I'm not good with rejection. (Laughs) I can't go audition. That's all ego, I know, but what can I say?

We just thought that the monologue you did at the bar with Kevin was just so like you, it was almost like you wrote it.

Well, I meant it. I didn't go upstairs and lie down with that man, but I am proud of every wrinkle in my face. I laid under Hawaiian suns, Palm

Beach—I mean, I may have had a rough life, but it was in a limo. (Laughing) So don't cry for me, Argentina.

Do you have any other movie projects lined up?
Well, you know, the director Andrew Davis has a project that is in his heart, and he is trying to make it manifest, and you know, you have to look for money and all that. That's the only one I'm thinking of on the horizon. I don't go out and hustle the bushes you know, but a hit record wouldn't hurt.

I think you have one, for sure. What's the most important thing in life?
Education. I mean, it's important to be a nice person, and da da da—but that's all taken for granted, do the right thing and blah blah blah. But if you're going to be in any kind of business, just know how to count your own money, okay? And keep track of where it is. You can't do that without an education, especially if you've never had any money. People who know how to keep their money will take your money. They know you don't know how to handle it. Just be able to handle your own success. That's brilliant. I just made that up. (Laughs)

Johnny Sandlin

Spring 2004

You can find his name in the credits of almost any Capricorn Records release from the 1970s—Johnny Sandlin, the remarkable producer, engineer, and musician who worked on many of the classic Allman Brothers Band releases, as well as countless others. We spoke with Johnny about his band the Hour Glass, working for Capricorn Records, and what he has been up to lately.

∽

How did you first get into the Hour Glass with Gregg and Duane?
Well, I was in a band called the Five Men-its with Eddie Hinton, Paul Hornsby, and I think at the time Fred Styles was playing bass. Anyway, we were playing, and we had heard of them—I guess at the time everyone in Florida had heard of them through the grapevine. We were doing a gig at this little place, kind of out of the way and right off the beach. It was a little Spanish village with a patio outside and a club inside. They had booked the Allman Joys for the patio, which usually attracted more kids. We were playing mainly for the sailors because Pensacola is mainly a navy town. That was the first place that I met them. We kind of kept in touch with them after that because they were the best guitar player and singer that I had ever heard. I had met Bob Keller who was the bass player.

But anyway, we all stayed in touch. Eddie Hinton decided to leave the band and go to Muscle Shoals and do session work, and that left us without a guitar player and singer. Eddie was both in our band. We called Gregg and them to see if they would help us find some people. In the interim, they sent Pete Carr up here, and we were going to start a band with him, but we never found a singer that worked out for us. We later got a call from them saying that their band had broken up and let's get together and jam and see what we could come up with. So they came up here to Decatur. We got together and rehearsed in our garage. So that's how we got together.

Were you in the Hour Glass the whole time they were together?
Yes.

Didn't they have another bass player called "the Wolf?"
Yes. Mabron McKinney, and we called him the Wolf because of his beard. I did leave one thing out, Fred Styles our bass player dropped out of our band the Men-its, and I am leaving lots of stuff out. Lots of things happened. When the Men-its came up here to rehearse before going out on the road, Fred left and went on to film school and we hired Mabron for the band. When we talked with Gregg later about joining forces, it was Paul, and me, and Mabron joining with Gregg and Duane.

It was later on that Mabron left and Pete came in on bass, right?
Well, when Mabron first left, Bob Keller came back and he played bass for a while. I don't remember how long, maybe for several months, and then he left on very sudden notice or without any notice actually. He just didn't show up for a gig. We were playing at the Whiskey, which was one of our big main shows out there [in Los Angeles]. Pete had been hanging with Duane and staying with Duane. Pete was the guitar player, but he had to change over to bass for a while. After Bob Keller left, Pete played with us until the band broke up.

Now, that clarifies something for me because two or three years ago I did an interview with Wolf and he had said that a lot of people had said that he was the one that left y'all quickly one night, but it was not him, it was the other guy?
Yeah, it was Bob Keller. We were thinking he might have killed himself or something, just to be blunt. We lived right across the street from where that HOLLYWOOD sign is. You see it in all the movies. We could go up behind the huge letters and look out over the city, and we thought he may have gone up there and jumped or something. I don't think we actually heard from him for about six months. We didn't know if he was alive or dead or what.

Did he ever say why he disappeared?
(Laughs) It's a funny thing because I was sitting in my apartment one day and the phone rings and it's Bob Keller saying, "Hey man, what are you doing?" (Laughs) Well, we are still waiting for you Bob. You missed a date didn't you? At that time I wanted him to be okay, and I was angry that he had left us. I thought he was my friend and didn't know if he was dead or

what. Anyway, that's my Bob Keller story. Things just didn't work out with him.

I wanted to ask you if there was any single story about the Hour Glass that sticks out in your mind as far as the things that you guys did. You got to play at the Fillmore didn't you?
Oh, yeah, we opened for Buffalo Springfield, and actually played on a show with the Doors, and at the Whiskey, Janis [Joplin] sat in with us. Eric Burdon and Paul Butterfield too. Anyone that heard the band fell in love with Duane and Gregg both, and they thought that they were great, which they certainly should have.

I am jumping all over the board here in this interview…
(Laughs) Well, I am pretty disjointed so just go ahead.

I feel like anything before today is fair game. I wanted to ask you about Capricorn and how you came to hook up with them in the beginning.
Well, before I was at Capricorn, I had a job in Miami and there was this studio there owned by Henry Stone. It was just a small, very small, four-track studio upstairs above one of the warehouses. Tone was a huge record distributor in Miami. They were extremely large—that was where the record stores got their albums. I played drums on demos, and Eddie helped me get that job. He introduced me to Steve Alamo, who was one of the people in charge along with Henry Stone and Brad Shapiro, the producer. I think that my very first session was playing on a single that was Betty Wright and Steve Alamo doing a duet. And at that time was a risky thing, black and white artists performing together. It was a neat thing.

Anyway, while I was down there, Phil had meanwhile started his studio in Georgia. That was in late 1969. He wanted to hire a studio band and do a Stax thing. That was my whole idea, you put a rhythm section together and work every day and get tight and put a distinctive sound together for your studio and your artists. That is exactly what I wanted to do, and Phil called me while I was working at Tone and asked if I was interested in working up there. I thought about it, but I felt like I was doing okay, and I liked my job there. In the meantime, the Allman Brothers had gone up there and signed a contract, and Duane called and asked me to come up and said that we could all do music together again. I took a trip up there, and when I was going home through Macon it just felt right. I loved the town, and it is one of the few towns I get around in easily without getting lost. So I came home and went from being out of work for six months to being offered about three or four jobs at one time. I was fortunate. I went back to Tone and put in my notice and moved up to Macon.

Did you start out at Capricorn straight away as a producer, engineer, or a musician?
My deal with Phil was that I wanted to produce and play on records, and we had agreed that I could produce and play the drums. I reserved the right to produce at a future date. Some of the first things that we worked on were demos with Jackie Avery. We did that for a while, and then Phil wanted to cut a record with Johnny Jenkins. Before that I guess the first thing was that I played on some Swamp Dog stuff that I love to this day. Then I got to do a couple of singles with Arthur Conley, who was someone that Phil managed at the time. Another reason that Macon appealed to me was I was a huge Otis Redding fan, and I loved everything he did. I had every record and even had worn them out. I knew that Phil had managed him and a lot of the acts. Phil was involved heavily with acts from Muscle Shoals.

One person I have been thinking about a lot lately is Tom Dowd. I did an interview with him just before he died, and I saw his documentary that is coming out, and it is absolutely awesome. I wanted to ask you as someone that had worked with him if you could tell me a little about him?
I knew a lot about Tom before I met him. He was always the man you wanted to see, and I knew a lot about Atlantic Records. I had bought every record that they had put out since I was teenager. You see the names on records and credits, and I knew who he was. Then when I got involved with sessions, I knew who Jerry Wexler and Tom Dowd were. He was the ultimate engineer in blues and rock and roll. I met him for the first time when the Brothers began work on *Idlewild South* record. I had done demos on them for most of those songs. He came to Macon to re-record some things, and I thought that I was supposed to be a part of that session. This was actually my most embarrassing moment. I guess as old as I am it's okay to tell this. (Laughs)

Phil and Frank at Capricorn told me that they wanted me to produce the second Allman Brothers album. Prior to this I had done production on the Johnny Jenkins album and been a critical success and sold records, but it didn't get lots of record sales. Then I did an Alex Taylor record. I had some demos on all or most of all the songs, "Statesboro Blues," "Elizabeth Reed," and lots of songs on that album. So they wanted me to do it and then felt like they needed Tom to come in and oversee it because he had more experience. We would do it together. That's how it was put to me, and it was never put that way to Tom. So when Tom came in to produce the album, in my head I was there to co-produce the album with him. I didn't know until the end of the first day when I was trying to discuss things with him, which you would do if you were a co-producer but you wouldn't do it as a bystander. He didn't seem interested in what I had to say. I felt like it was strange. Then at the end of the session I think it was Gregg who said that Phil had decided that Tom should do the record, and I felt like the biggest ass in the whole world. I had never been told that I would not be involved in it until I had made a fool of myself. Here was my first introduction. You could imagine, here is my hero, and he felt like I was an asshole, but I had not done anything that I really knew was wrong. That was the story.

Did you do anything else together with him?

I did play on some sessions for him, and I mixed a lot of stuff for him. Then I did a Cowboy album, and when I produced it I took it to Miami and he mixed it for me and I was able to watch and learn a lot from him. Then on the *Eat A Peach* album when they had finished recording it, or just about finished it, Tom had another project, and I went in and mixed and did some of the overdubs on it. So we worked together, apart.

You know when you go down to Macon now, it is hard for me to imagine seeing all of my heroes hanging out and eating at Mama Louise's and recording at Capricorn. Could you tell me a little bit about what it was like to work in the studio down there in the heyday?

Every day you never knew what would happen, and it was usually something wonderful. It seemed like as the days passed more and more people were getting interested in the music, and it was getting more recognition. One of my favorite things was when Jeff Beck came in there and he was looking to put a band together, and I think that was where he hooked up with Jimmy Hall. Jimmy ended up on some of Jeff's records. I was down there to record the rehearsals for several days. We would go see bands at night. When the Brothers were home, they would be at Grant's Lounge or sitting in somewhere, or there would be a bunch of us going out to jam. Boz

Scaggs lived there for a while, and Berry Oakley. I would go out and jam at clubs. There was always something happening, and we could get into all kinds of trouble.

I guess I have most of the Capricorn albums that came out at that time, and I love reading the liner notes and credits. I love the camaraderie and brotherhood of those musicians playing on each other's albums.

It was wonderful because Duane would just stop by and ask if we needed him to play on anything. He would just drive by, and he would stay if there was something going on. The studio was sort of a meeting place or hang out for a lot of people, it was so centrally located, and we had a lounge area up there where people could sit and stuff. It was a good-sized studio.

Dick Cooper said that there were astrological charts cast for recording in Muscle Shoals at times. Did you ever see any of that going on in Capricorn studio?

No, I think that we were interested in astrology but I don't remember it being used in reference to recording times.

Why did they name the label Capricorn?

It was because Jerry Wexler and Phil Walden were both Capricorns.

Now, can you give me a few words on some of these people in your life? Beginning with Duane Allman.

He was one of the most interesting, exciting, and alive people that I ever knew. He was one of the most intelligent as well. Most of the time he was great to be around, and he was so dedicated to music, and it was a central thing in our lives. It was that way with [Oakley] Berry too. Whenever anyone played with Duane, he would bring out the best in them. Not that it was a competition, but he was an inspiration. He was one of the best that there ever was.

What about brother Gregg?

I love Gregg very much. I enjoyed working with him at times, and then there were times that I would have never put myself through if I had known what it was gonna be like. I hear that he is doing well now, and I sure am glad. I do love him to death, and I have known him since we were seventeen eighteen years old. He sings as well as anyone when he is on, and he has a huge voice. He always did. When we were rehearsing with the Hour Glass we did a bunch of blues-based stuff, and his voice was as good as it ever got. It was strong, convincing, and real. He is not a prolific writer, but when he writes, he is talented. One classic song is better than fifty that don't get out there. (Laughs)

How about Bonnie Bramlett?
She is the best white female singer out there, and the best that there ever was. The first time I saw her live was at that thing at A&R Studios in New York where Duane was playing with Delaney & Bonnie. That was such a great performance for them. When that was over, I went back there and told Phil to please sign Bonnie Bramlett because I wanted to produce her and work with her. Finally, it came about that he did, and I thought the world of her then, and she has gotten even better today. I can't say enough about her. I love her to death.

Eddie Hinton?
He was a buddy of mine from way back in the Five Men-its, and we both loved the Stax music and got along so well. We both loved Otis, and it is obvious because of the way Eddie ended up singing. We kind of both came to love Otis from different directions, and the love of that and Muscle Shoals, and the music coming out of there was just "our music." I loved being on the road with him. He was crazy as hell at times. We used to take two cars and a trailer, and no one would drive with him because he would be driving in the winter in Illinois with the windows rolled down. He would scream to rough up his voice so it would have that growl to it. (Laughs) I could hear him screaming or singing when I drove up beside him. He was also the best producer that I have ever seen, and he knew how to work with musicians in the studio. He had lots of ideas and brought the best out of the other players. He was just a great singer and songwriter and guitar player. He did a version of "Sha-Na Boom Boom" that was one of the finest records that has ever been done.

Here's one out of left field for you. Didn't you produce the Gregg and Cher album? Tell me a little bit about Cher.
I felt kind of strange going out there because she has this reputation of being a big movie star, and there was all this controversy around the disputes of her and Gregg through the tabloids. She was as nice as she could be to

me. I really enjoyed working with her. It was a crazy time, and Gregg doesn't like studios. I don't think he gets along with them real well. They were having their good and bad days, and their bad days were bad for everyone. Gregg would end up disappearing, and I would end up taking her home after the sessions and dropping her off at her place and stuff, and she was always super nice and good to work with. I was proud that I got to meet her. Then a few years later when I was on the road with Delbert (McClinton), I would run into her again. She was always super nice to me and treated everyone around her very well.

Lots of people wondered if that album would be a good match between Gregg and Cher. If you listen to it, you find out it is a pretty good record, you know.

There are some things on it that are good. I will have to get that out and hear it again soon. A funny story that Bill Stewart told me because he was playing in the band—they were preparing to go to Japan, and Cher came in and wanted Gregg to learn a Doobie Brothers song to sing with her. I just thought that was so funny. I don't even have a comment on it, and don't really know what it means, but it struck me as very funny.

How about Colonel Bruce Hampton?
I just talked to him a few nights ago.

He is a fun guy to talk to. We love him.
I didn't get to know him real well until 1991, before the Aquarium Rescue Unit album, and it was about the time when I was doing Widespread Panic. I met him way back in '69, and in Chastain Park in Atlanta he was playing with the Grease Band, and to be honest with you at that time he scared me a little bit. A lot of it is not true, but you heard lots of shocking stuff about him, kind of like Ozzy [Osbourne] biting off the bat's head, not quite to that extent, but things that were shocking for that time. I never got to know him very well then, but in '91 we got to know each other, and he is a great guy. His heart is with the music. He knows what is good and who is good. That band, the Aquarium Rescue Unit would not be who they were without Bruce.

Anybody that Bruce gets together with ends up being extremely good. Like the Codetalkers—who he is with now—they are just awesome. Before

that, Derek Trucks was one of the guys he worked with, and Oteil, and of course Jimmy Herring is in the Dead now.

Yeah, he keeps them real. The Aquarian Rescue Unit was as good a band as has ever been. They had the joy of the music and spread the good feelings around. Every one of them were great, and Bruce kept them from going off the edge, you know, into stuff only musicians and Martians could understand. (Laughs)

I grew up in Spartanburg, South Carolina, around Marshall Tucker Band, and I wanted to know if you had any dealings at all with Toy or any of those guys?

Of course, I went to see them when they first came to audition with Phil, and they played at Grant's Lounge, and they would come in there and say, "Mr. Walden," and, "Mr. Sandlin" (Laughs) and I don't know if anybody had ever called me that before. They were just such nice and decent guys. I did some demos with them, and then Paul [Hornsby] did some better demos with them that got them signed. Toy was great. I used to love when we were doing some of the Cowboy albums—and there were several that he played steel on—he was just great to work with. Most of my dealings were with him. I remember going skeet shooting with him one day, and he was right-handed and left-eyed. They had this weird shotgun that had a cutaway stock, and he could put the gun up to his right shoulder and move his head through where he was looking down the barrel with his left eye. It was a weird situation. (Laughs) He was a good player. Great guy.

One of my best all-time favorite albums was *Highway Call*. Tell me a little bit about that album and what it was like working with Dickey Betts and Vassar Clements and everybody?

I loved working on that album because it was slightly offbeat from what we were doing up until then. Dickey had written all these great songs for it, and I got to know him well over this album because we would sit around in my office after recording sessions and play stuff. I had just gotten turned on to Billy Joe Shaver. He had the *Honky Tonk Heroes* album, and we would listen to it almost every night. When we finished sessions at two or three in the morning, we would go listen to music and strum guitars all the rest of the night until daylight. I loved doing it, and having the band with Vassar, John Hughey, and Dickey, and of course Chuck Leavell. There was a lot of soul in that band. What a group of people. Some of the sessions were real quick. We met the Rambos, and they were great singers.

Oh, yeah, Dottie Rambo. Back in those days I was a gospel DJ and used to play them on the radio; you know, Southern gospel musicians, mostly the Rambos and the Happy Goodmans. They were such good singers. It was a whole different vibe back then, a really warm feeling. Dickey was happy, and his singing was very happy.
Wasn't that around the time *Brothers and Sisters* came out? I remember them both being on the charts at the same time, and I think it was a little bit later. Dickey's album didn't come out until later, after Gregg's *Laid Back*, but I am not positive. (Laughs)

How would you compare the music of today with the music of the late '60s and early '70s?
Which music of today?

The popular music that the kids are all listening to now.
Britney Spears stuff?

Yeah, Britney, Fifty Cent, etcetera.
I don't think that there is much of anything musically offered to anybody anymore. All of that is made to sell CDs, and I read something in an interview recently, and the guy said something about how the major labels are pimping our children and doing records that are made to sort of bring out the worst in our kids instead of any values. Now, I am not a big moralist or a prude of any sort, but there is nothing of musical value to what is coming out now. I don't see any use for it. Rap music is something I have no use for either. All of my influences were black artists and they knew how to write, arrange, and were great players and singers. Now the stuff is all electronic and just pushing buttons. Not with everyone, but the majority. Everyone is talking about the demise of record companies, and unless they do something, they need to be demised. I am not sure that is phrased very well, but it is true. It's sad but true. I just watched a biography on Sam Phillips of Sun Records, and he would not sell Sun Records out to the majors until twenty or thirty years after it was done with. Unfortunately, most of them are selling out bigger and bigger, and they will not develop or support bud-

ding artists, but instead bring their talent down to the lowest denominator and sell it to twelve-year-olds.

Yeah, you have pretty much summed it up. I feel that way.

That's where it has all come to. Music should be uplifting to the human condition. Another thing that I saw recently was Martin Scorsese's *The Blues*, and they were talking about in the very oldest days of the blues, the blues gave people something to hope for in the hardest of times when they were so oppressed. People always want something to hope for and to have something more for themselves. It certainly can do that because it did that for me.

What are your thoughts on Widespread Panic now that they are huge?

Yeah, they *are* huge. It was fun to do those records with them. It was when Phil had first put Capricorn back together, and I remember the Georgia Theatre in Athens was where I first saw them. I was so impressed with their strong rhythm section. John Bell is one of the finest rock and roll singers that has ever been, too. He has this huge, scary voice. Mikey [Houser] had this totally unique way of playing, approaching music, and writing and singing. He had a great voice. He didn't sing all that many songs, but he and John sounded great singing together. It was a joy to work with them in the studio, and they would come in and work until we found something that grooved and felt good for everyone. Dave [Schools] is a fine bass player. The first album had T Lavitz playing keyboards on it, and he was a hoot to work with. (Laughs) Then Jo Jo [Hermann] came in for the second album. Their music was a little different. Jamming to them is a little different than when I came up. It is a whole different approach to it, but it was certainly a good approach and absolutely as valid. It was just different. I loved working with them and wish I was still working with them. I think that they are working with John King now, and obviously they are doing well there.

Another friend of mine that I would like you to elaborate on is Microwave Dave.

Oh, yeah, Dave did his first album in the mid '90s with very little budget, but we pulled it off. I loved working with Dave. We did some with Roger Hawkins and David Stewart playing. Then, we felt like we had something that might do something. We didn't think it would be a huge hit record, but that it would sell well. Anyway, the record companies hated it and held onto it for a year and wouldn't release it. Then, they would not sell it back to us for what they had paid for it. What a situation (Laughs)—they said they didn't like it, but would not sell it back or put it out. Eventually they did put it out and sold it as a blues album, and it did sell well.

He went to Europe several times with it, and it was amazing that it did pretty well. Dave is a true blues man, and he is into it and knows who did what. And he is a great player and very talented. He is an extremely intelligent guy and has been schooled very well as a musician. He can be stubborn sometimes, but I love him to death. (Laughs) We don't agree on some things sometimes, but we have always managed to resolve those things, and I would not take anything for his friendship. He lives close by in Huntsville and is a great disc jockey as well. He has a college blues show that is very good. When he is on, they play good stuff. The sound of the station is good.

There are two other guys that I wanted to ask you about. I was a big fan of Cowboy, and I wanted to see if you could tell me about what Scott Boyer and Tommy Talton are up to these days.

Sure, Scott is living in the Shoals area and lived in Decatur for a while. In the late '80s we put a band together called the Decoys, and Scott was the guitar player and singer and Brian Wheeler was in the band, who died recently. He was a good friend and great drummer who went on to the band in the sky. Scott is writing lots of songs, and we had one song that he co-wrote with his partner and Donnie Fritz. We had a country cut on called "24-7-365." This was one that Gregg cut on the album that was done in '95. Chuck did one of his songs on his Christmas album. I see Scott often. In fact, he was over here two days ago, and someone was talking about using a Cowboy song on a movie, and we were making a CD of it. Tommy I am working with now on an album. He is living in Atlanta and is writing and working some during the day. We have had about eight tracks cut and four songs demoed that we are trying to get some interest in. And we have some good people playing on it. Folks like Bill Stewart, Brian Owens and a bunch of bass players, from Oteil to David to me and Charlie Hayward came down and played on three songs. We did an album called *T. Talton, B. Stewart, and J. Sandlin* for Capricorn back in '75 or '76, and it was sort of a continuation of that but thrashed out a little bit.

That's one I don't have, I will have to get on eBay.

Happy To Be Alive was the title of it. Lucky, would be more appropriate. (Laughs)

What are you working on currently?
I have been doing some jazz albums with the Watters Brothers, Ken and Harry Watters's band. Ken plays trumpet and Harry trombone, and there are usually four or five pieces with upright bass and drums, and guitars and piano—or guitars without piano. I have been real lucky that all four albums have made the jazz charts, and one of them was in the Top 25 on the jazz charts. That one was called *Brothers III*. I love working with them, and they are very good players. Doing this thing with Tommy is interesting, and the Skeeters are working on their second album. I was telling you about Billy Joe Shaver coming down and playing on that album. For the moment that is all I have been doing, but you never know what will be coming tomorrow.

Johnny Sandlin, along with Paul Hornsby, Scott Boyer, Tommy Talton, and the rest of the gang from Capricorn reunited as the Capricorn Rhythm Section and recorded a fine live album. Sandlin still works as a producer and engineer at his Duck Tape Studio in Decatur, Alabama.

Paul Hornsby

January 2001

Paul Hornsby's name is synonymous with Southern Rock, as both a musician and as a producer. The following interview was a real treat: a nice, casual interview with a man who was a band mate of Duane and Gregg Allman and who produced albums by the Marshall Tucker Band and Charlie Daniels, among countless others.

&

Who influenced you musically?

The earliest, I suppose, would be my dad, Ed Hornsby, and his cousin James Tindol. Dad is an old-time fiddle and guitar player. My earliest musical memories are of being dragged around and watching him and James play four-square dances.

At about fourteen, I began to play guitar and listen to Chet Atkins and the Ventures. Man, I wish music could sound that good to me again! Everything was brand new! A few years later, I branched out and started playing organ and then piano. I listened to a lot of Jimmy Smith, the great organ player. Then it was Booker T. Jones.

It wasn't until several years later that I really tried to be a piano player. And there really is a difference. Much more involved than just having similar keys. Organ playing has more to do with sounds. Working the drawbars and the fast-slow Leslie switch. I'm rambling a bit here. My piano influences were first Ray Charles, then Dr. John.

Speaking of Dr. John, please share your thoughts on Mac.

Well, I think Dr. John is the greatest piano player in the world. That's a lot of territory, I know. I had the pleasure of playing [the Hammond B-3 organ] behind him for a while in the early '70s. That was a paid scholarship in a sense for me. That really lit a fire under me where piano playing was concerned. I'd be sitting behind the B3 on stage, and at the same time looking over his shoulder trying to see what he was doing. I think anyone who hears my playing will notice his influence on me. Chuck Leavell also played with Mac for a while. Mac left his mark on him as well.

Tell us about The Five Men-its. Elaborate on the late Eddie Hinton a bit.

The Five Men-its started as a college band in 1964 in Tuscaloosa. We had put something together to go down and play in Panama City for the summer. The group fell apart at the last minute, just as we had given up our day jobs. Out of desperation, I, along with Fred Styles and Paul Ballenger drove up to Muscle Shoals to look for a drummer and sax player. I was on guitar then; Fred Styles was on bass, and Paul Ballenger was on piano and vocals. We got a lead up there on a sax player who was down in Decatur, Alabama, named Charlie Campbell. We called him and he was interested in meeting us. So we drove down there [from Muscle Shoals]. When we mentioned needing a drummer, he told us about Johnny Sandlin, who also lived in Decatur. Anyhow, we all got together, "woodshedded" a few days, and struck out for Panama City. We didn't have any gig prospects or anything. The place we were supposed to audition for with the original group had already filled the bill for the summer.

We couldn't find a gig in Panama City, so we went over to Pensacola. To make a long story short, we got a job playing at the Pensacola Beach Casino for the summer. That fall-winter-spring we continued back in Tuscaloosa with the same band lineup, playing college fraternities, etcetera. The following summer, we decided to go back to Pensacola. We added Eddie Hinton on guitar and vocals. I think Paul Ballenger dropped out at that time. After the summer, Charlie Campbell and Johnny Sandlin left. Bill Connell joined us on drums. We were then a four-piece group, which we continued to be till the end. I guess you'd say we were the four Five Men-its.

The next summer [1966] Bill Connell left to join the Allman Joys, and Johnny Sandlin came back. We played that summer back in Pensacola Beach at the Spanish Village. That fall, Fred Styles left, and we hired Mabron McKinney on bass. We took this version of the band on the road. This was the first time we were able to play music full time for a living. Boy, this is where you find out about "paying dues."

The Allman Joys were friends of ours—you might say we were an "extended family." They had gotten us on with their booking agency out of Nashville. We two groups chased each other all over the South and Midwest for a few months, playing the same clubs.

In early 1967, Eddie Hinton decided to quit the road and pursue a career as a session guitar player in Muscle Shoals. At about the same time that we were looking for a replacement, the Allman Joys broke up. The remnants of both bands joined up, which I'll talk about later.

As for Eddie Hinton, books could be written about him alone! Eddie was the "blackest white boy" I ever knew. He had a vocal and guitar style I haven't heard since. Other than his music style, Eddie was in a club all by himself. No one else seemed to be invited. On the road, he always drove his own car by himself. The rest of us carpooled. He preferred it that way. It wasn't that we didn't get along; he was just very much a loner. Hinton was one of those guys that just had charisma. In a room full of people, he stood out. That also carried across on stage.

Eddie's career had a lot of ups and downs. He went from being a first-call session player to literally sleeping on park benches. Maybe that was a form of success to him. I think being down and out was something Eddie thought you had to do to be authentic in playing R&B. I said he was different. Anyway you look at it, Eddie never was really appreciated during his lifetime. Which is the way it usually is. He left us a few years ago at the age of 51, with some great unfinished demos in the can.

Tell us a little about the formation of Hour Glass, the combined efforts of Allman Joys and you guys, the players, and recordings you guys did.

Now, to continue with the Hour Glass portion of the program. As I said, Eddie Hinton left the Men-its to be a session player. One bleak day in the middle of starvation, Duane Allman called me up and asked, "Paul how would you like to have me and Gregg in your band? Well, it really wasn't "my" band, but I thought it over thirty or forty seconds and said, "Why, hell yes!" So, it seems we immediately started woodshedding in the Sandlin's garage in Decatur, Alabama.

Within two weeks we had our first booking at Pepe's-a-GoGo in St. Louis. That had been a big town for the Allman Joys. We played there for a month. I don't remember if we used the name Allman Joys or not. We had kicked a few names around. We all figured that a new name was in order by now, but hadn't really settled into one as yet.

During that month, Mabron McKinney, our bass player, was at the St. Louis airport when he ran into the Nitty Gritty Dirt Band. In those days [1967] you naturally noticed a fellow "long hair" and felt a natural kinship. He had never heard of them, as it was before their first hits. They were on a promotion tour for their first LP. In the conversation, he invited them to come by Pepe's to hear us play while they were in town. This they did, accompanied by their manager Bill McEuen. After the first set, McEuen ran to a phone and called someone at Liberty Records in Los Angeles. He told them that he had just discovered the next Rolling Stones. Come to think of it, I guess we were pretty good, at that!

He convinced us to come out to California and promised to get us a record deal. This we did, he did, and the rest is history. We cut one LP for Liberty. Then, Mabron McKinney left the group. He was finally replaced by Pete Carr. Pete was a guitar player friend who just happened to be visiting us when the position came available. He had never played bass before. However, after a little bit of arm-twisting, he jumped right in and continued on bass till the end of the group in 1968. We cut one more LP for Liberty in 1968.

At this time, "Beach Music" was the thing on the west coast. Here we were, a band of Southern cats with a blues-oriented sound, like you might expect the predecessor to the Allman Brothers Band to be. You might say we were the first "Southern Rock" band in the classic sense of the word. The producer and record company didn't have a clue as to what to do with us. Our producer had just come from a few hits with Jan and Dean, Bobby Vee, etcetera. As we had a "black" or "blues" sound, he kept referring to us as a "Motown" band—wrong side of the country. Our first record was filled up with horns and black chick singers. We were just eager to please. Anything they suggested, we went along with. We were just a bunch of country boys; what did we know? We did know how to make music! Most of the stuff they had us play on those records, we never played live. We had a set of mostly blues and R&B-sounding stuff that we had put together during the past year together and inherited from past bands we had all been a part of.

We played all up and down the California coast: the Fillmore, Avalon Ballroom, opening act at stadium concerts. The Fillmore was beginning to be noticed in all the rock magazines as the headquarters for the "Frisco" bands like Jefferson Airplane, Big Brother, etcetera. Bill Graham was the owner of the club and also managed the "Airplane" and several other bands who played there. Bill had not as yet received the "legendary" status that he later acquired after his death. He was just a guy who gave the bands a place to play and the people what they wanted to hear. He seemed to know what those fans wanted though.

At the time, I never gave much thought to Bill, no more than any other club owner. I do know that he was a personal fan of the Hour Glass. He kept having us back time after time, even though we didn't have a charted record. One thing in particular I remember about Bill was one night after a weekend at the Fillmore, we were struggling with my Hammond, carrying it down those steep steps out in front of the club. A bunch of stragglers were hanging around after closing time. He yelled out, "Give them cowboys some room. They just played their asses off and now they're trying to get their own gear out." I don't know why, but he seemed impressed by that. I've toted it many times since.

We were practically the house band at the Whiskey-a-Go-Go. That was a prestigious place to play back then. We sort of started a custom of jam sessions when we worked there. The biggest acts in the country, when in town, would come out to hear us play and sit in. One such unforgettable night, Janis Joplin, Eric Burdon, Steve Stills, Neil Young, Buddy Miles, and Paul Butterfield, joined us on stage there. The club had to pull the power plug to stop us that night, as there was a 2 A.M. closing curfew. Most of these acts we had opened up for, and so we had developed a reputation of sorts. This was all without the benefit of a hit record to help us break out of California.

By the middle of the summer in 1968, we had become disillusioned with the whole L.A. thing. Duane wanted to come back east. We did try it back in the old haunts again for a month or two, but it just didn't work out. The band disbanded in August of 1968.

Is it true Nitty Gritty Dirt Band helped Hour Glass get signed?

As I have mentioned, the Nitty Gritty Dirt Band, accompanied by their manager Bill McEuen, came into the club to see us play in St Louis. After we arrived in L.A., we lived for a couple of weeks with the Dirt Band in their band house in the Hollywood hills.

Let's talk about the band you formed next with Chuck Leavell. Is that right?

Actually I didn't form the next band. After the Hour Glass broke up, I went back to Tuscaloosa, to sort of regroup. That was always a town renowned for its musicians.

There was a little ol' joint called "The Chef Lounge" across the river in Northport where all the best musicians in town played. It was mostly an old redneck place, but there wasn't that many places to choose from if you wanted to play in that area.

The house band was called "South Camp." I don't know if they ever put it in print or anything, or even cared, but that's what they were called. Each night, the band varied as to the lineup. But, among them were Johnny Townsend [later of the Sanford-Townsend Band], Tippy Armstrong [later session guitarist], Bill Connell [former Allman Joy, Five Men-its drummer], Lou Mullinax [later drummer for Alex Taylor, Dr. John, who left us far too young], Charlie Hayward [later bass player for Charlie Daniels], and many others of equal and lesser fame.

Well, this was an obvious next stop-off for me. Some of the most magical, musical moments of my life were spent at that place. Being a part of those musicians will always be like a family to me. Eventually, I tried to consolidate the group into a more of a stable organization from the jam band that had existed heretofore. Out of this environment developed a group consisting of myself on organ and guitar, Bill Stewart on drums, Glen Buttes on guitar, Richard Kent on vocals, Charlie Hayward on bass, and a sixteen-year-old high school senior, Chuck Leavell, on piano and vocals. I think we kept this lineup longer than any other previous incarnation of the group.

How did you meet Phil Walden and tell us about the Capricorn studio band.

After I had been back in Tuscaloosa for nine months, Duane Allman called me from Muscle Shoals, where he had been playing sessions during this time. He had come to the attention of some Atlantic people, who had heard his work on the Wilson Pickett cut, "Hey Jude." After finding out who this guitar player was, they—I think it was Jerry Wexler—expressed an interest in forming a band around Duane and had brought Phil Walden aboard as Duane's manager. In the phone conversation with Duane, he asked me if I would come up to Shoals and play on some cuts with him and see what would happen.

I did go up there, and over the next few days, Phil Walden came in. Johnny Sandlin and Pete Carr were also called in for the sessions. Duane also brought in Jaimoe and Berry Oakley with whom he had recently been jamming with down in Florida. Out of these sessions came some well-known cuts that later appeared on the Duane Allman *Anthology* LPs.

Basically, Phil wanted to put the Hour Glass band back together, in a sense. Well, for me, Sandlin, and Carr, we had been on a virtual rollercoaster for the last two years and were in the middle of looking into other musical interests. A rehash of what we had just gotten out of seemed to be walking backwards.

Walden suggested that if the three of us wouldn't be a part of this group, maybe we would consider coming to work as the rhythm section for a new recording studio he was building in Macon. At that time, I had never heard of Macon. I remember asking him what state it was in.

Over the next couple of months, he called a lot, and each time the deal got a little sweeter. I think what really clinched it for me, though, was that Johnny Sandlin and Pete Carr had decided to accept the offer. We had always sort of stuck together. I was finally convinced, though, and 4 July 1969 I moved over to Macon to become a full-time studio musician.

Phil Walden had, until this time, had most of his success with R&B acts like Otis Redding, whom he had managed. Also, he had a booking agency that had booked most of the major R&B acts in the nation, for instance Sam & Dave and countless others. Many of these acts had been recorded at the Stax studio in Memphis. At the core of this studio was the rhythm section, which really was Booker T. & the M.G.s. Having drawn from these experiences, he wanted to put together a recording studio staffed by musicians along the lines of the Stax group.

So, presto. Johnny Sandlin, Pete Carr, and myself, along with Robert Popwell, became the staff musicians at the new studio in Macon, called Capricorn Sound Studios. Popwell later went on to play bass with the "Jazz Crusaders," of well-known fame. We literally glued acoustical tile, built baffles, and added hands-on construction to this studio.

At this time, we recorded behind such acts as Arthur Conley of "Sweet Soul Music" fame—we didn't make that particular recording, however—Eddie Floyd, and others.

How did you come to produce all of the great Southern albums of the '70s that you did?
Within the first year, the Allman Brothers Band had sort of taken off. The Capricorn record label was established. The move was made toward signing more rock and roll acts. Livingston Taylor had his first success, recording in the Capricorn studio with the rhythm section. We also began seeing more self-contained groups coming into the studio who didn't need studio musicians on their recordings. Coming to work every day in the studio was a natural progression to experiment with all the recording gear. I

guess what started my producing career was when Phil asked me to produce some sides on a local Macon group called "Boogie Chillun."

Well, for me this was really an experimental project. I could see the handwriting on the wall as far as a limited future as strictly a studio musician. We recorded this group for nearly a year, with the group breaking up and reforming probably five times during that project. Near the end of it, I think we were down to maybe one or two members of the original group. I then called some of my old buddies I had played with in Tuscaloosa.

We had a unique situation here in reverse. Usually, you form a group, play for a while, then cut some demos, then if you are lucky, get signed to a label. Here we had already started the record with no group to finish it off. So, I convinced Chuck Leavell, Lou Mullinax, and Court Pickett to move over and step into a ready-made record deal. We did get to finish the project, though piecemeal, with some pretty good stuff thrown in by these new members. Capricorn didn't release it, but sold the rights to the short-lived Ampex record label. It came out with the group renamed "Sundown."

That was my first attempt at producing, although I had been doing studio session work for a number of years. A pretty good experiment really. The next project had better results. Not that it was a hit, but that it got good reviews and was noticed. That was a group from Texas called Eric Quincy Tate. They were probably the best "bar band" I ever heard. They played a lot in Macon at a place called Grant's Lounge. There was a tremendous following here for the group as well as in Atlanta, where they re-located. The LP was entitled *Drinking Man's Friend*.

Please reflect for us on some of the bands you worked with and include any memorable anecdotes.

Shortly after the Wet Willie Band was signed to Capricorn, they played with a band in South Carolina that really impressed them. They came back and told Walden about them, and an audition gig was set up at Grant's Lounge for the Marshall Tucker Band. Phil liked what he heard, and a demo session was set up. Actually, Johnny Sandlin did the session. For some reason, he didn't wind up producing the group, so I was asked to take over.

The Marshall Tucker Band had previously cut some demos in Muscle Shoals. Nothing had become of that. Now they had cut more demos at Capricorn with only lukewarm results. When you saw them on stage they presented a freight train full of energy and excitement. There had to be some way to get this across on studio tape. This was my third attempt at producing. The first was a failure, the second was more promising, this one had to be the one! As far as having a scientific approach, I had none. I had very little producing experience to draw from. What we had going for us was some great songs that Toy Caldwell had written and a band who were the easiest to work with I had ever met. They brought their enthusiasm with them and played their asses off like they had been doing for the last few years. Not much thought was given for an "image." We took each song individually and added whatever we thought fit that particular cut. On "Hillbilly Band" there was a fiddle added. Toy played steel guitar on several cuts. If you read the musicians' credits, you'll see that Jaimoe played "gitongas" on "Can't You See." Actually, that was just him beating on the back of an acoustic guitar instead of using congas! Wherever there was a "crack" left, I filled it with a keyboard. Everyone got to explore their ideas and try what they wanted. I don't think we left one spot open for anything.

Well, we spent eight weeks in the studio, there were many fifteen-hour days. At the end we came out not knowing what we had. I had been so close to the project and spent so much time on it that I didn't know if it was great or terrible. I don't have any idea of what the band thought.

When we handed the tape over to Capricorn, it wasn't clear what they really thought either at first. The label was brand new, and with the success of the Allman Brothers, maybe they thought this project would be cut from the same mold. Well, it wasn't. It had more country influences—steel guitars, fiddles. The term "Southern Rock" was yet to be coined. By the time those two words were used in conjunction, it was perfectly normal to use all of the above ingredients within one band.

Anyhow, Capricorn was somehow convinced to release the LP. It was simply entitled *The Marshall Tucker Band*. One of my favorite definitions of "luck" is "being good at the right time." The Marshall Tucker Band was that! At the time of the release of that LP, they were opening act on tour with the Allman Brothers Band. What a perfect audience to showcase a band like that. It allowed thousands of people to get a taste of what the band had to offer on that record. It was practically a hit right out of the shoot!

Something I might comment on was the attempt to get a hit single out of the band. Well, they were famous for long extended "jam" songs, sometimes over six or seven minutes. The record label would ultimately come up and ask me to hand them a three-and-a-half-minute version that the radio would play. No mean feat! I got a lot of practice with razor blades—cutting tape—trying to get a verse, a chorus, a bit of guitar work, and finishing off with the chorus, then fade, all within the constraints of three-and-a-half minutes.

Well, just before we started the *Carolina Dreams* album, I was in a gig dressing room somewhere with the band. I had not yet heard any of the new material for the upcoming album. I asked Toy if he had anything ready for the next project due to begin in about a month. He said, "Listen to this and see what you think." He had a practice/tuning amp in the dressing room. He started to play and sing a new song. Doug and Jerry chimed in on the harmony. I was blown away. I told him right there, "That will be your first hit single!" It was "Heard It In a Love Song." From the first day in the studio, we approached that song as being the single. We purposely kept it short, with just the required guitar, flute, piano licks added. This was such a melodic song. I wanted every note, whether played or sung, to stick in every listener's head. From the opening flute lines to the final guitar licks, I think everybody who was around to hear music in the '70s can hum it. And that was indeed the band's biggest selling record. It went to #10 on the pop charts in *Billboard* magazine. The group and I continued to work successfully together through 1976, with that last LP *Carolina Dreams*, which was released in early 1977.

One of the great groups that the Marshall Tucker Band began touring with, was the Charlie Daniels Band. They had become friends, and so now that we were "allowed to put fiddles on rock and roll records," we had Charlie come in as a guest on all the Tucker albums that I had a part in.

Charlie approached me after the first Tucker LP and said he liked what we had done and asked if I would be interested in working with his group. Up until this time, Charlie had one hit: "Uneasy Rider." I liked Charlie a lot and agreed to go and catch some of his shows and get a feel for what he was doing.

If I had one criticism of his band, it would be that he was doing a lot of stuff that sounded like the Allmans. He did it great, but it wasn't anything new. At the end of a show in Tuscaloosa, I remember that for an encore he brought out his fiddle and did "Orange Blossom Special." After a set of guitar-oriented, Allman-Brothers-influenced material, that fiddle during his encore made the fans go crazy! I could see an obvious direction taking place here. We did several albums together, and that fiddle sound remained prominent on all of them.

I think the easiest and one of the biggest records I ever cut was the first Charlie Daniels Band we did together called *Fire On the Mountain*. From pre-production rehearsal, to tracking, overdubbing, and final mix took eleven days straight. Oh yeah! I always remember this: During this album, we had sort of a deadline to meet. The band had to get back out on the road for some dates. Also, I think the budget was pretty low, so we didn't have a lot of studio time to waste. We had some pretty good tunes cut as we went along on this project. One was an instrumental, which we called "Fiddle Boogie." Well, it was pretty good, but I didn't think it was strong enough to stand alone as an instrumental. Charlie assured me he would stick some lyrics into it eventually. Well, "eventually" was limited to eleven days. Every day when we came in to start the session, I'd ask him if he had finished writing any lyrics for that "fiddle thing." He would always reassure me not to worry. I'm a naturally born worrier, and I knew I didn't want that thing on the album like it was. Every day it was the same story, "Have you finished the lyrics?"—"Don't worry," etcetera.

It got right down to the last day for mixes, and we had no lyrics for "Fiddle Boogie." I said, "Charlie, this is it. We got to have something." He said, "Just give me a few minutes. I'm going up here to a quiet place in the front office [of the studio]. I've got a few ideas. I'll be back shortly." We took a break. He came back in about fifteen minutes and said, " I got something I want to run by you fellows." We put the track on, and he went out to the microphone and began to sing something about "Dickey Betts playing on that red guitar, and "ol' Lynyrd Skynyrd's playin' down in Jacksonville." We all fell out. That obviously was "The South's Gonna Do it Again." No more worries here!

Well, again this was in my early days, so to speak, of producing [1974]. I thought there were several pretty strong cuts on that album. However, when they informed me that the first single to be pulled would be "The South's Gonna Do It Again," I thought they were crazy. Then then told me to tune in to WLS in Chicago, of all places. They were playing the hell out of it! We followed the jock's lead, and that was indeed a hit single.

Today, that album *Fire On The Mountain* is one of the musical high points that I'm proudest of. There have been many other moments, but that one is very strong. After twenty-six years it still hangs right in there and keeps selling. I suppose among all the records I did, the rival to that one would have to be the Tucker's *Where We All Belong*. I thought that was really a classy collection of music. Incidentally, both albums were done back-to-back in 1974. I think just as I was finishing the Tucker LP, we overlapped the beginning of Charlie's album.

Another group that I was a real fan of, were my old Alabama compadres, Wet Willie. I did two albums with them: *The Wetter the Better*, and a live thing called *Left Coast Live*. I would have liked to have continued with them, but after *The Wetter the Better*, the group made a label change to CBS. CBS wanted to take the group into a more of a disco direction. That left me out entirely! So ended that musical relationship.

Grinderswitch were a great bunch of guys. They had been friends of Dickey Betts whom he had persuaded to come up to Macon. Joe Dan Petty had been an ABB roadie off and on. We had become friends and began to jam a little, so back in 1974 I began to go out to their band house in Perry, Georgia, outside Macon, and kick around a few tunes. They at that time, consisted of two guitars, bass, and drums. I would throw my Wurlitzer in the trunk of the car and go out there and jam to all hours.

We finally got around to putting some things down in the studio. The record label [Capricorn] liked what we were doing, so we churned out an LP of some of the finest boogie stuff I have every heard. They could play a "shuffle" better than anyone I knew. After several LPs, the group just never took off. I think of Grinderswitch as the "trench soldiers" of the Capricorn roster. They never got the push a lot of other groups got. But they had heart and never slowed down from touring/gigging. Through all of the hard times a group like them endures, they kept the best sense of humor of all to keep them going. There isn't a day that goes by that I don't think of some hilarious line quoted by their bassist, the late Joe Dan Petty.

I really liked the Kitty Wells LP you produced (*Forever Young*) that had Toy Caldwell on it. What do you remember about that session?
Capricorn had growing pains around 1974 and made an effort to become more diversified as a label. They decided to open a country division. The first artist they signed was Kitty Wells. She had always been touted as the "Queen of Country Music." This was before the days of female megacountry stars like Shania and Faith Hill, so she seemed like a good first signing.

For some reason, Johnny Sandlin was asked to produce her album. Well, Johnny had never really been a country fan. I expressed an interest in the project, and Johnny offered to co-produce it with me. Anyhow, we got started, and then Johnny pulled out half way through the project. I think he really didn't realize just exactly how "country" Kitty was. The whole thing was just really a challenge for us. Kitty had not had a hit for some time, and we had never produced a truly country artist before. It was sort of like, let's see what we can get away with here, just how progressive can we take her? We cut stuff like Otis Redding's, "I've Been Loving You Too Long" [which I think was the best cut on the LP], and Bob Dylan's "Forever Young." You know a good song is just in the interpretation. Due to her legendary status, practically the whole Capricorn roster was eager to add a note or two on that album. It remains a memorable experience for me.

One of the best Capricorn LP's ever in my opinion was *Rock Your Socks Off*, by Bobby Whitlock. Please reflect on that LP, the folks involved.

I thought the Bobby Whitlock LP *Rock Your Socks Off* deserved more attention than it got. For some reason, the label never got behind it. Bobby is a great songwriter and singer. I also thought Jimmy Nalls did some of his best work on that project. What a great guitar player! Bobby and I were great friends. His daughter and my daughter were born about the same time. Both our families hung out together, our kids sharing parties. Unfortunately, we only go to do that one LP. Together, there weren't that many musical memories we could share. He moved back to Memphis shortly after that record.

Besides producing, didn't you play piano on some Marshall Tucker tunes?

On all of the Tucker albums that I did, I also played the keyboard parts. As I have said, I only tried to fill in the "cracks." I didn't want the keyboards to be noticed all that much, since they were mostly a guitar band.

I must confess though, a bit guiltily, that we did get Chuck Leavell to play on one cut. I can't remember the particular song right now, but Chuck had always expressed an interest in playing some on their albums. I felt "guiltily" because there was this one song that I just couldn't get a feel for, or any ideas for a keyboard part. I thought this would be a great chance to call in Chuck and see what he could do with it . Well he came by and didn't flinch one bit. He just sat down and played the hell out of it! I should have thought of that sooner.

What did you do after leaving Capricorn?

From 1969 to 1974, I was on staff with Capricorn as first a studio musician, then as engineer, studio manager, and producer. In 1974 I decided to go out on my own as an independent producer. I had had a couple of hits with the Tuckers and started to get a few offers from other artists on other labels. It really didn't change much in regards to where I worked. I continued to live in Macon. Also, I continued to work with Marshall Tucker and other Capricorn groups, using the Capricorn studio as headquarters. But in addition, I had the advantage to work with other people outside the label like Charlie Daniels.

When did you open Muscadine Studios? Tell us about the studio?

By the late '70s Capricorn had gone out of business, and there was no studio to work out of. I also took about three years off and rested up. It seems that I had not slowed down for one minute for the past several years. I badly needed a rest and to spend time with my family. During this time I put together some simple recording equipment at my house just to play around with. One day, a friend of mine, Randy Howard, called and asked if he could come out one afternoon and lay down a few demos. I thought he meant just an acoustic guitar and vocal. Well, he showed up with his entire group.

Well, we pushed the furniture around a bit, stuck an amp in the closet, put the drums in the spare bedroom and turned on the 8-track recorder. Over the next few days we turned out some surprisingly good stuff. One cut that always got good response at clubs for Randy was "All American Redneck." Well, we cut that song at the house, then took a recorder to the club and recorded a "two track" version with the mics only on the audience. We brought this back and synced it up to our "studio" version so that it turned out to be a "live" version. That song got us a record deal with Warner/Viva. The *All American Redneck* LP went to #41 in the *Billboard* country charts. This was a kick in the ass for me. I had been off for three years, and now, with a "bedroom" demo, we had gotten this success. I began to look around for a building to put my recording gear in. I found a place where it still is located, and put my 8-track recorder and 8-track mixer in. Eventually, I knew if I was going to be in the studio business, better gear had to be added. Over the years we have arrived at 24-track digital.

What projects are you involved in at present? Future plans?

As you can imagine, I record a lot of local acts, but as well, people from all over. Some of the recent acts that are well worth mentioning are Chris Hicks, a great blues singer and former Marshall Tucker guitarist. A couple of chicks I worked with this summer are Atlanta-based Anne Marie Perry.

Her group is called Jane Ivey. No Spice Girl here, just good stuff. The other lady is E.G. Kight. She's been around here for a while, but has now found her niche in the blues. What a singer! I guess you could say that every time the doorbell rings, I'm wondering if it's another Marshall Tucker Band with another "Heard It In A Love Song." It's about time we had another one of those!

Any final comments, Paul?
At this time, with the indulgence of the readers, I'd like to add the following personal note: I feel that I've been extremely fortunate to have been in the company of such a roster of talented players and performers throughout my career. However, there is one important person that some might not be aware of.

Near the beginning of this story, I met a beautiful young lady named Jeanne. She had caught my eye and became my biggest fan. Every time I played on stage, I played directly to her. Not very long after, she became Mrs. Paul Hornsby. We were together for the next twenty years. She remained a fan and through the years never failed in her support for my career and the music I was involved in. I know it was because of her support that I continued in this difficult business of music. Besides being the mother of my two oldest children, April and Jesse, she added her contribution to all the music I participated in. Though we lived apart for the last several years, she was my constant council, and had been the song in my life. We lost her suddenly on 9 November 2000. It is to her memory that I dedicate this interview: Jeanne Lowry Hornsby, 1944-2000.

Alan Walden

January 2002

Anyone who has read anything at all about the history of Southern music is familiar with the Walden name. Phil Walden and his brother Alan did more for Macon music during the '60s and '70s than perhaps anyone else. In this interview from 2002, Alan spoke candidly about brother Phil, Otis Redding, the Outlaws, Lynyrd Skynyrd, and more.

∽

Alan, tell us how you first broke into the music business, and a little about your relationship to Phil.

My brother booked a black band for his high school fraternity, and it went over so big all the frats began calling him to inquire how to book more of them. As he scouted around, he discovered a band called Pat Tea Cake & the Mighty Panthers who had Johnny Jenkins on guitar and Otis Redding and Bill Jones as vocalists. They soon became a favorite of the fraternities and sororities, and when a dispute arose within the band, Phil formed another band and named them Johnny Jenkins and the Pinetoppppers. I booked them for my high school dance and would often help Phil get them to their dances and parties. I became the high school representative for Phil's new agency, Phil Walden Artists & Promotions. Also, I doubled as a Coca-Cola soda jerk at the local club where we promoted bands like Doug Clark and the Hot Nuts, the Delacardos, and Maurice Williams and the Zodiacs. We were almost arrested for presenting Doug Clark and the Hot Nuts because of their controversial songs like, "See the man all dressed in green, he lost his quarter in the rubber machine."

The company grew and expanded into booking bands for colleges and high schools all over the Southeast. Phil operated from a one-room office [which Otis painted], and even had our mother answering the phone for him while he was in class at Mercer University or working his main job at Ben Jones exclusive men's store.

Business was good, and Phil wanted to develop his favorite band into a recording attraction. "Love Twist" was recorded by Johnny Jenkins and the Pinetoppers, and "She's Alright" and "Shout Bama Lama" by Otis Redding.

Neither did well nationally but became regional favorites, and "Love Twist" sold enough regionally to capture the attention of Atlantic Record's promotion man, Joe Galkin, who quickly became one of the our closest friends and also our mentor in the recording industry.

A second recording session was scheduled for Johnny Jenkins at Stax records in Memphis. Otis drove Johnny up for the session. After a long day with little results, Otis, with the help of Al Jackson of the M.G.s was allowed to put down two sides, "These Arms Of Mine" and "Hey Hey Baby." The owner of Stax, Jim Stewart, was not impressed and literally gave away his half of the publishing on these songs to John Richboug of WLAC in Nashville. The record had been released for nine months before it started to sell. Hamp Swain at WIBB in Macon and John R at WLAC in Nashville continued to "burn" this record for the entire time, refusing to give up on it. "These Arms Of Mine" became Otis Redding's first release to hit *Billboard*'s Hot 100.

I was away at college at the time and remember some of my friends laughing when I said Otis had a hit record. They did not believe it was real and went as far as to say, "I like Otis, but I don't know if he can really sing!" After completing my first year at college, I transferred to Mercer University and began my first quarter when I received a call from Phil. He had graduated from Mercer and was commissioned a second lieutenant in the army, and in those days even Elvis Presley served.

Between 4 P.M. on Friday and 4 A.M. on Saturday Phil trained me to be a booking agent and the manger of Otis Redding. Twelve hours to run a company singlehanded for the next two years! The first year it was very rough. Phil told me he left $5,000 in the bank, but failed to mention $10,000-worth of debts.

I had to first try and break the racial barrier with the black acts and gain their trust. This was not easy for a nineteen-year-old white kid fresh out into the black music scene. I have to say my inexperience became an asset at times. I made mistakes and found myself deeply in debt not to banks or finance companies, but to my relatives, the Waldens. I was not old enough to borrow from the banks yet. Bankruptcy was out of the question and not practiced in those days like it today. Besides, Waldens paid their bills, especially to other Waldens.

During these trying times, I often slept on the sofa in the office just so I would be there early in the morning to answer the phone the next day. The agency became my whole life. While my friends were going out to have fun and dating, I was mostly at the office even bringing my dates there instead of to the movies. During this time, Otis and I became very close friends. When he was not doing shows on the road he would hang out at the office with me. Otis enjoyed being involved behind the scene as well as performing. He and I often grabbed a twelve-pack of Bud and spent most of the night writing songs, answering mail, booking, or making promotion tapes for the DJs and radio stations. We were one of the first integrated companies employing both white and black secretaries. We traveled together, and this was prior to the Civil Rights Bill. Yes, we encountered racists but it only fueled our determination to make it work more. Some of them were very cruel, but we wrote them off as crackers, rednecks, and dumbasses.

After the first year we began to show a profit, and my father even came to work for me. By the time Phil returned from Germany, Otis and I had a string of hits. "I've Been loving You Too Long" was in the top ten of *Billboard*, and "Respect" was already in the can [recorded]! Phil and I became 50-50 partners and immediately began an even stronger push to expand. We built the largest working stable of black artists in the world. The only other large management company was Motown, and their artists never worked except for the Motown Reviews and a few selected dates. We were the kings of the one-nighters, with our acts only taking ten days off in a year if they were hot.

Who were some of the clients y'all were handling at the time besides Otis?

In addition to Otis, we represented Sam & Dave, Percy Sledge, Clarence Carter, Johnnie Taylor, Etta James, Al Green, Booker T and the M.G.s, Arthur Conley, Joe Tex, Eddie Floyd, Joe Simon, Bobby Womack, Albert King, Albert Collins, John Lee Hooker, Clarence "Gatemouth" Brown, James Carr, Tyrone Davis, and many more. We opened Redwall Music, which was one of the first publishing companies in the South and unheard of in that era. Plans were made for the recording studio since Otis had begun to produce other artists. Then tragedy struck. Otis was killed en route to his gig in Madison, Wisconsin, 10 December 1967.

So sad. How did you cope with that?

The whole world stopped cold for me that day. My star and my best friend were gone. I had never known pain like that. He was the first man I loved outside of my immediate family. I still cry sometimes for Otis. I might be reading a story or hear a song, or just remember some of the good times, and it will rip through me like it was yesterday. Predictions followed. THE WALDENS WERE OVER WITH!

What happened next? Did you guys start Capricorn then?
My brother and I were crushed by this terrible accident, but we were still determined to go on and on and on. Soul music died almost the same day as Otis. It began a very fast decline over the next year. We began to look at the rock and roll bands. Phil and I had already purchased the building for the recording studio, and we decided to go forward with it. With our new direction he signed Duane Allman, and I signed Boz Scaggs. Into rock and roll we went. We founded Capricorn records bringing in our other brother, Blue. Now with the studio opened and a whole new adventure underway we hit it hard again.

Most of the money in those days went to finance the Allman Brothers Band, and Boz began to get discouraged. He and I had become good friends, and he even moved into my log cabin near the Big-O Ranch.

Financing was short, and we were building some very large debts again. This strained my relationship with Phil, and one night in New York he said I was riding on his coat tails! I had been a manager, an agent, a publisher, a record company [executive], and even tried one session as a producer! In addition to all of those hats, I was the office manager and supervised the books. Ironically, I accounted for 62 percent of the income to our companies while hanging on that coat tail and knew it very well. I also felt we could take one or just a few bands and pursue every avenue and make just as much money as handling twenty and not having enough time to do it all. This led to dissention, and I finally resigned in 1970.

What did you do next, and how did you come to record Lynyrd Skynyrd?
I opened Hustler's, Inc., on April's Fool Day 1970. There was no magazine at that time, and we named it for "hard worker," hence, let's hustle! I set it up as a publishing company number one, and a management company number two. I went on a talent search for that "special" band and auditioned 187 bands in one year, and I only kept one! The thirteenth band I auditioned was Lynyrd Skynyrd! I changed my lucky number from 5 to 13!

I took them to Muscle Shoals and recorded them with my friends, David Johnson and Quinn Ivy at a studio named Broadway Sound. Then I took them to my other good friend, Jimmy Johnson at Muscle Shoals Sound. Jimmy really sunk his teeth into the band and literally taught them how to record. He gave them great advice and pushed them hard to get the best sounds. He helped polish their whole concept while working with them. After living there for five months trying to get something going, I found myself broke again. The Allmans had broken wide open and business was booming at Capricorn. I have to admit, I wondered, "What to hell have I done?"

Nine record companies had turned us down! I don't mean, "We like you but you need better material." I mean, "Not interested! No need to contact us again." Atlantic, Columbia, Warners, A&M, RCA, Epic, Electra, Polydor, and even Capricorn all passed after hearing "Free Bird," "Gimme Three Steps," "Simple Man," "I Ain't the One," and about twelve other originals. Their comments were, "They sound too much like the Allman Brothers!" Now I ask you? Put them on back-to-back and tell me they sound alike? We all came from the South, played hard, had long hair, drank and chased women. But we did not sound alike! The Allman's had their jazz influences, and we were a straight ahead juking band! I remember one executive telling me to turn that noise off while I was playing him "Free Bird."

I had one hundred dollars in my pocket when I left Jimmy and Muscle Shoals. I had encountered problems with some of the other partners and was looking at starting all over again. I got about thirty miles out of town when the old Cadillac broke down with a bad fuel pump. The wrecker service left me out there waiting until after 5 P.M. so he could charge more. There went all but ten dollars. Add $90,000 in debt back home, and you might understand how bad it was. I walked out into a cotton patch shaking my fist at the sky, shouting, " I am going to make Lynyrd Skynyrd happen even if it kills me!" It was my solemn oath.

We had to hit the clubs again. We played a hell hole called Funochios, which was a real fruit and nut bar. The booze was good, the women were wild, and we stayed until I thought I would die there. Then we had a run in with the manager. Ronnie's grandmother died and he did not want to sing. When Ronnie and I went to see him to tell him the band would still go on and Jeff Carlisi was also bringing his band, the manager's reply was, "The old bitch is dead and you go on!" When it was the last song ("Free Bird") on Saturday, Ronnie started throwing amps onto the dance floor, smashing chairs, and breaking bottles. He totally wrecked the joint! People screaming and running, cops rushing in. I reached him just as the cop was about to bust him with a billy club. I screamed, "His grandmother died! Help me, don't hurt him! We got him outside with the help of the police only to find out I had to go back and collect the money for the week.

During these years Lynyrd Skynyrd rehearsed constantly. When they were home, they went to rehearsals like most go to straight jobs. Judy Van Zant, Kathy Collins, girlfriends and families supported them. They had a place in the swamp called "Hidden Hills" and a deal with the local police to turn off by 5 P.M. every day. They may have always been broke but they still knew how to have fun with each other. We continued to improve our equipment and our shows. We would write, rehearse, and then try the new ones out in Atlanta or Jacksonville or Gainesville, Florida. The good songs stayed in the set, and the bad ones went to the trash can. I wish I still had copies of the bad ones. They were great too!

We changed members several times but there was always Ronnie, Allen, and Gary. And Ronnie was the undisputed leader! He was a natural poet with the gift to write about what he felt, what he knew, his life, and the things he understood. No fantasies. The REAL DEAL! We became the Ten Musketeers! All for one and one for all! Wild, crazy, drinking, fighting Rednecks with a capital R and proud of it! I had drank with some of the best with Johnnie Taylor—the best—but when I met Skynyrd, whew, I went under the table. Those guys could drink. Straight from the bottle—and they were still teens at the time.

We met Al Kooper while still playing the clubs. He was starting his own "Southern label," Sounds Of the South. Even though it was short-lived, we used it as stepping stone. When we signed the recording contract on the hood of my pickup truck in the Macon Coliseum parking lot, Ronnie asked me in front of the other musicians what I thought of the contract. My reply was it was the worst I had ever seen. Worse than most of the old R&B contracts.

His reply was, "What else we got?" "Nothing," I said, "Gimmie that damn pen," as he reached for it. We could wait no more. The band could not starve anymore. We had already been in the clubs too long. They signed, and he went back to Jacksonville and started writing "Working for MCA!"

I knew from the beginning we needed MCA on our side. I made sure we gave them a deal that would give them a chance to make millions. We recorded *Pronounced* for $22,500. Can you believe it? We did not try to borrow a lot of money. We did not call every day. We were a working machine fully tuned and oiled. Independent! When I met Mike Maitland, he was shocked. I was all business and not into hanging out in the Hollywood scene like most. With him I laid out some of the best marketing and promotion plans ever. I got the Who tour when all others failed! I got the best dates for the band and built a foundation the current band lives on! Take away "Free Bird," "Gimmie Three Steps," "Sweet Home Alabama," "Simple Man," "I Ain't the One," and what do you have left? If these songs were dropped from the set, would you pay to see them?

I did very career-minded booking while their manager. I had the long run in mind constantly. I caught a lot of crap from the band sometimes because they wanted to make a certain amount all the time! Once we played a $10,000 date they thought all the dates should be $10,000. We might play Nashville for $35,000 and the next day be booked for $3,500 in a market undeveloped. Then once they said no more under a certain price, they complained of working the same cities over and over. They should have concentrated on the music and the shows and left the bookings and business to the pro. It amazes me how bands hire a manger and as soon as they get hot want to tell him how to do it. Or fire him because he is too smart for them. They should stick to what they know best! Music!

During this time, I also was thinking of their latter days when they would no longer tour. Like now maybe? I had set up profit-sharing and pension plans for their older years. I got them life insurance. Things they did not want to keep at that time. They wanted it all in cash! One visit to the road I discovered $90,000 in a briefcase. Smart. I took it home and straight to the bank. I tried to remind them it wasn't that long before that we all had been broke. The wheel of success had turned. I was the money miser. And they just knew the success would never stop.

Pronounced was a smash and *Second Helping* was as well. MCA was thrilled and now had reps meeting us in every city. *Second Helping* came in for under $30,000. Both smash albums for under $50,000. No wonder MCA loved us so much. I was setting them up for the kill. We had not borrowed money, and it was a prime time to renegotiate their recording contract. It would have been a multimillion-dollar deal. My biggest to date.

We were also getting prime concerts now with the Allman Brothers in Atlanta at Braves Stadium, Clapton in Memphis, ZZ Top in Nashville, and heading to pick off the Eagles at the Orange Bowl in Miami! The band was now the showstoppers! They killed and killed. No one could hold up behind "Freebird!" Along the way Ronnie had recommended I sign a band called the Outlaws, and I did. He said they had themselves a "Bird." That turned out to be "Green Grass And High Tides." Now I had five of the best guitar players in the world!

We were at the Orange Bowl with the Eagles, and I was doing an in-depth interview with *CREEM* magazine. They had spent two days traveling with me, and this was going to be the big story! Ronnie told me he need to talk to me right after the show, and he and I went back to the room together. When we sat down he informed me the band had voted to replace me as the manager of the band. The wind went out of my sails. I can't tell you how bad and shocked I felt. This had been my whole life for the last four years. No one loved the band anymore than me. Not Ronnie, not Allen, not Gary, or any of the rest of the band. Ronnie had been best man at my wedding. The only people I invited were the band. I thought of Ronnie as my closest friend. There was anger, hurt, pain, fear, and numbness. Ronnie said I could beat the hell out of him, that he would just cover up the vitals and let me have a go at him. I couldn't. He asked me if I wanted to know who voted what. I was still wrestling with the verdict. I knew Ed King didn't like me, but the rest of the guys were supposed to be my friends too. I knew I had done a superb job for this group. But something had gone wrong! Here we were with the whole world at our feet and now BOOM! I must admit that also came a feeling like concrete blocks falling from my shoulders. Now I did not have to worry about their future like I had been doing. The truth of the matter is no one was looking after mine or seemed to care but me.

I went home to Georgia to lick my wounds. I have never been the person to stay with someone if they did not want me, and this was my biggest disappointment in life. Not for all the money in the world. Now they wanted that big Hollywood super manager to take them on to superstardom. I waited a couple of days, prayed over it and then called Ronnie. I offered to meet with them and try to correct any problems, and I did go out to see them. But it was not the same group of guys. They were now "the machine" as Ronnie called it. No more brotherhood. My control was gone, and I knew it. I could have stroked them all and maybe stayed in the picture a while longer, taken a cut in commission and become the yes man. Gary, Dean, and Ronnie came to the Capricorn Picnic that year, and Ronnie and I ended up in a room alone again. I won't go into details, but I lost it with him this time. Here was the guy whose back I had been covering for four years, even when we were up against very bad odds. And now he's letting them all stab my ass in the back! I knew Ronnie could kick my ass one-handed, but I was so angry this night that it did not even matter. I was furious, and after I had my say I saw a tear coming down his face. Then I lost it and left with tears flowing as I left the hotel. I knew for sure then it was all over for me with them.

The next day he asked me if I knew I had a bull by the horns the night before. I knew exactly what he meant. Now that it was over I made the suggestion instead of us ending up with a big lawsuit we should try to find the new manager together and keep the lawyers from getting rich. I had seen these guys rise from poverty and work every inch of the way. I still loved them and tried to understand why they were doing this. I had been around enough acts to know these things happen sometimes and there is not much you can do to stop it once it gets going. No one ever doubted my honesty at least. They did say I was a money miser, and I do count money well. Forgive me, but isn't that what a manager's job is? Would you rather have one who could not count? I did not want to see some idiot come in and totally ruin everything I had worked on, and I wanted him to have to buy my contracts.

I recommended Peter Rudge. I had met him on the Who tour. He managed the Rolling Stones, the Who, Golden Earning, and Tanya Tucker. I figured if he could deal with Mick Jagger's ego and Keith Moon's insanity, he could surely manage my little Southern band who were not totally out of control yet! I took their offer of some cash and retained the publishing on the "old" songs that had already had their big earning days. The cash did not equal what I would have made off the negotiation of the record deal alone. It was a drop in the bucket compared to what I could have made in the next three years. It would all equal to about 1/100 of what I would have made. But even with trying to keep things cool, bad blood still developed. Rumors spread that I only wanted the money. I find that ridiculous and totally untrue. I wanted to love what I was doing, and it wasn't fun any more. Not only that but I went to see the movie, "The Longest Yard," which had the only song I had helped write with Skynyrd in it. When the credits came on the screen there was Ed and Ronnie and no Alan. I came up with the title and the plot to "Saturday Night Special," and they took it from me. At this time I made another solemn oath. "I will be back and beat you at your own game. Music! One year later the *L.A. Times* review said, "The momentum of the show had dropped until the return to the stage of the Outlaw's Hughie Thomasson and Billy Jones, where a friendly competition of the guitars roared" along with numerous others on the thirty-seven day tour where the Outlaws never let up!

I took my publishing catalog and made it a valuable commodity. When I sold my Skynyrd copyrights many years later, I once again heard they were upset I had done well on the deal. I made the deal where I was promised their songs would be pumped directly into movies. The first movie after the signing was *Forrest Gump* with "Freebird" and "Sweet Home Alabama" in it. Do you have any idea how much money that made the writers? The "bad man" did it again! I finally had an opportunity to sit down with Gary alone one night, and I did not beat around the bush. I asked him if all the rumors were true, that they still had all these resentments about the publishing. At least he was honest and told me he did think I had gotten the best of them with this. Then I told him I was sorry he felt that way, but that I wanted to add, though, that I thought I had made them all rich. I met with Gary another time in Atlanta and he asked me to help him make a strong publishing deal, and he even signed a piece of paper saying I had the deal! When I tried to call him later to tell him of the interest, I had found he never returned the phone call. I hear he is clean and sober now, and I am so happy for him. I am, too, for three years now, and a brand new father to my first son, Christian Walden. I hope one day we can sit and talk as just friends.

I went on to work with the Outlaws for twenty five years until they completely disbanded. We had three gold and one platinum on Arista Records. It was not near as successful as Skynyrd, but I am still very proud of what we did with them! Henry Paul has proven to still be a major recording artist, still in the mainstream, and he was asked to leave the Outlaws under very similar circumstances as mine.

I began with Otis Redding, who remained my favorite and accomplished more than them all put together. He put the "S" and the "O" in soul music. It never got any better than Otis! He was the king of them all, y'all! A statue of Otis is to be placed in the new park right next to the Otis Redding Bridge in Macon. It is the first statue of a black man in Macon, and maybe the first in Georgia. Otis's "Dock of the Bay" just also received an award from BMI for seven million airplays. Only seven writers from America in history have accomplished this. Thirty-four years after his death, his records continue to sell more now than when he was alive.

I heard you were nominated for the Georgia Music Hall of Fame. Were you inducted?

This last year I was nominated for the Georgia Music Hall Of Fame, but L.A. Reid of Arista Records was inducted. I hope I may be nominated again and be inducted in the next few years.

Would you care to share your thoughts on the H&H Restaurant and Mama Louise?

Here in Macon we are very proud of the H&H, still a favorite spot for the hungry musicians and fans alike. Not only is the food still down-home great, but the Lady of Class, Mama Louise who owns and runs it and does the cooking, is one of the sweetest, kindest, finest people in the world who makes you feel good all over inside and out. And her collection of posters and photos is outstanding, and the jukebox still smoking!

What was the scene like around Macon during the heyday of Southern Rock, early to mid 70s? Capricorn?

Macon will probably never know another era like the '60s to the '80s when you could meet everyone from Cher to Joe Frazier on Cotton Avenue. There was never a dull moment, and you never knew who was coming in the door next. Music was plentiful all over town with bands lined up for a chance to play a joint named Grant's Lounge. Free music in the park almost every Sunday. The annual Capricorn picnics were a major event, with people coming from all over the world. Bette Midler, Cher, Andy Warhol, Lynyrd Skynyrd, the Allmans, Marshall Tucker, Jimmy Carter, Bill Graham, Don King, Bonnie Bramlett, Dr. John, the Outlaws, and Wet Willie, just to give you an idea of the variety of people. Music, money, and more beautiful women than you could shake a stick at. This town was humming around the clock!

What's next on your agenda?

My future plans are to write my own book, work my publishing catalog, and I still believe in a guy named Chris Hicks! His day is still yet to come but believe me it's coming!

Robin Duner-Fenter

October 2014

After literally years of campaigning by his son Robin, Frank Fenter was been voted into the Georgia Music Hall of Fame. It is an honor that no one deserves more than the late record man.

Fenter was a music industry executive who was the first European managing director of Atlantic Records, helping sign Led Zeppelin, Yes, and King Crimson. He's also credited for introducing R&B to Europe with the legendary "Hit the Road Stax" tour, including Otis Redding and Sam & Dave in 1967. Later, he was a co-founder and partner in Capricorn Records, and instrumental in breaking many Southern Rock bands, including the Allman Brothers, the Marshall Tucker Band, and Wet Willie.

I spoke with Robin Duner-Fenter about his dad and his legacy.

༄

Rob, tell us about your family, your mom Kiki and Frank.
My parents were really the best. I respected them and never talked back in a bratty way, as you see kids doing; and if I ever did, my stepfather would most certainly take me onto the front yard and show a few of his boxing moves. Frank, who was my stepfather but I considered him my real father, was strict with me on getting good grades, doing household chores, encouraged me to do sports, and insisted I work during summer holidays. He taught me in the school of "tough love," and liked to say, "you might hate me now, but your gonna love me later". Both my mother and Frank were urbane, cool and sophisticated; they could relate to any age group and were comfortable in any social circle, although they came from completely different worlds.

My mother's side of the family came from Sweden, and as a kid, we would spend a month in Sweden every summer visiting my grandmother, who lived on a lovely farm with beautiful wheat fields that stretched for as far as the eye could see. My late mother had a heart of gold and a gift of making everyone she met feel special; she was understated and unpretentious, simply known, in Macon, as "Kiki," her nickname, although few people knew she had the title of Baroness with quite a privileged upbringing.

There was a movie about our family, *Out of Africa*, adopted from the book by Karen Blixen on her life in Africa with my great-uncle, Bror Blixen, in the 1920s Kenya. Her uncle Bror was a larger-than-life safari hunter, who lived life to the fullest and, interestingly enough, "The Great White Hunter," phrase originated from him, based on his legendary oversized personality while living in Kenya. Ernest Hemingway, a good friend of Bror, loosely used him as his main character in the book, *The Short, Happy Life of Francis Macomber*.

Now, "Frankie," as I used to call him, was my stepfather, but as I already mentioned, he was also my father, as he was the man who brought me up; he came from a completely different world than my late mother, where there were frequent dinner parties and you could use roller skates to get around the house due to its size. Frankie grew up in Johannesburg, South Africa, in a small house on the other side of the tracks with a tin roof and no electricity; however, without lights, my father avidly read books with a flashlight and listened to American blues music on his battery-operated radio. Frankie became a great boxer out of necessity—he had to walk to school crossing through other kids' turf, and would have to defend himself. In fact, he got so good that he became a Golden Glove boxer and, had told me, was a contender for the Olympics. The guy he was going against was someone he had beaten before, but on the trials, the fight stopped due to Frankie having gotten cut, qualifying the other guy to go on to the Olympics. Later, Frank did a stint in the Air Force, before making plans to leave South Africa.

Frank's biological father was a butcher, and his stepfather an electrician; the family expected him to follow in his stepfather's footsteps, but that was not in Frank's master plan: he always intended to leave South Africa and move to America, where his love of blues music and Hollywood movies came from, and to also seek "fame and fortune." He left South Africa in 1958 on a two-week boat ride, having a blast on the voyage he would later share, but was broke when he arrived on the shores of England, while not knowing a soul. The original idea was for him to become an actor; he got a few gigs, the most notable being a BBC science fiction series called *The Big Pull*. He later co-wrote, acted, and produced the first South African rock 'n' roll movie with the first integrated cast called *Africa Shakes*.

Discovering that acting did not actually pay the bills, he began booking bands, and eventually landed a gig heading up Chappell Music Publishing and later Chess Music, prior to becoming European managing director of

Atlantic Records. Frankie met my mom in 1963 when he was still, as he would later say, "between being a hustler and a starving actor," at his coffee shop in London; it was love at first site, although the relationship would not be consummated for several more years. While my parents' backgrounds were completely different, they complimented each other perfectly—my mother, perhaps, giving Frankie some polish and understated sophistication, and him keeping it real; their relationship was a testament of their good taste in each other, and I was very lucky to have both of them as my parents and role models.

How old were you during the Capricorn years?
My father came to Macon first, I believe, sometime late summer or early fall of 1969. My mother and I took a boat to America in December. I was six, and remember being very disappointed, looking through my binoculars, to not see cowboys and Indians as we approached the Manhattan skyline..., but to answer your question, I was six through sixteen during the Capricorn years, if we count the end of 1979 as the end date.

What are your fondest memories of Capricorn? ...of Macon?
I would have to say going to the Capricorn office over school holidays. I loved hanging out in my father's office; he listened to demo tapes and new Capricorn acts through a reel-to-reel. I enjoyed watching and listening to him on the phone with his wonderful theatrical hand movements and expressions, cajoling and entertaining others over the phone while getting business done. My father had a very charismatic and larger-than life personality, and, as a kid, I found it fascinating how he conducted business with such verve and excitement. He made work never seem like work, but fun.

What was Phil Walden like?
Like my father, Phil was also charismatic, funny, and persuasive. Going to the office or doing sleepovers at Philip's [Phil's son] house as kids, I remember him being passionate about movies and setting up the projector for little Philip and me to watch these very obscure 1940's horror movies or seeing *Blazing Saddles*, which, I believe, was his favorite comedy. When I would go to the Capricorn office as a younger kid, he was playful and had a verbal banter with me about girls, school, and also wrestling—he called it the "Indian Treatment"—knuckles hitting my chest methodically to a 1, 2, and 3 beat, making me laugh more than anything; Frankie watched in amusement

as I would try my best to escape from Phil's attempt to pin me down. Phil also had quite the temper, which I witnessed more than once; he also struck me in a way as shy and someone who could be reserved, despite having what appeared be an extrovert personality. My father and Phil were very close friends and shared a similar sense of humor, deference to the status quo and their vision for building a multi-faceted company together while, I am sure, having a great time doing it.

Like you said, you were friends with his son. Were you the same age? Share memories of Phillip.
Yes, Philip and I were best friends growing up. We were only four months apart in age. He and I had a similar sense of humor and lots of fun getting into innocent trouble. We literally did everything together, and he was a brother I never had, and I think he felt the same way. As he has said himself, Philip literally stayed more at our house over the long summers than with his own family. We were very close, and it saddens me to think he is no longer with us, but the childhood memories will never go away, which were so many…our first double dates together; going to our first concerts, and going backstage to get autographs; spending long, hot summers in Macon at our pool; walking to Nu Way; trying to flirt with girls at the Macon Mall, and usually not being successful; working one summer at Philip's aunt's ice cream shop in Valdosta; spending a summer together in Sweden at my grandmother's house; spending summers at the Capricorn house in Hilton Head; camping in the woods; going to our first camp together in north Georgia, are only a few of the many childhood experiences and memories we had together that I will always cherish.

You've worked hard to get Frank into the Georgia Music Hall of Fame. What drove you so hard to see this through?
Good question. It was important for me to see it through since my father does not have a voice to share his own wonderful and amazing life and his many accomplishments. Since he passed at forty-seven, some thirty thirty-one years ago, he has been forgotten for the music history he helped create, and as his only son, I felt it was my fiduciary duty to make everyone aware of his vital role in it all; not least that he was an amazing father who believed in me when few did, having severe dyslexia growing up and not being able to read or write until I was sixteen. His love and belief in me as an

insecure kid was so important to who I am now that the least I can do is return the honor.

What does it mean to you now that he has been inducted?
It's a wonderful feeling to know that Frank is finally getting recognized for his amazing legacy, although long, long overdue. His induction is a confirmation of everything I knew about his career, and it's nice that he is finally getting the public recognition he so richly deserves. His legacy and life story is now permanently recorded and will be known by future generations, but most importantly, for my daughter for when she is older and wants to know more about her very colorful grandfather's life.

For those who are under the impression that Phil was the only guy steering the Capricorn ship (simply because he was the public face, whereas Frank ran things behind the scenes), please explain what Frank brought to the party.
Frank and Phil were Capricorn Records, just like Ahmet Ertegun and Jerry Wexler of Atlantic Records; each being essential to the success of the company. As you know, Frank ran Atlantic in Europe, building the label into prominence abroad by getting signed some of the most important late British invasion acts, including Led Zeppelin, YES, and King Crimson. Frank brought to the table his experience and expertise in knowing how to run a music company where Phil's background was in artist management and booking. Each man knew their talents and their respective role, and, together, eventually made Capricorn the most successful independent record company in America.

Frank also brought international cuisine to Macon. Tell us about Le Bistro.
One of Frank's first gigs in London was as a dishwasher, and the guy who hired him was a man by the name of Peter Marriott, who cooked fantastic French food for much of London's music scene throughout the 1960s. Between acting and odd jobs, Frank got promoted, and later, Peter and Frank briefly partnered in the restaurant were Frank learned to be a great cook. Years later, when Frank moved to Macon, he was frustrated with the limited restaurant options when entertaining out-of-town business associates, so he recruited and financed his old friends Peter and Paul Harpin to come over from London and setup Le Bistro, which, incidentally, was the

first French continental restaurant in Middle Georgia. It became very successful and was the main hang out for Capricorn artists, executives, out-of-town business guests and celebrities, including Cher, Andy Warhol, Don Johnson, Nick Nolte, Bette Midler, and Jimmy Carter. Le Bistro was ahead of its time as French food was quite exotic for Macon; back then, you did not eat anything that you could not pronounce.

What were Frank's feelings about Capricorn? What was it like when the ship began to sink?

Frank was a maverick, and he always knew he would break from the large corporation of Atlantic, even though he was groomed under Ahmet Ertegun, the chairman of the company, to become his young protégé and work closely with him in New York; he would have had a very, very bright future; but to be a part of something that he would co-own and help launch was his dream, particularly after hearing the rough demos of the Allman Brothers. He was proud of Capricorn's success, having been a huge part of building it, although he was very modest about his integral role. He and Phil were not just partners, but great friends, more like brothers, and very much enjoyed working together and making what Capricorn became.

I think the downfall of Capricorn was very tough on Frank, although he was the most optimistic person you could ever meet and was very good at not showing his concerns. I recall Alan Walden saying, "Frank could make you believe there was sunshine when it was pouring outside," which really says it all. I think the excesses of success along with the indulgences had an impact on Phil and Frank; they lost their hunger and drive, I believe, with the luxurious and comfortable lifestyle they had attained; it was a true rags-to-riches story, and along the way I think they got out of touch and lost their edge. I also think they believed that their preferred style of music, Southern-style rock, would continue forever, without thinking or adapting to new music trends. And when they did, it was too late.

What did he do after Capricorn?

Shortly after Capricorn folded, but still retaining his ownership in the label, Frank setup a production company called Fast Forward Productions with A&M Records through a guy named Jerry Moss, the chairman of the label and the "M" in A&M. Their first release was a band called the New Riders of the Purple Sage, which had some success. Frank also setup a distribution and marketing deal with Polydor through his old friend, Freddy

Hine, who was head of the label, to release an old Capricorn act, White Witch.

When did he pass away and from what?
My father passed on 21 July 1983 at the Capricorn studio, from a massive heart attack; he and Phil Walden were together with the Atlanta Rhythm Section. Frank had just secured a distribution deal with Warner Bros.' Mo Ostin, chairman of the label; he was to fly out the next day to Los Angeles and sign the papers that would have revived Capricorn.

What are your fondest memories of Frank?
Our Saturday and Sunday breakfast talks and his fascinating, and often, funny stories about his life and his own philosophy of life and living. I learned a lot about life at that kitchen table.

What's the best thing you learned from him?
There are many, but most importantly, his love and passion for living life to the fullest and always seeing and bringing out the very best in others. He taught me to believe in myself and that you can do anything you set your mind out to do.

What is the main thing you'd like for the history books to remember about Frank?
I'd like for my father to be remembered as a maverick and an innovator who played a significant role in rock 'n' roll music history here, in the United States, and when he was abroad in England.

Jimmy Hall

September 1999

When the stage is his, Jimmy Hall, the dynamic, Mobile-born singer transforms himself into a Southern preacher who melds the blues and rock and R&B into an exciting gumbo. Back in 1999, I spoke with Jimmy about the past, present, and future of his music. Hall has had a long and fruitful career that has included touring with acts such as Aerosmith, the Allman Brothers Band, Grand Funk Railroad, and the Grateful Dead, and his Grammy nomination for Best Male Rock Vocalist (he was a featured performer on Jeff Beck's *Flash* album) is an honor he still considers a personal best.

Hall's career began with the birth of Wet Willie and has been a nonstop musical joyride since the band's move from Mobile to Macon in 1970 to record for Capricorn. After the demise of Wet Willie, Hall moved to Nashville to work with producer Norbert Putnam on a solo project with Epic. Putnam had played on Arthur Alexander's "You Better Move On," and the pair hit it off immediately. Putnam's salesmanship brought Hall to Music City for good.

Hall's new home became the birthplace for other lives: the founding of Jimmy Hall & the Prisoners of Love; the embracing of the position of band director for rogue country star Hank Williams, Jr.; and the eventual reunion of Wet Willie.

When we met with Jimmy in 1999, he was as busy as a bee, working with Hank, Jr., the Prisoners of Love, Gregg Allman and Friends, and half a dozen other various and sundry projects, including a solo album on the—at that time—newly risen Capricorn Records label.

~

Many people think Wet Willie formed in Macon, Georgia, but it was really in Alabama, right?
We were in Mobile in '68 and '69, putting the band together, and then in '70 we headed for Macon.

Do you think there will ever be a full scale Wet Willie reunion?

We've played a lot together between 1990 and last year. We've had some good experiences, but right now we're in a holding pattern.

Is your sister Donna, from the Wet Willie band, doing any recording right now?
She did a local project in Mobile, a live thing with a friend down there. She was also doing some work with the Beat Daddys, and working on some solo stuff.

What's your take on the '70s, and your time as lead singer of Wet Willie?
I wouldn't take any amount of money for the time in which I was born, and the time in which I grew up. I wouldn't take anything for the situation I was in. Doing what we did—rocking in the '70s —it was the best of all worlds. It was like being indestructible. I was in a rock band; we had records, and we were on the road playing with everyone we'd ever idolized. How can you beat that?

How does it feel to be a part of the reformed Capricorn family?
I just revisited a video from the early '70s, *Saturday Night In Macon*. It was a Don Kirshner production. Those days mean a lot to me. But, now I feel I've stepped up to another level as a performer and have remained true to what was driving me all along. Being back with Capricorn is the best. For Phil and I to wind up working together after all these years is great.

What was the vibe like around Capricorn Studios during the '70s?
It was a real cooperative atmosphere. Almost like a workshop. People were interacting and learning from each other. If you were recording your record, you didn't close your doors and lock out other musicians. The bands encouraged the bands and the other Capricorn artists to drop in and listen to what was going on and give some feed back, maybe contribute to a song. It was a real community feeling. We were in a place that you wouldn't think that kind of music, or that much music, would come out of—tiny little Macon, Georgia. A town with only one recording studio at the time. It was that community spirit, brother helping brother, that I loved. All of us being down there, getting our studio chops together.

I just spoke to David Goldflies, and he was telling me about a supergroup y'all had for a while: Betts, Hall, Leavell & Trucks (BHLT), with Dickey, yourself, Chuck, and Butch. Too bad you guys didn't record.

(Laughs) I know! My son pulls out the *Dreams* album (the Allman Brothers box set), and he says, "Dad whatever happened to this band?" I had a friend up in New York the other day who asked if I had any board tapes of BHLT, anything. It was amazing, with that lineup, and playing for two years, we never recorded anything. Nothing. I think there's a tape somewhere from Charlie Daniels's Volunteer Jam, and a couple of demos floating around. That's about it. It's pretty rare.

I was just watching a video of *Saturday Night In Macon*, myself, with y'all, the Marshall Tucker Band, and the Allman Brothers Band. When did you first encounter the Allmans?

The first time I saw the Allman Brothers, it was way back. They were playing The Warehouse in New Orleans, opening for Albert King. I was knocked out by their songs; I mean, I had bought the first album. It was their first album that caused Wet Willie to start setting our sights for Macon and Capricorn. One thing I remember about that night was Berry Oakley. Some good-looking girls were standing at the front of the stage, and he made an off-the-wall comment that would be considered sexist today. He looked at them and said, "Forget about hamburger; we're having steak tonight!" (Laughs) Also, when I think about them playing there, that's where we recorded *Drippin' Wet Live*; that was New Year's Eve, 1973.

I know you've been a regular on the current Gregg Allman and Friends Tour. How's that been for you?

It's been great. Gregg is in top form, feeling good. And it just keeps getting better and better. We've had some good people playing, of course: Jack Pearson, who's with the Allmans now, and Danny Chauncey from .38 Special, and Mark McGee. We were in Japan in April. We were on the West Coast in February. In November we took a one-month tour of the Southeast. We played Athens, Georgia, and Myrtle Beach at the House of Blues. We play "Rendezvous with the Blues" from my solo album, which Gregg also recorded. He's been great to share the spotlight. We do "Keep On Smilin'," and I sing with Gregg on "Midnight Rider." It's been great.

There's always so many rumors floating around about Gregg, I was going to ask you how he's been lately.

The bottom line is, he's been sober for over two years now. He's very healthy, and his attitude is great. He's working hard—he inspires all of us.

It's been documented countless times that you were pretty much responsible for discovering the Marshall Tucker Band. Do you recall the events of that history-making night?

We were playing Spartanburg, at the Ruins. We were booked there as the headliner. We didn't really pay attention to who was opening until we got there. But we sat out front and listened to them. They just knocked us out from the beginning. It was a sound that was totally unique to my ears, and to the other guys in the band as well. It had a lot of the elements that we were into—good Southern music, good rock and roll. But there was so many things that set them apart from the others.

Were you friends with the band?

I was pretty close to Doug. We related on the lead vocalist position that we both had with our bands. I can remember talking with those guys when they recorded their first album. My girlfriend at the time worked at Capricorn, and another friend of ours, Carolyn Harris, was an engineer there. During that first recording, my girlfriend was in the studio a lot with them, and I'd come down too.

What do you remember about working with the Charlie Daniels Band?

I remember first seeing him in Tennessee. (Of course!) I was very impressed. He had elements of both the Allman Brothers and Marshall Tucker, and I like that territory. Two drummers, two guitar players. He forged his own way playing country, rock and roll, and rhythm and blues. He's always been a gentleman and a fine friend. We were managed by the same guy for a while. We toured with him in 1981 and '82 with my solo group, and of course, Wet Willie played with him a lot. I'm happy to say we're still friends, and I want to say that Charlie did a great thing with the Volunteer Jams. I participated in most of those. The last one I participated in was, I think, October a year ago, here in town.

These days you are also blowing harp and sax for Hank Williams, Jr.'s Bama Band, and you did the Volunteer Jam 1999 Tour. How was that? Were there any special moments?

I don't know if you were there for this one, but jamming with Marshall Tucker was great fun. And Doug [Gray] was so gracious to tell the audience about my involvement with the beginnings of the MTB, and getting them signed to Capricorn. He invited me to play on the set, and I ended up jamming on harmonica on several tunes. I have really enjoyed playing with Hank, Jr., and jamming with Charlie is always fun. That first night we were together was in Greenville, and Rick Medlocke was jamming, and Charlie brought me out on "The South's Gonna Do it." What fun. He asked me to sing the line with, "Ol' brother Willie's gettin' soaking wet." Charlie came up to me after and said, "Jimmy I love you, and I'm real glad you're on this tour." Just being around Charlie is an up. He's just a positive influence to everybody.

So what projects, besides the tours with Gregg and Hank, are you involved in at present?

I have my own band called Jimmy Hall & the Prisoners of Love. We're going on what's called The Sandy Beaches Cruise. It's headed up by Delbert McClinton. This will be the fourth or fifth one. It's a week, and it goes to the Grand Caymans, Cozumel, and the Caribbean. He's got Asleep at the Wheel, about a dozen acts that rotate. It's already sold out. In January of 1998, that was the first one I did. We had done a show here in Nashville in the summer of '97, a B.B. King Blues Festival. We did the show with Delbert McClinton, the Neville Brothers, and Kenny Wayne Shepherd. At that point, Delbert asked me to do his cruise.

We did our first cruise in January of '98. It was to Puerto Rico, the Bahamas, and St. Croix. It was a great experience, and I'll tell you what, I'm hooked! We did one with Lee Roy Parnell, Asleep at the Wheel, Marcia Ball, Big Al Anderson—we had about a dozen groups. Monte Montgomery is a great guitar player from Austin; he was there. In 1998, I went on it, and my band couldn't do it, or some of them couldn't, so I called up to find out who was going to be on it. Lee Roy Parnell was going to be on it, and I'm an old friend of his. I know his band guys, the Hot Links, I've jammed with them before, and they knew some of my material. They said, "If you don't have a band, we'd like to do it." We had a great time, and my wife fell in love with the whole situation. This time we took my sister and my brother-in-law and another couple, some friends of mine from Macon. And I brought my kids, my three boys. Actually, before it was over, two of my boys ended up onstage, but my oldest, who is seventeen, is a keyboard player, and he was rocking. It was Jimmy Hall & Son. He had a ball, and I still have people contacting me on the internet and saying, "Tell your boy we still have a fan club for him."

Are all three of your sons musicians?
They are all gifted in a lot of different ways. All three of them have had piano lessons, and my oldest has had piano lessons since he was six, for about eleven years. He also plays guitar. We got him a Fender Strat one year for Christmas. The fourteen year old has a set of drums he got at the same time. The youngest plays piano and likes to sing. He's been onstage with me a few times, playing tambourine.

You must have a lot of fun with the boys.
One of the most fun things was working up all of these songs I do with my band, with my son. We have an acoustic piano, and we just sit around it and sing, which is just a joy. Then I might break out a saxophone. One time, I pulled out a soprano sax, and he turned to me and said, "Do you know 'Black Magic Woman' by Santana?" So we started jamming instrumentally on that. Classic rock is a big deal—it's something they all lean towards—as well as Charlie and the Allman Brothers, Wet Willie...

I know Capricorn is reissuing all of the old Wet Willie albums on CD. Do you think there is a market for that old Southern Rock music as we approach the year 2000?
I really do. A lot of people are wanting to replenish their collections. I know of fans right now that have said, "I wore my vinyl out. My copy of *Drippin' Wet* was completely worn out. I was on my second copy."

Besides all of the Wet Willie albums, what are some of the other records that you've appeared on?
One of the bigger ones, or at least the most noteworthy, was the Jeff Beck release, *Flash*, in 1986. That was a major milestone in my career. I think I sang five of the vocals. There were only a couple of other vocals on the album, and one of them was Rod Stewart singing "People Get Ready." We did the video called "Ambition," which went into heavy rotation on

MTV. I got a lot of mileage out of that. I toured with him in Japan in '86, and the album was nominated for several Grammys, and I was nominated for Best Rock Male Vocal that year. Jeff was nominated and won for Best Rock Instrumental. Now I look at it and say, I wish we could do more of the same. That was a great album, and it was great working with Jan Hammer and Simon Phillips. The band was incredible.

How many solo recordings have you done?

I have had three projects. The most recent is *Rendezvous with the Blues*, which Capricorn put out two years ago. Between 1980 and 1982, I did two solo albums for Epic. The first one was called *Touch You*, and the second one was *Cadillac Tracks*. They are not available on CD at this time. I'm working on material for a new one now. I've been woodshedding and trying to get the material done. And I've been talking to Capricorn about producers, but we haven't decided yet. The songs are 99 percent there. I think I need to just jump in there and say, "Let's get it done now." I think I work best under those conditions.

Frank Fenter and Phil Walden in Holland, 1976.
Courtesy Robin Duner-Fenter

The Allman Brothers Band, 1969.
Courtesy The Allman Brothers Band Museum at the Big House

Then Governor of Georgia and future U.S. President Jimmy Carter gets his cowboy on with George McCorkle of The Marshall Tucker Band.
Courtesy George McCorkle

Toy Caldwell of The Marshall Tucker Band and Jimmy Carter.
Courtesy George McCorkle

Elvin Bishop with Capricorn's Mark Pucci at Capricorn picnic.

Courtesy Mark Pucci

Frank and Kiki Fenter flank Tom Dowd.

Courtesy Robin Duner Fenter

Bonnie Bramlett burns up the stage during her Capricorn years.
Author's collection

Frank Fenter with Dickey Betts
on the day Dickey married Sandy Blue Sky, 1973.
Courtesy Robin Duner Fenter

Backstage with Doug Gray, Jerry Eubanks, and Paul T. Riddle
of The Marshall Tucker Band, in the mid-70's.
Courtesy Mark Burrell

The Marshall Tucker Band. One of their earliest Capricorn promo photos.
Author's collection

The Marshall Tucker Band performing in Manchester, England
during the Capricorn European Tour of 1975
which also featured Grinderswitch and Bonnie Bramlett.
Photo by Peter Cross

Phil Walden and Jimmy Carter.
Courtesy George McCorkle

Doug Gray performs with The Marshall Tucker Band at the annual Angelus benefit in Tampa, Florida in 2010.
Author's collection

The author with friend George McCorkle during recording sessions at Mill Kids Studios in Huntsville, Alabama, 2005.

Photo by Bruce Wall

Tommy Talton and Johnny Sandlin of The Capricorn Rhythm Section perform with Gregg Allman.

Photo by Bill Thames

Cowboys reunited: Pete Kowolski and Scott Boyer of Cowboy.
Photo by Bill Thames

Chuck Leavell.
Photo by Bill Thames

Jimmy Hall.
Photo by Bill Thames

Bonnie Bramlett.
Photo by Bill Thames

Randall Bramblett.
Photo by Bill Thames

Tommy Talton.
Photo by John Charles Griffin

Paul Hornsby.
Photo by Bill Thames

Tommy Crain jams at the Angelus benefit in Tampa.
Author's collection

Taz DiGregorio during one of the late night jam sessions at the Angelus event.

Author's collection

Donnie Winters performing with the author at the Southern Festival of Books in Nashville, 2015.

Photo by Colleen Knights

Phil and Alan Walden.
Courtesy Alan Walden

Scott Boyer

2009

We met up with Scott Boyer at his home in Killen, Alabama, near Muscle Shoals. His dog Rusty was running around playing and having a high old time, while Scott sat behind a keyboard in his home studio to open up about his band, Cowboy, the Decoys, Duane Allman, and a lifetime of good music.

❧

Tell me about where you were born and raised.
I was born in upstate New York, right outside of a town called Binghamton, New York, in a small community called Shenango Bridge.

A Yankee? I'm sorry Scott. This interview is over. (Laughing)
I get that sometimes. (Laughing) I am a Southerner by choice, and they have accepted me in Muscle Shoals, and by God if they will accept me here then I guess I can pass anywhere. (Laughs)

When I was five my parents moved to Louisville, Kentucky, and I went to grade school there through fifth grade. Then I went from sixth through high school graduation in Florida, and then went to Florida State in Tallahassee and lived there for a while. I got into a band called the Travelers. How is that for an original name. (Laughs) Then got up with David Brown and Butch Trucks, whom I had gone to high school with, in Florida State where I was a viola major. This was when folk rock had gotten going.

David Brown had the idea to go to Butch—they had been in competing bands in high school, rock bands that is. So they felt like we should all get together because I knew the words, and he knew all the rock, and we could turn all the Bob Dylan songs into rock songs.

We made a ton of money. We were making $300 per night in a three-piece band back then. This was in 1965. I bought a Jaguar ,and we were playing three or four nights a week. I dropped out of college at the end because I was making good money. I could probably do well as a viola player somewhere, but I enjoyed this kind of music. (Laughs)

David Brown went on to play with Boz Scaggs. We had a band with Butch Trucks called the Bitter End at first, and then were later called the Tiffany System, playing in Kentucky and Tennessee, around Chattanooga and Knoxville. This was when bands like the Strawberry Alarm Clock were big. We were a Spinal Tap kind of thing, acid rock. After that we became the 31st of February—it was me, Butch, and David. The three of us and Duane and Gregg Allman did play with us for a little while. I believe some demos were cut in Miami, and they came out later as *Duane and Gregg, the Early Years*. That was some stuff we sent to Vanguard, which was our record label at the time, to secure a budget for a second album. Vanguard did not approve the budget, so then we broke up. Duane started hanging out in Jacksonville, and there were jam sessions happening a lot shortly after. I think someone at Vanguard must have lost their job after letting the Allman's go. (Laughs) Gregg had a couple of tunes, one was called "Well I Know," and then there was another called "God Rest His Soul." They were good songs, and whoever listened to them at the label felt they were not that good.

You gotta love record label people. There was a lot going on in Jacksonville at that time. Can you tell me a bit about that?
Lynyrd Skynyrd was around then, but they were called the One Percent, and there was a band called the Second Coming with Berry Oakley, and Dickey Betts, and Dickey's wife. Reese Wynans was their keyboard player. They were a great band. There were several things going on at the time as well. The Illusions were a band that was kind of like the Beach Boys.

Tell me a little bit about how you got Cowboy together, meeting Tommy Talton and all that...
Well, I was living in Gainesville with our keyboard player, Bill Pillmore. We were living with a guy that was...shall we say...not making his living legally. (Laughs) We were hanging out and picking on some guitars, and I had met Bill at Florida State, and there was another friend Pete Kowalke, and the two of them were on the swimming team at Florida State. Pete came and saw us, or did a gig with us at some point in Gainesville and said that he knew this guy that was a very good songwriter and that we should meet. I went and met him in Orlando, and that's when Tommy and I met. We sat up for several hours picking with each other, and by the time the night was over we decided to put a band together. At the time, Bill and I

were playing guitar, and Pete was a guitar player, so we mixed with Tommy who had been playing with a drummer and bass player. The drummer was Tom Wynn and the bass player was named George Clark.

So we ended up with a six-piece band, and it just so happened that everyone played the right instruments, except we had too many guitar players. So Bill went and bought a piano, and he learned how to kind of play it. It all worked out well for us as long as it lasted.

How did you get signed by Capricorn Records?

Pretty much because Duane showed up on our doorstep one morning. We were living in an apartment house that had been sectioned off into an upstairs and downstairs apartment. We had a practice room downstairs in this old house. About 7 A.M. one morning, someone comes pounding on the door. It was Duane, and he was driving a camper on his way back from Daytona to Macon. He wanted to hear us play something. So I woke everyone up and scrambled down into the music room to play a few songs for him. The next thing I know, Johnny Sandlin, whom I previously knew from Miami, showed up and we did a set for him. After that we were called up to Macon. We had a place in Cocoa Beach, a little split level home in suburbia, and these high school girls that lived there thought we were cooler than heck, but their parents didn't really want us in their community. So we called Phil Walden, and he said to come on up because they had a band house. We went up there and got there late at night, and we were taken to this grey house that had cots, similar to army cots, and we all fell asleep on them. At 3 A.M., we were awakened by the police, who wanted to know what we were doing in there. We explained to them that we were musicians for Capricorn Records and had been put up there. Nevertheless, it was a harrowing experience.

After that, the band moved to Cochran, Georgia, and we had this huge farmhouse. There were only three bedrooms but they were fifty-by-fifty feet. There was someone living in the corner of each bedroom. We had the band, which was six people—Tommy, myself, Tom Wynn on drums, George Clark on bass, Pete Kowalke on guitar, and Bill Pillmore on guitar and keyboard. Those are the original six fellows. We lived in Cochran for a while, and the neighbors down there would come out and sit on the hoods of their cars on the weekend and just watch us because we had long hair. These were just good old country folks, and they had not ever seen hippies before, and they would just sit out there and watch.

There was a junior college in Cochran, and you couldn't hold hands there—and males were constrained from carrying females' books. That's how conservative it was there. The landlady came over and said that we had to go after about three or four months, and by that time a lot of our friends from Florida had come over—about twenty-five or thirty—and never left. (Laughs) I remember us driving back from New York one night, about a fifteen-hour drive, and we were all exhausted. I went into my room, and there were about three people sleeping in my bed. I woke one of them up, and the guy made the mistake of asking me who I was, and I went on a tirade about how that was my bed and he wouldn't live long if he didn't get out. The landlady said that we all had to go, and we went to get some apartments in Macon.

Tommy sent was a couple of good pictures of that old house. One had the Allman's playing in the front yard for a few people.
Oh yeah. It was called the Shedd House. It was some of the Brothers and us, jamming. Duane and Berry came out there, and we had twenty-five people living there, and on a nice day we would just sit outside on the porch and play because it was fun for us. We all learned from each other that way. It was just a fun thing to do to get together to play. Sometimes a song would come out of it. Back then it was fun.

I know the Allman's had a house as well.
Yeah, they had a place called Idlewild South. I lived there shortly after the band house broke up. I moved in with Chuck Leavell and Charlie Hayward and a fellow named Barry Brandhorst after we had those apartments for a while. Chuck and I began to look for a place to live and coincidentally we got a place's address, and it turned out to be Idlewild. The brothers had moved out by then and bought some land in another place in Macon. Funny how that happened.

What are a couple of highlights you recall from the Cowboy days?
Well, I think it was seven or eight years that we were together. We got together in '69 and broke up in '75, but ran until '77 with a last rendition. The highlights were many. One was the first time we played at the Fillmore East. It was Cowboy's first time in New York, and our road manager was driving our Ford station wagon like a maniac on the way to the Fillmore to the hotel. And I remember him making a comment about, "That's how eve-

ryone drives up there." We got into a wreck, just a fender bender, but we were late by five minutes, and we ran in to get our instruments. Bill Graham is yelling his brains out at us, and we were running to get to the stage and play. I remember running down the stairs to the stage with Bill right on my tail, cussing me out. "How dare you be late for a gig at my club!" (Laughing) That is a very vivid memory, and we had a great show thank God.

Another memory of the Fillmore was the next time when we went there, and I can't remember the name of the headliner, but maybe it will come to me in a minute. It was some large act that had been booked there a couple of times and not shown up—so many of these fans had been holding their tickets for some time to see whoever it was. So we walked out onstage to a chorus of boos from the audience, then Bill Graham came out from backstage and stepped up to my microphone and said that the people that did not like the music that he presented could go up to the front door, get your money back, and go home and listen to your 45s. Some guy in about the third row yelled, "Fuck you," and Bill Graham jumped off the stage to get the guy, but about the time he got there the security had grabbed him and dragged him out of his seat and pulled him up the aisle with Bill kicking him in the ass as he was being dragged. We only played Fillmore East two times and then Winterland with Gregg. Many years went by, and I ran into Bill Graham when he was having lunch with Phil Walden, and he remembered me. I was amazed at his ability to remember people.

We played a pretty good show that second night, and I think we were billed with Bloodrock and Spirit.

"Please Be With Me" may be your most popular song ever. Do you remember when you wrote it?
Oh, yeah, we were doing the second Cowboy album, recording *5'll Getcha Ten*, and the studio was being redone at that time in Macon. Johnny wanted to finish the album. He convinced Phil Walden to let us come here to Muscle Shoals Sound Studios. At one point they came in and we did a few tracks, and I was done for the day. The other guys still had parts to do, and our road manager—who is another story entirely—took me back to my room. They were supposed to come and get me for dinner, and they forgot me and left me there. Suffice it to say that I grabbed a pen and started writing. I was doing free association in my head, and then I looked at all the verses and started putting the verses in order the way they rhymed, just sort of a Zen way to write a song. This was just busy work because I got left at

the hotel. I was not trying to write the next classic tune. Duane came in the next day and wanted to play. Well, we had three guys on guitars already. He wanted to know if we had something new and we tossed out a few tunes, and finally I played "Please Be With Me." Duane said, "Yeah, that's the one I want to play on," and I remember that Johnny Sandlin looked at him and said that he felt that it was a beautiful song.

So I was a little puzzled, I didn't think I had written any masterpiece. I didn't really care that much about it, but have, over the years, grown quite fond of it. (Laughs) It has treated me well, and I am grateful to have written it. The motel over here where I wrote the song is now run by folks from India, and they live in that particular room, so I can't go back over there to try and write another song and see if history repeats itself.

How did you feel when you found out Eric Clapton was going to record it?

I didn't believe it. Johnny Sandlin called me while I was living at Idlewild South, and I was going through one of those times that musicians go through when you have nothing. Didn't know where the next meal was coming from kind of thing, okay? I got a phone call from Johnny, and those guys at the studio in Macon were really practical jokers. Paul Hornsby had found out on my birthday one year that I had crab lice, and he wrapped me up a nice package of three bottles of A-200 and a fine-toothed comb. I opened that up in front of about twenty people on that birthday. (Laughs) We got Johnny a duckbill cane one year for his birthday. We just mess with each other. So one day I got a phone call from Johnny, and he said, "Man, you aren't going to believe it; Eric Clapton is going to record your song, "Please Be With Me!" I told him that wasn't funny because I was having a hard time. Johnny was having to convince me that he was not kidding and it was for real. It took him a minute or two to convince me it was not a practical joke. It was a year after that I got a check, but my line of credit improved immensely—and dramatically.

Was that on *461 Ocean Boulevard* album?

Yeah, and I know it is the best-selling album he has to date. They have reissued it several times, and I can tell a difference when it is re-released. That's the songwriting business. I know the guy over here, Don Von Tress, who wrote, "Achy, Breaky Heart." He was hanging drywall. He cut the demo on that, and about two years later it was recorded. In his defense, I would like to say to the people of the United States, who hate the song as much as I hate the song, his original title to that was, "Aching, Breaking Heart." It was the producer who wanted to change it. Don is a very fine songwriter, and he has had several other good songs recorded as well.

Tell me a little bit about the Decoys.
That's something I love doing. They are a band that I love. Johnny Sandlin called me up in 1988 when I was in the Convertibles with Topper Price—and Tommy Talton was in it for a while. My wife and I were in the process of separating. I didn't have anything holding me in Mobile, Alabama. Johnny called and told me he was putting a band together up here. I had been one of the primary guys in the Convertibles, doing a lot of the work in the band, driving the band, really at the forefront of the band. So when Johnny called, he says he needs a rhythm guitar player. I could just go up there and play the guitar, simple as that. So I was ready to go and brought the drummer from the Convertibles up with me. I was looking forward to not being the lead singer, just the rhythm guitar guy who sings some harmony parts and doesn't have to do all the set up and physical work. The people who were fronting the band separated from us after a few months. I was left at the forefront. Johnny felt the band was going to break up. I felt like I couldn't just give up after bringing everything up from Mobile, and so I became the front guy in the band. That was nineteen years ago, and we have gone through a host of people, but there are two other mainstays, Kelvin Holly on guitar and N.C. Thurman on keyboards, and they have been in the band since 1990. We are the core of the band, and we have had several drummers and several bass players, but we have David Hood right now on bass, and I don't think you can have anyone better there. We do basically R&B stuff that is classic—Al Green, Delbert McClinton—and David is just great on that stuff. He has played on so many of those classic records that he can't remember. (Laughs)

In the past couple of years, I have been turned onto the music of Eddie Hinton. Can you tell me something about him as an artist?
Eddie saw things from a different perspective. He was as he was, and there was not much he could do about it. He was a wonderful talent, and one of the blackest white singers I ever heard. There is no question that most people hearing him think he is black. He did so much for so many guitar players by sort of pioneering the parallel fourth. He taught Glen Frey

how to do that, and then the Eagles had a hit on the song called, "I Found Somebody To Love." You can go back and listen to that song and see if it doesn't sound like Eddie Hinton playing guitar. That is because Eddie had showed him the parallel fourth. I am not sure if there is anything I can tell you that others have not already revealed. I do remember right before he did the *Very Extremely Dangerous* album he came to Macon and did some janitorial work in the studio. He would come in and clean the floors, empty trash and ashtrays, and I remember seeing him in there when we were working on the third Cowboy album. I talked with him and asked him to come up and play on the album with us. He was saying to me that he wanted to just stay in the position of cleaning at that time. He just had a different way of looking at things than anyone on the planet. He deserved much better than he got.

Tell us about the new Cowboy album.

Basically Carl [Weaver] came to me, and I have been doing Capricorn Rhythm Section thing for the past few years, well, during that time he has mentioned to me doing another Cowboy album. I was basically doing other things and not even in a position to respond to it. The fourth or fifth time he asked me, I told him that if he could get it all together, Tommy and I would be up for it. We have planned to get the original band members together and record with some other folks that we are playing with currently.

The music that Tommy and I are working on are some new tunes and then we have some songs that Tommy had written in the past we may use. Then there are some other songs I have written that I may be able to choose from, and another song from Bill Pillmore. We have a potential of about thirty songs to pick from. We will probably record in November and have it done by the end of November. I have not talked to Johnny about it because there is a lot to get coordinated, getting the songs together and people here. And Carl said something about wanting a spring release. I have done lots of albums, and it never happens as planned, but I am not saying that won't happen. That's an awful lot to try to get done, but it's doable. Rock and roll has a way of changing it's own schedule.

Tommy Talton

2009

One of Capricorn Records's finest bands during the 1970s was Cowboy, an outstanding country-rock band headed up by Tommy Talton and Scott Boyer. During the past few years, both Talton and Boyer have reunited with Johnny Sandlin and the other members of the Capricorn Rhythm Section to record a live album and play some shows.

Talton has also been busy performing with his own Tommy Talton Band and has recently begun writing with Boyer once again for a brand new Cowboy album. We spoke with Tommy by phone from his home in Georgia.

&

Where were you born and raised?
I grew up in Winter Park, Florida. Winter Park and Orlando is like Marietta and Atlanta. Winter Park is a quiet little place next to Orlando. I always thought this was funny, and most people think it makes a lot of sense, but I was born in the "Orlando Hospital and Sanitarium" [Florida Sanitarium and Hospital].

(Laughs) Really, that was predestination.
Right! I think my mother was in the hospital section, but uh, that is where I was born. Winter Park. I heard that at the time Winter Park was one of the places where, per capita, most of the millionaires in the United States lived. The chairman of the board of 3M company and guys like that. When I was fourteen or fifteen, we would play at the youth center, and there was one main street there in Kissimmee. We would drive out on what we thought was a really long drive out into the sticks or cattle country. Now I hear that Kissimmee has more hotel rooms per square mile than any other place on earth. Look at where the world has gone...

Things change, don't they?
Yep.

How old were you when you had your first band?

I was in the ninth grade, how old are you in ninth grade, 23? (Laughs) I was in the ninth grade, and we started a little three-piece thing, actually two guitars and drums, no bass. My good friend Walter Neils and I started a band called the Chessmen. The first name we had was the Keyes. We played Kinks songs and stuff, and even then we were already writing songs at thirteen and fourteen years old. We got that little band together and were writing our own stuff, and I remember the very first gig we did at the Junior High School, and we did some meeting in the auditorium, and we made five dollars each for that. We added a bass player and had a great drummer then named Scott Ytturia, and his parents just hated the fact that he played in a rock and roll band. They wanted him to go to dental school. I talked to him about fifteen years ago, and he did become a dentist, but he was a great drummer who was actually more into a jazz-oriented thing. Joe Morello, a drummer with Dave Brubeck, came through town a couple of times in Orlando, and Scott met him and played for him. Joe Morello gave him one of his floor toms. That is pretty impressive at age fourteen for a jazz legend to give you his floor tom. You know?

Yeah, I would think so...

It is because he was that good. Do you remember "Take Five" by the Dave Brubeck Quartet? Well, Scott at the age of thirteen or fourteen had had that whole incredible drum solo down, verbatim.

That's pretty intricate stuff.

Yeah, he had it down like it was his, not like he was copying something he had learned. Well, I guess a lot of people are glad that he became a dentist, the people who go with rotted teeth to see him... (Laughs) Then I joined from there another band in town called the Nonchalants. They were the happening band in town. Did that for a year and a half or so, and then joined forces with a band called the Trademarks from Leesburg, Florida, that became We the People, which to this day is like a pretty crazy thing. I have seen more publicity and talk about We the People than I have about Cowboy in the past few years.

I have been reading that book by Greg Haynes, *Hey Hey Baby Days*. It's a giant coffee table book.

Yeah, I met that guy in Macon one night. They were having a party, and Paul Hornsby told me he was in the book. I don't know if they covered the central Florida area. There is a great website that I have seen that some guy from Central Florida has and is a real good catalog of Stephen Stills, Gram Parsons, Tom Petty, and We the People, the Offbeats, Ron and the Starfires, the Romans who used to back up Tommy Rowe from Tampa, and the Canadian Legends—that was a real good band that did lots of Everly Brothers stuff, and might have even been the Everly Brothers backup band for a while. They were incredible. They were the ones that blew me away.

We the People began in 1966 or late 1965, I was in there until 1967, and we had a contract with RCA where we recorded. I met Chet Atkins and Felton Jarvis, who produced Elvis, and I believe Elvis bought him a kidney.

It was better than a Cadillac...

(Laughs) It was a pink kidney, and it was good one. Didn't have a lot of mileage on it.... (*In the manner of Elvis*) Thank you very much.... Yeah, I got a lot of great stories from Felton about recording Elvis. But Felton produced We the People, and we were quite popular in France in 1968. There is a vinyl LP out with all the recordings. There is a double CD on Sun Dazed Records, with forty songs of We the People. In the world of garage band memorabilia, I have heard that We the People are among the top three bands.

The bands that I mentioned, the Keys and the Chessman, we would play at the Tiger's Den in Cocoa Beach with the Allman Joys, and that is how Gregg and Duane and I met. We didn't know each other very well because we were separate bands on stage for a night or two, and then we wouldn't run into each other again for a while.

Just last September We the People did a reunion show. I had to drive to Orlando from Macon when the Capricorn Rhythm Section played in Macon with Bonnie Bramlett. I checked out of the hotel that night and drove down to Orlando, and when I got there did not go to sleep from the night before and rehearsed for an hour and a half with We the People, whom I had not played with in thirty-eight years. David Duff the bass player, who was incredible, had not picked up an instrument since 1976, and he did it man.

It just shows how he was one of the most talented guys that anybody had seen in central Florida back then. When this guy was eighteen years old and he could sing James Brown, and then he would go to the Everly Brothers, then from Everly Brothers to singing something by Gene Pitney. Anyway, they had a central Florida band reunion last year on September 16, and I was able to make it down there, and I was pretty burned out. But We the People played for thirty-five minutes, and the crowd went wild. There were about six- to eight-hundred people there, and they loved it. We had won the Battle of the Bands down there, and we were the ones to go see there for awhile. We did a lot of Young Rascals stuff, Beatles, and blues, and Stones stuff. But I just couldn't get into doing one whole night without doing anything that either I, or someone in the band wrote, you know?

Let's take off on the history of how and when you met Scott Boyer and how Cowboy began.

When we met, it was through a mutual friend named Becky. I don't know what she said to him, but she told me that there was this guy I needed to meet that she had met from Jacksonville and he writes his own songs like you, and plays guitar, and sings really well. At that time, it was hard to find someone that wrote their own songs. It was not like it is today because everybody now writes their own songs.

I had just come back from California in late 1969 and had been living in L.A. for a year, and I was writing a lot. I was doing solo gigs in coffee houses and folk clubs. I was doing some Dylan songs and then my own stuff. Becky says that there was this guy I needed to meet. She introduced us, and we both had our guitars. I know this sounds made up, but this is exactly what happened. We sat down and pulled our guitars out, and Scott played me "Livin' In The Country," which was a song we did on the first Cowboy album. I felt it was so neat to find someone else that also wrote their own music and that the music was good. I forget what I played for him, but after I showed him a song we just sat down and asked each other who could we get in the band.

We got together with a friend of mine, Tom Wynn, a drummer for We the People, and I had grown up with him, and he was also in a band called the Nonchalants and the Offbeats that I joined that turned into We the People, and he was the original drummer in Cowboy. And George Clark, a friend of mine from Orlando was playing bass, and Scott knew a piano player named Bill Pillmore from Jacksonville, and we all met up and literally within the next three months of our meeting we were all living together in a house in Jacksonville and doing nothing but working up original songs and playing all day and all night long.

We were throwing newspapers at 2 A.M. to pay the rent, and young kids would come by our rehearsals. These thirteen- and fourteen-year-old kids with some name like Van Zant or something.

No kidding?
Ronnie and them. They would come in and listen to us, and we would just constantly play. Then a guy named Duane Allman came through while we were living there, and he was with Capricorn Records and Phil Walden at that time. We stayed up until early in the morning a couple of times and played together. Duane went back to Macon, and I don't know what he said to Phil but we had all those contracts back in the mail. Phil had never met us or heard us, but he knew that Duane knew what he was talking about. It must have been something fairly acceptable. (Laughs) It was pretty neat.

Capricorn Records has always been fascinating to me. Tell me about the atmosphere around there. Dickey and others have told me in the past that it was a brotherhood kind of thing.
You can call it that, a brotherhood. But it is something that will never exist again. That is too bad, and the way the world of the music business is now and, quite frankly, the way videos have taken over and all that—I don't want to get off track here; I have a tendency to wander—it was a brotherhood. Capricorn studios was a house that we could go to. It was someone's living room that we were fortunate enough that Phil had put that together. He had had success with Otis Redding and had the money to have that establishment built.

The way Cowboy was entered into the situation, if you can imagine that two people would meet and within six months after meeting be in the studio recording and doing all original songs and having free reign over what you do musically. Not having businessmen in suits coming in telling us that it won't work. Johnny Sandlin was at the helm producing. Like one night we would be recording a Cowboy record, and then Chuck Leavell might walk in and put a piano on a tune. It was literally that loose. There was no request to have him booked to put a piano on two songs at 4 P.M. for Cowboy. It happened because it was all a spirit of camaraderie and, as Dickey said, a brotherhood, and that word was not used until after the fact, after you had been through it. We didn't call it anything. Someone would just have a new song to do, and it was fun.

Tell me a little about the Talton, Stewart, Sandlin album, *Happy To Be Alive.*

It's all my songs except for one cover, "Working in a Coal Mine." The way that whole album came about was me, Bill Stewart, and Johnny Sandlin were sitting around, and Dickey was supposed to come in and do some overdubbing on something he was working on. Well, Dickey didn't show up for a while, and Johnny just said, "Hey, Tommy, you got any new songs?" I said, "Yeah." So Bill, and Johnny, and I recorded this song called "Help Me Get It Out," and we recorded it and just off the cuff, Johnny showed it to Phil a few days later after he had mixed it. So Phil said it sounded pretty good and that we should just go ahead and do an album. (Laughs) This was while Cowboy was still together, but I was also doing sessions with Kitty Wells.

Oh, the *Forever Young* **album.**

In fact, I am the one that brought "Forever Young" to Johnny, and to the husband/manager she has, and the way that happened, Scott and I had been in Atlanta up from Macon, to do a photographic session for the Boyer/Talton album. The guy who was doing the cover was from New York, and I believe his name was Richard Mantrell. Richard and I were talking in between shoots about album covers. I told him that my favorite cover was by Thelonious Monk and called *Underground*. I asked him if he had ever seen it, and he told me he had done that cover and had won a Grammy for it. (Laughs) So anyway, he had in his possession at the time *Planet Waves*, Bob Dylan's album, before it was released. I am not sure where he got it, or if he was doing some work for Dylan as well, but he gave me that album. I heard "Forever Young," and took it back to the studio, and we were doing Kitty Wells in two days, and I showed it to Johnny. We did "Forever Young" with Kitty Wells. It was actually released as a single maybe two days later after we recorded it. What a wonderful, nice, beautiful woman she was, and at that time she had done forty-three country albums. She was the queen of country music.

Tell me about writing music for the Billy Bob Thornton movie that never happened. It was based on a favorite book of mine, *Joe,* **by the late Larry Brown.**

Phil Walden wanted to see me when I got back from Europe, and I went down to his office here in Atlanta, and it was just him and me for about two or three hours talking about old times and what he had been doing. He was trying to get a movie together for Billy Bob Thornton and asked me about it and if I would do a song for it. He gave me his only copy of the book to read. It was written by Larry Brown, a fireman in Oxford, Mississippi. I loved the book. You should read it. They'd already spent $250–$300,000 on the rewrites for the screenplay of it. I wrote this tune about one month later, because I had initially had no ideas at all.

Then one day in the shower, a line came to me, and I got out of the shower, and sat down and wrote it. I felt it might be better to do it on the piano, because you come up with different chords than you do on guitar. It's much more theatrical. Anyway I wrote this tune—it has a low Tony Joe White style vocal, the reason being he said that Tony Joe would be singing some of the tunes on this movie. It's a great story about the seedy underbelly side of the South. You know drunks, thieves, and you just have to read the book. It's easy to find, and he received many Faulkner awards. But he died about seven months later after we had talked about doing this movie and I had written the song. I had even gone over to Johnny's house and recorded it. That's the version I will show you. It never came about, and I don't think the money was there anyway. I spoke to Donnie Fritts who is a friend of Billy Bob's, and he said he would do it, but they had not come up with the money or anything, so it never happened. It's in the same vein as *Slingblade*. It was one of my favorites.

How did the hook up happen with the Gregg Allman '74 tour and album? That was interesting that an artist would have another artist featured on their album. I have never seen anything like that. Cowboy was spotlighted on Gregg's album.

That all came about for the same reason we were speaking of earlier: the camaraderie, the brotherhood, and the house. You can just call Capricorn the living room. Gregg and Scott knew each other forever. I didn't know Gregg as early on as Scott because they were both in Jacksonville, and they knew each other a little bit better. Gregg loved Cowboy and loved our stuff. Gregg and I actually became really close during that time when we were on tour and recording.

He recorded "All My Friends." I don't know if you ever listened to the Boyer & Talton album? Essentially, if you look at the Boyer & Talton album, everyone from the *Laid Back* album was all the same. Except Gregg sang instead of me and Scott. It wasn't some outside idea that happened. It was all the same people. Cowboy started the show, and Randall Bramblett was in Cowboy then, and David Brown was on bass— he also played with Boz Scaggs and Commander Cody later.

So what's this you were telling me about a new Cowboy album and reunion?
I just got back from spending time with Scott. We started writing some new stuff. Scott and I did not write that much together in the past. Like Lennon and McCartney, not to compare, but Lennon would write a whole song, and then McCartney would edit some of it, and they split everything down the middle. But you can tell when Lennon wrote a song and McCartney did a song. We started trying to do that last Thursday, just get the ball rolling and some ideas flowing. I left him some songs of mine for him to listen to, and he can say, "Why don't we change this or edit that," or rewrite. Editing among friends. It looks like it's probably going to happen. We are looking at beginning to record in September, hopefully. We have talked to the "capital-O" original members of Cowboy, and we plan on doing a few songs with them, and the rest with other friends.

The original band members are alive and still playing music. Tom Wynn, the guy we were talking about in We the People that was the originally drummer in Cowboy, and George Clark the original bass player is down in Orlando as well, and they play with bands around there. It's not their main income thing, which is smart on their part. George is a master carpenter and very good with wood. I like to do that, too, but don't have the equipment. I love woodworking as well. I had some lyrics about it from when Cowboy was living together in Cochran, Georgia, just south of Macon. There is an old, old shack out across the street, and it was an old slave's quarters. At the time it was $75 a month for our rent, and there was four hundred acres and a house built in the 1850s. I found this old shack on the property. The line was, *"There is an old, old shack out across the street/ I am going to get it fixed up as sure as I walk on my feet/You can learn a lot from the hammer's sound/it takes a lot to get it built up but nothing to tear it down."*

"She Carries a Child" is the name of the song. It's on the *5'll Getcha 10* album. Anyway that's where that line came from.

Tell me about the song "Please Be With Me."
That was one of those songs that just came out. It came out of Scott. I believe the level of honesty that you live your life in will open up the tube that connects you to the muses and to the other side. Any information that

wants to be communicated to those of us who are still here in the physical world comes through that tube if you open it up. It's called creativity, but in actuality it's just copying what someone's telling you through the tube. That is how "Please Be With Me" came through. That's how my song on the first album called "Josephine Beyond Compare" happened. I got up at 2 A.M. and wrote the entire song immediately and then went back to sleep. When I woke up, first of all I was thinking Josephine, where did that come from? The writing was not mine, very female, with that feminine look.

You channeled that right through...
Yeah, definitely, and I never edited that song, never changed a word of it from what I wrote at 2 A.M. out of a deep dream. Many people have come up to me and said that song meant a lot to them, and that it was real strong. I credit it to the fact that I didn't fuck with it.

You didn't overthink it.
I paint a lot and like music, writing, and such; the hardest thing to learn is when to stop.

I have always felt that white space is very important. Same with my own songwriting.
Sound cannot exist without silence.

That's beautiful and true. What do you think about today's music?
It's all video-oriented, and the world has become image. I believe that there is a generation of kids now that is finally getting into acoustic music and a depth of lyrics, lyrics about something that matters, other than something like...

With the resurge in Southern Rock, it's a good time for a Cowboy reunion.
I agree. You know, Cowboy was never really Southern Rock. I always hated that label Southern Rock, especially in connection to Cowboy. Marshall Tucker was Southern Rock, if you want to call it that. They are Southern, county rock. Cowboy was country rock. Many people have said that we were ahead of the Eagles in what we were doing.

Yeah, it stemmed from Gram Parsons.

Yeah, folk music electrified. Dylan and Tom Rush, Fred Neil. He is the artist that I bet Stephen Stills would be willing to tell you that he got a lot of his inspiration from. Fred Neil wrote and sung "Everybody's Talking at Me" with a very low voice. You know Larry John Wilson?

Yeah.

He is a good friend, and we used to sit across from each other in Nashville in 1980 and play for hours, and his voice from three feet away on a wooden floor would vibrate my chest. (Laughs) That's where Buffalo Springfield came from, and Cowboy was folk-rock. I have never been able to answer the question what kind of music do you play?

I saw one time Leonard Bernstein was accepting an award and said that he had worked with Paganini, Beethoven, Bach, and on and on, and he said that he had learned that there were only two kinds of music: good or bad.

That's also what Tom Dowd told me in our interview because he said that is what it all comes down to, good or bad.

That says it all, doesn't it.

Thank you for your time, Tommy. We'll be watching out for more from the Tommy Talton Band, the Capricorn Rhythm Section, and the big Cowboy reunion.

Thank you Michael.

Tom Wynn

2009

One of my favorite bands to come out of the Capricorn Records era was the band called Cowboy, a group that originated a sound that other bands such as the Eagles and Poco would later utilize. Scott Boyer, Tommy Talton, and the band recorded some dynamic albums for Capricorn, and enjoyed several years of fame. They remain a cult favorite, and many folks still name "Please Be with Me" as one of their all-time favorite songs. In this exclusive interview, Cowboy's founding drummer Tom Wynn recalls the Cowboy days, the Allman Brothers Band, Macon, Georgia, and much more.

∽

Were you born and raised in Florida?
Yes, in Orlando, way before Disney and all the major tourist stuff hit. It was a sleepy little town back then. It was very pleasant, as I recall.

What was your first exposure to music, and when did you say, "Hey, I want to do this myself!"
I used to listen to the local AM stations all the time—always "Top 40" and the R&B station. There was one of each. Even the radio stations were segregated back then, two entirely different playlists and never any crossovers. Two different records stores too, but eventually I found the R&B store downtown on Church Street next to the train tracks, and I'd go to both.
When I was twelve, I heard live rock 'n' roll music for the first time. It just blew me away. It was a group of local high school guys playing covers. The band was named the Icemen. I was mesmerized—yep, that was it. Not only did I want to do that, I had to do that. Within a couple of months, I had a used set of Ludwig drums.

How did you come to join We the People? Tell us a little about that rockin' band. Also, did you know Tommy Talton before that?
I'll answer the second question first. Tommy Talton and I were next-door neighbors when he was one and I was two years old. So yes, I've know Tommy for a really long time. And yes, he's always been three or four steps

beyond cool—some guys are just born that way. We the People was a reforming of various members from two popular groups from Central Florida. Both groups had been managed and booked by Ronnie Dillman. Ronnie kept a lot of us busy every Friday and Saturday night for years.

Ronnie had been the manager for several bands I had invited the members to join for five or six years prior to We the People. The first of those bands was the Nonchalants; the second was the Offbeats. Tommy joined us as a member of the latter. David Duff was also a member of those groups; and he, Tommy and myself joined with Randy Boyd and Wayne Proctor of the Trademarks to form We the People.

What did you do between We the People and Cowboy?

I moved to Miami—played in some terrible bars in the industrial section of town. I finally got a decent gig playing at the Wreck Bar in Miami Beach. That was Miami's hot spot then. Wayne Cochran and the C.C. Riders played right across the street. Jimi Hendrix came to the Wreck Bar and sat in once when he was in town and blew up the guitar players' amp—no one minded. I was there six nights a week for a good while. Also worked on some side projects and kept an ear open for whatever else I could find to do. Hippie-dom was just getting started in Florida.

I had stayed in touch with Tommy while he was in California after We the People had broken up. When I heard he was moving back to form a band with Scott Boyer in Jacksonville, I knew I wanted to be a part of that band just based on my history with Tommy. Somehow we agreed I should move to Jacksonville to be part of what was to become Cowboy.

Crazy when I think back—I left a solid gig at the Wreck Bar to move to Jacksonville to start a band with no intention of doing covers or anything else that might indicate we could make a living. But, as I mentioned, hippie-dom was getting started—we had to do it. So, Tommy Talton, Scott Boyer, Bill Pillmore, George Clark, and I all moved into this big, old house together, played eight or ten hours a day, every day. We did that for months. We learned a bunch of original songs. Life was good.

We had no money, only one running vehicle between us. Scott had a job delivering newspapers, and we'd take turns helping him on the route. On payday, we'd go to the farmers' market and buy dozens of eggs. Fried eggs on peanut-butter sandwiches were a delicacy. We were all very thin.

Tell me about how the band came to sign with Phil Walden and Capricorn.

As I recall, Scott had played in bands with Duane and Gregg Allman when they were all in high school five or six years earlier. The newly formed Allman Brothers Band had just been signed with Phil Walden's Capricorn Records in Macon, and they were starting to gain a little altitude. Capricorn was looking for new groups to bring forward, and Duane told Phil Walden about us because of his history with Scott. Duane had never heard the band at the time—actually, no one had heard the group yet as we had never played out.

At some point, Phil asked Johnny Sandlin to come to Jacksonville to hear the band. He did, and when he went back to Macon, he apparently told Phil Walden he thought we had something worth hearing. So that was it. Duane told Phil; Phil sent Johnny; Phil signed the band; Johnny was our producer, and Duane got famous. The lesson must be: Always help your friends.

What are your memories of recording that first album?

We went into the studio and did what we had been rehearsing in our little practice room for months. We played everything live, and my memory is that it didn't take long at all. I don't think the basic tracks could have taken more than a week or so. Some of the vocals were overdubbed here and there, maybe a guitar part or two, but mostly just went down live—all of us playing at the same time—usually two or three takes. Johnny has a way of keeping things drama-free, and I'm sure that helped a lot. In retrospect, seems kind of like a dreamscape. Did I mention hippie-dom was just starting? I think we actually captured some of it on tape. Breathe deep.

What was the vibe like down in Macon and around the studio in those days?

What can I say other than it was very cool. But, you know, you don't really know things like that when you're in the midst of it. It seemed amazingly normal. We were a rock 'n' roll band doing what is normal business for that. Come to think of it, I guess that's not really normal, is it?

The studio was just plain funky. It was housed in an old storefront building right in the middle of downtown. There was no sign; and walking up to it, it looked like just another dust-crusted vacant building. The front was vacant; the studio area was a big room with a control booth in the back of the building. That area must have been used as the warehousing for the retail store that originally used the building. Most of the other buildings in the neighborhood were vacant. Seemed like they probably had been vacant for a long time. I remember getting up the nerve to actually eat there. I remember the red neon lights on the mission building's cross that said "Jesus Saves" would glow huge in the fog. We could see it from several blocks away coming out of the studio late at night. It was the heart of old Georgia.

The studio sounded good. We didn't bother much with instrument isolation back then. We were playing the tracks live, and the room was large with a high ceiling, and we didn't play too loud so it wasn't too much of an issue. I think there was an 8-track recorder at the time, if memory serves. It was a decent machine at the time, and later it was changed to a 24-track, I'm pretty sure. The control room was large enough for the whole band to be in for playback. Johnny had a number of different speakers he could choose for that. Some were audiophile quality, "as-good-as-you-could-get" type, and some were half-blown automobile speakers so we could hear what it would sound like coming out of the radio driving home from school or work. We could hear either one by flipping a switch.

I think one of the most interesting, and possibly instructive, memories I have of the place had to do with Chuck Leavell. Chuck was hanging around a lot. He was playing with anyone who needed a keyboard player, and according to his discography, Cowboy's *5'll Getcha Ten*, was the fourth album he ever played on. But the amazing thing I found out was that Chuck had a set of keys to the studio, and every day he'd go down there and practice all by himself for at least six or eight hours. Nobody else around, Chuck would be at the grand piano practicing. Totally focused, totally straight, he would just practice his instrument. Not too amazingly, people noticed.

What were your impressions of the Allman Brothers at the time, especially Duane, but also as a whole, and were you friends with fellow drummers Jaimoe and Butch Trucks?

I liked them all. They were good guys, focused, massive nads, and they seemed to goad each other pretty aggressively, but it was much more of a warrior feel among themselves than Cowboy ever dreamed of. One listen to each band's records pretty well reveals that. Duane was definitely the sparkplug, and there were zero questions in anyone's mind about that. He was massive, raw energy. I liked him a lot.

It was interesting and not my imagination—and I don't think Duane would mind me saying—but I saw Dickey blow him away on more than one occasion. As a matter of fact, I'm sure that's why Duane wanted him in the band. Duane really did care about the music first and his ego second. Sure, probably a pretty close second, but the music was first for him. He was a big-hearted guy with a big spirit. So, Dickey was not a threat to Duane. Dickey helped make the songs better.

It was always mighty impressive to watch the same skinny guys you'd just been backstage with, especially Berry Oakley and Duane, and watch them totally dominate an audience of ten thousand people. They made a point of getting up on the tightrope every night, and people had no choice but to watch—and try to keep breathing. It was powerful. And Duane always led the charge.

I have to say, Jaimoe was the Allman Brother—though you know he's not really related, right?—that I remember most fondly. He was one of the big guys to me, much more than the rest of the guys. They were just guys. But Jaimoe, he had been on the road with Otis Redding before the Allman Brothers. He had already been doing it for a number of years when the Allman Brothers were not even a thought. Jaimoe was one of the big guys.

Jaimoe was cool, and he loved his job. Once, when both bands were in New York at the same time, we were all staying at the Chelsea Hotel. Somehow I ran into Jaimoe as he was getting ready to go across town to his favorite drum shop. He invited me to go with him. He was looking at some new drums, and the guys at that shop would customize them in ways I had never heard of. He was excited fine drummer, very delicate touch, and the fire seems to come out of nowhere. But, come, it does.

What are your memories of playing the Fillmore. Please share any stories about Cowboy and also your impression of Bill Graham.

It was definitely the real deal. The theater was an old, probably 1870's opera-house theater. I'm not sure, but my guess is the room would hold about three thousand people. It had very ornate Victorian-style plaster carvings and moldings in the lobby and public spaces. Heavy, high-theater curtains, the old recessed footlights at the front of the stage. And it had all been taken over by us—the hippies laid claim. We created a major commotion, and it was wonderful!

The sound system was enormous, and all tube-type amplifiers and folded-horn speakers. The sound was physical; it would shake your core, but it was clean—no distortion, no over-exaggerated bass. The sound was huge and clear. I had heard "loud" before, but this was more than just loud. It was better than the best stereo I had ever heard and a lot bigger.

The first time we played there, Black Sabbath opened for us. They weren't my cup of tea. Still, an interesting bill: Black Sabbath and Cowboy. What a concept. And I think Jethro Tull headlined that night, and that seemed a more reasonable fit.

I think Bill Graham was only present at one of our shows there—my memory is of a very busy guy who was focused on putting on the best show he could. I remember thinking that he was seeing everything. He was at the helm of a pretty unwieldy ship, and he made it work week after week. He and his crew developed a system to make sure hundreds of groups like ours got in and out with a minimum of fuss. My guess is they would do shows for twenty or thirty acts every month; it was an efficient operation. I believe it was sold out every time we were there—that speaks to customer confidence. Even if the audience didn't know every act on the bill, they would come. The audience knew Bill Graham wouldn't let them down. It was the Fillmore.

What are your memories of recording the second album?
Muscle Shoals—Muscle Shoals Sound—home studio of the baddest musicians in the world. And we got to be there. That studio was popping out hits at the time. The rhythm-section players, Barry Beckett, Roger Hawkins, Jimmy Johnson, and David Hood, owned the studio, and they were playing on everybody's records. Paul Simon, the Staple Singers, Aretha Franklin are just a few. Say what you will about musicians, but those were some pretty smart guys.

The studio was usually booked twenty-four hours a day. When we did our record, we had the day shift and Leon Russell had the night shift, so we'd cross paths sometimes at the shift change. That was cool for me because Leon had Jim Keltner playing drums for him on that session. Jim is kind of the gold standard of drumming for me, so to be in proximity to him really impressed me. The guy is so solid and steady and still creative within that steadiness, it's no wonder he's played on so many hits for the last forty years.

I guess the most memorable moment from that session was when Duane came to sit in. He played slide acoustic Dobro on Scott's song, "Please Be With Me." I think the tag work he did at the end of that song ranks right up with some of the best licks in rock 'n' roll history. Those final notes could slice through stone. He had heard the song for the first time thirty minutes earlier, played it through two or three times, and then he did that. His game could not have been any higher.

We were all saddened by the loss of George Clark last year. Please share with us your connection and any stories of your buddy, the other half of the Cowboy rhythm machine.
George was one of the steadiest, most consistently excellent guys I've ever known. George constantly humbled me. He was extremely competitive, rarely with others, but unendingly competitive with himself in the things he found important. Whatever interested George, he did well. He was an excellent musician, fisherman, golfer, and woodworker. He was patient, except with those who had no patience, and he wasted no energy debating them. He would simply be somewhere else, doing what he thought was important.

George and I worked together for a long time, both playing music, which continued until the week before he passed—he played great that night, as usual—and in the custom woodworking shop we shared for a number of years.

His daughter, Courtney, was tremendously important to him, and she was never far from the front of his heart and mind. George had recently been excited with the news that his daughter was to have a daughter; he was so looking forward to meeting his first grandbaby. I am sad for them both that the joy of that meeting must be postponed. Courtney and her new daughter and husband are doing great, and I'm confident the distance that separates at this moment has not dampened the uncharacteristic strut that seemed to overtake George when he would talk about the new grandbaby-to-be. With that much love beaming her way, she can't help but do wonderfully.

When I met you guys during recording at Johnny Sandlin's last year, it was just a thrill for me, and the reunion album you all recorded was sounding excellent. Now, due to whatever problems, I hear it may not be released. What are your thoughts?
It was a privilege to meet you too, Michael. And I've enjoyed our correspondence since then and look forward to more of the same in the future. It's actually a little humbling to have people fondly remember things we did so many years ago and to realize that lives were actually touched. Thanks for

your kind words about the album. I was pretty excited with the songs—I think people might like it, if given the opportunity to hear. Maybe there's still hope it will come out, but a lot of other people have decisions to make about how all of that works out.

    I think recording it was a special time for all of us. To have all of the original Cowboy players together with our original producer, Johnny Sandlin, was wonderful. Who could have predicted that would be possible? But it happened. And the thing that struck me was just how good those guys have become on their instruments. We played a couple of tunes together for the first time in more than thirty-five years when we got to Johnny's studio the first night, and it felt to me like we were home. Real familiar but way more refined, dare I say it? Yes, mature. Bill Pillmore's piano playing is so smooth and articulate. Why, it's as if he's been playing all of his life. And he's a pretty old guy, you know. (Laughs) And Pete Kowalke. I know you were there too, but do you remember when he was doing some guitar overdubs? He would play a six-measure run of sixteenth notes more fluidly than anything I had ever heard; then he'd say, "Wait! Let me do that again but with less emphasis on the second note of the third measure." Then, he'd do it! Totally freakish! Who can he do that kind of stuff? Both of those guys are just awesome players. Not just a little better—miles better from back in the day. It may be true to some extent for all of us, but those two deserve the trophy. The whole experience was great. But there's music, and then there's the music *business*. We go from the sublime to the ridiculous in that transition. It's always interesting to me how something that starts out as a free gift to the writer—the *song*—turns into the focus of so much contention and disagreement. And here we are. I've not heard every side of the story for sure, but I'm guessing it has to do with somebody feeling as if they are about to be taken advantage of.

    I think if everyone would back off a little and remember to have confidence in the source that originally gave the song, things would all work out. Then the public could decide if they actually want another Cowboy record. I think too many people think they know the answer to that question; I think there may be some arrogance attached to that thought...or maybe someone is too afraid to test for the real answer in the real marketplace. So what? Either way, let's find out. The record's sitting there, two whiskers from finished. Most of the money that needed to be spent has been spent to get it this far. The finish line for this part is three easy steps downhill. Who's going be the one to keep his hand in the air longest saying, "Yep, it's me. I'm the craziest. I'm not going to let this happen." I hope everybody gets tired real soon and does whatever they need to to let it come forward.

From my point of view, it is some combination of arrogance, fear, or stubbornness that will keep this record from coming out. None of those are reasons I would want to justify. Who knows? Maybe a little nudge from some of your readers will help. The record company's name is Rockin' Camel Records.

Like I said, I don't know every side of everyone's story, so I'm not pointing a finger in any particular direction. All I do know is that agreements need to be reached among those people. Right now, everyone is sitting with 100 percent of nothing—that doesn't seem reasonable to me. Gee, I hope I haven't hurt anybody's feelings with all of this.

Let's talk about your kids. I deeply enjoyed the Wynn Brothers CD you gave me, and have just gotten turned on to Thomas's current project, and the samples online sound amazing. Tell me everything about your musical children.

You are really opening up a can of worms when you ask about the children. Five of them, and three grandbabies. All of them have an active artistic life in one form or another. The oldest, Angela, mixes being a great graphic artist with the other parts of her life. She lives in the Tampa area. Leah, the next oldest daughter, is a talented artist and musician in addition to being a truly gifted preacher for Jesus. She and her husband, Larry Ramirez, run a ministry school and have their own church, which is making a difference in the Orlando area. Their two kids, Juniah and Judah, are a major blessing to us all.

You mentioned the Wynn Brothers Band, thank you for that. I'm glad you enjoyed it. It's pretty real, all original stuff—two, maybe three takes for each track live. We slammed that puppy dog. Could be cleaner, could be a lot of stuff, but it's pretty good, and that's the way we sounded. So, I'm glad you liked it.

Musically, emotionally, spiritually, it was a whole lot of fun. We had the band together for about three years up until about May of 2007. While we were together, the band stirred up a pretty good commotion. We played a lot, and it was one of the strongest bands I have ever been a part of. That kind of statement is more rare than you might imagine, unless you've ever tried to get something pumped up in this business. Even with two resident old guys in the band, the kids in the audience really responded wonderfully.

I had not imagined that would be the case when I told my sons I'd sit in until they could find another drummer. It just worked, so I stayed. If the opportunity to play in public or private with your kids ever presents itself, I highly recommend it.

The band changed lineups from time to time, but mainly it was Jordan, Thomas, Olivia, and Lee Simpson and myself. Lee is an old friend of mine who is a wonderful guitar player; he played some really great things on that record, some so good it'd make you cry—just beautiful. Lee and I were the resident old guys and mostly hung out in back while the kids fronted the band. CDs are still available on CDBaby.

Jordan, our oldest son, has recently become a father and has a band project together with his wife, Heather Lee. They have a MySpace page that is well worth checking out. It is great original music in the folk-gospel vein. Jordan is a mighty good guitar player and one of the wittiest and original bass players I've ever played with. He is just great. His wife, Heather Lee, is a talented writer, great singer, and guitar and piano player. And most of all, she is an exceptionally good mom to our new grandson, River.

Son Thomas and daughter Olivia have an absolute powerhouse band together. It's called Thomas Wynn & the Believers. They are working to be in the position to do music full time, so they're working it pretty hard these days. They just finished an album with old friend and producer, Tony Battaglia. Their record sounds spectacular. Thomas's vocals, songwriting, and passion are key, brought forward by hair-raising harmonies and a fiery band. They are all solid musicians, and their live show is just downright impressive. I'm excited for them. They seem to be getting close to the edge of going to the next level, and I'm confident they're ready.

What's next for you? Any musical projects? Other projects?

As I mentioned, I've been a custom woodworker and furniture designer for many years. I closed that shop several years ago and now specialize in kitchen and bath design and project management. It's a better fit for my body, dragging a mouse around a computer screen instead of sheets of plywood and lumber around a shop floor. And, it's not nearly as dusty. Got any projects for me?

I'm also working with a young sculptor in Central Florida doing some mold work for him and seeing what we can do to generate lots of business for his new foundry, Inspired Bronze. Do you need any bronze cast?

And musically, right now I'm excited about a new project that's showing every sign of being a lot of fun. It's been percolating since the Wynn Brothers Band broke up. It's kind of an old R&B and soul-type project that will be vocally driven with those all-important "nuances" gently massaged and nurtured. But we certainly won't be prissy girls or pretty boys about it. You may count on that, my young buddy.

We're gathering material right now, and the tunes are starting to take on a pretty compelling sound. We have two remarkable girl singers, ZZ Ramirez and Tammy Shiestapour. Brian Chordikof, guitarist and founding member of the Orlando group the Legendary JCs, is our guitar player and a massive force of "positivity." And, our secret weapon, David Duff, is playing bass and singing. David and I played together for years as kids. In fact, we were in We the People together. It is a major thrill to get to play together with David after all these years. David took a break from music altogether for about thirty-five years, and as a result, he has not been corrupted by too much of what's gone on musically during that time. But time has come again, and it's a major delight to hear him open the time capsule of his memories. They really don't do it like that anymore, and hearing David is such a treat. His touch is masterful and his vocals continue to be astounding.

Would you do a Cowboy reunion if asked?

Sure…well, probably. What do you mean? Will they have bran muffins? But, along the lines of old musicians playing great stuff, I heard the Tommy Talton Band a couple of months ago over in Lakeland, Florida. Outstanding! Jimmy Hall from Wet Willie joined Tommy's band that night, and Jimmy's vocals are just stronger and better than ever.

Yep. Jimmy is still the man. And Tommy's band is one of my very favorites these days.

And who, of all people, would I get to hear playing drums for Tommy? Bill Stewart! He absolutely blew me away—he always has. Bill is so solid and deep in the pocket, and then, out of nowhere, he'll take the top of your head right off with the most dynamic fill you've ever heard, then he's back in the pocket, real content, like nothing ever happened. Bill is spectacular. Bill's album, *Drum Crazy*, is a must-have in every music lover's collection. So, in the absence of a whole Cowboy reunion, go and see the Tommy Talton Band and hope Bill's playing with him that night. It will be a night you'll remember.

Yep. Well Tom, thank you for sharing your time and stories with us.
This has been a real treat, Michael. Thank you very much.

Pete Kowalke

2009

Pete Kowalke is one of the founding members of Cowboy, the coutry-rock flavored band that was among the earliest and best of the Southern Rockers to come out of Macon, Georgia's Capricorn Records label. With close ties to the Allman Brothers Band, Cowboy enjoyed several years of national tours and excellent recordings.

In our exclusive interview, Kowalke talks about his youth, his influences, and bands prior to Cowboy, as well as sharing many great Cowboy, Duane Allman, and Allman Brothers memories.

༷

Where were you born and raised?

I was born in Fort Sheridon, Illinois, up on Lake Michigan, just above Chicago, on 21 May 1947. I was an air force brat. My dad was in the air force at the time, so I moved a lot. We moved from Chicago to Milwaukee, then to Japan for two to three years. Then to three places in Ohio around fourth grade and on to Baltimore for the last of the fourth grade, landing in Winter Park, Florida, from fifth grade on through high school.

So I was raised up north in those places, but spent a longer time in the Central Florida area. That is where I had a lot of fun. A lot of water skiing and crazy high school stuff, you know. I had lots of friends and good times.

Then I went to Florida State [University] in Tallahassee. I met Scott Boyer, Butch Trucks, Bill Pillmore, David Brown, the bass player for Boz Scaggs, and a few others there. I started playing some with Scott, and Butch, and Bill, sometimes going to dropped out of FSU and started juking around Florida, playing a bit of music and starting to find out that that was what I wanted to do more than anything.

You were once asked to join the Allman Brothers Band?

At one point when I was in Daytona Beach, we—Scott, David Brown, and me—were at the Allman Brothers house, and they wanted to start a group and invited me also to join. Silly me, my response was, "You got Duane, what do you need another guitar player for?" (Laughs) Oh, well, live and learn. (Laughs) Later on at another time, I was playing the Daytona Beach Pier, and Duane came by and gave me his Fuzz Face—you know, the round effects pedal—Jimi Hendrix used one sometimes. I tried it a few times and determined that I didn't like the sound of it and proceeded to go to Duane's house and give it back to him. Can you believe it? He looked at me kind of funny like, "Why would you give it back?" (Laughs) I hear that Fuzz Face is in Duane's biography book, but no one got this part of it's history in there.

Anyway, one time way back then, I took Gregg Allman home to my Winter Park family home and took him water skiing on my local lake. I barefoot skied for him, and he was way impressed. (Laughing) Then sometime later, don't remember how much later, I went to an Allman's concert. I think it was after a few years, after the original Cowboy had broken up. Anyway, here comes Gregg out of his dressing room with a great-looking girl on his arm, looking rather high (laughing), and I go up to him and say, "Hey Gregg, how you doing man?" He still has a glazed look. "Hey man, it's Pete from Cowboy. Remember me? He turns and looks at me, and in a voice similar to W.C. Fields, says, "Sure do, best damn water skier in the world." (Laughing) And then I must have had a funny look on my face too, as he didn't remember me in Cowboy, just the water skiing! (Laughs) Funny stuff.

What was your first exposure to music, and who influenced you the most?

I took piano from six to twelve years old as a kid 'cause I expressed an interest. I also remember a Benny Goodman record when I was in fourth grade, and it had an opening clarinet lead on it. It was so cool, I played that part over and over until the beginning fuzzed out. (Laughs) Of course I listened some to the radio when I was young, and then albums, commercial radio not that much, but some of course as we all did. My brother Vern actually got me started on guitar when I was sixteen. I first heard of folk music as he was into that also: Peter, Paul, and Mary; Kingston Trio; Eric Darling. From there I started learning rock and roll, listening to the Beatles, Rolling Stones, Cream, Led Zeppelin, and of course Bob Dylan, a real favorite. And the Band as well. Then I got into the country side of rock, Gram Parsons, Flying Burrito Brothers, the Byrds, and of course I followed Eric Clapton then and now. Jimi Hendrix—I'm a fan. I have a huge, huge love for his music and influence.

Lots of other listening to a smaller extent—Emmylou Harris, Joni Mitchell—then more blues of course; a smattering of Muddy Waters, B.B. King, Freddie King, Lightnin' Hopkins, and others. Oh, yes, soul music, too: Junior Walker, Temptations, Smokey Robinson, James Brown, and more. Then later, I kind of quit listening to others as much—for a while. Now, of course, I love everything Derek Trucks does. It goes without saying my love for the Allman Brothers. I enjoyed and learned so much from being around them. That reminds me of a story.

Once I found myself over at the Allmans house jamming. Just me on guitar and Berry Oakley on bass. I wasn't quite getting free; I felt a little stuck. We are jamming, and he is just shaking his bass at me and pushing, pushing, pushing me until I finally broke through! What a guy! Then he ended the song with a huge shake of his bass, almost to shake off the final junk, set his bass down, and we finished the jam.

Got another story?

Okay, a Duane story. Once, when we were out on the road and [playing in a] theater-type place just lettin' it eat! Everyone is sitting in their theater chairs, and I am standing about halfway down in the aisle watching. They take a break, and Duane comes walking pretty briskly down the aisle. I am still standing there, just him and me in the aisle. He stops right in front of me, turns my way, and says, "Pete, this band only knows how to play one way: full tilt!" Then he turns and continues his brisk walk on down the aisle, without another word. (Laughs) I was still standing there kind of smiling to myself.

Oh, here's a good one. We are at the recording studio in Macon, I come out of one of the doors further on down, I look back about hundred feet, and there is Duane sitting on his motorcycle chatting to a few friends. So, smart ass me has a little quick blurb of a thought, something like, *oh whatever, big motorcycle*— just a quick kind of smart-ass thought—and Duane flipped his head around just as I thought the thought. He picked up on the thought instantaneously! He proceeded to kick start his bike and punch it in my direction, of course not to hit me, just to show me a bit about the bike indeed. So I stood motionless in the same spot I was in while he roared right past me, oh about a foot or a foot and half away it seemed. Man, he was roaring and going fast big time. Once again, slightly taken aback and kind of smiling to myself and going to myself, "Yep, that is one fast hunk of bike he's a riding!"

What were some of your pre-Cowboy bands?

After taking piano lessons, I started learning guitar from my older brother Vern. I played mostly at home, practicing and learning. I did do an acoustic bit on the stage in high school for something or other. I actually saw Tommy Talton on that same stage with We the People, I believe. Then on to college, where I played in a group called the Matchbox, playing rock and roll—actually Bill Pillmore was in it too. We played frat parties and some local beer joints. I was in Plant Life for a while, a Winter Park group; George played bass in that one, plus my friend, drummer, Tom Pool, and Randy Williford jumping and screaming up front. (Laughs) Really, the next band was Cowboy. Can you believe it?

Tell me how you got together with Cowboy.

Back to high school. Actually, Tommy Talton and I went to the same high school. I just knew of him and occasionally maybe would say hello. He was a year or so younger and ran in a different crowd than I. But we were there at the same time. I knew Tom Wynn and George Clark in kind of the same ways, as they had the same situation as Tommy as far as me knowing them went.

After college, when I was in Daytona and other towns in Florida kicking around, I ran into Tommy a bit again, and of course I already knew about Scott. And I am gonna have to say here that the idea of Tommy and Scott being great musical players together kind of first spawned in my head, cause I knew Tommy from Winter Park and Scott from FSU and Jacksonville—no one else did—and I put the idea out somewhere to someone, maybe one of Tommy's friends, that he and Scott should get together. I don't know who I told this to, maybe even possibly someone on Scott's end. Maybe even Scott. It is all a haze, but I do know I originally had the idea of those two, and then someone got a party together and they finally met, and there you go. Yep, I did have that original "flash" in my head. And then when Tommy brought George and Tom along and Scott brought Bill and sort of me, and Tommy sort of me also, I was asked to also be in the group, but I was hung up on a girl and went to New York chasing her and playing with this other fella. It was a low time of my life, sleeping on the floor of a friend in NYC and pining away over this girl, while the others were in Macon making their first album.

At some point I realized I was fading up there in New York, and I called Tommy up and wondered if there was still a place for me in the group. He was so cool, and said, "Come on down." When I got there it was like warmth and love to the max: friends, Southern charm and hospitality, music, recording in the studio. Man, I was so much better off immediately! The guys were all great. And I wrote a song with Billy that got to be the first tune on the album, *Opening*. I wrote the first part; he did the second.

So then there we were. I always felt I was the crazier one who wanted to hard rock it, and here we were doing this great new country rock, which I loved and enjoyed. Still, I was a little nuts, and I think that they consciously or unconsciously wrote some of their songs about me. My guess, of course, but the influence in there definitely. In songs like "Everything Here" and "Right On Friend."

Anyway you know the rest of that story, a bit more than two years later the original band broke up, and Scott and Tommy continued on with other players. We were young and had a lot to learn, but I still feel that for the most part the original band had the greatest feel of any players they played with after us. Although they did do some really cool stuff of course, 'cause them boys is talented and brought some great players in. Also, they did the Gregg Allman tour and album. They probably did more than that but I can't recall at this point—it's the Reagan syndrome. (Laughs)

Tell me about your band mates.
All the guys were great. Each with their own personality, of course. But everybody was very cool.

We were all saddened by the loss of George Clark last year. Please share with us your connection and any stories of your friend.
George was from the same town I lived in, Winter Park, Florida. Although we didn't hang out regularly, we really liked each other and had great mutual respect. George was very wise and always laughed a lot. I was really glad he was one of the ones in Cowboy. I'm also very glad we had some time with our friend George before he made his exit to the next realm. Sail on, George. We miss you! I actually felt him the other day when I was working on some bass parts. I think he came around to help me get it right.

What are your memories of recording that first Cowboy album?
Ah, yes, memories of recording the first album. Nice ones indeed. Once I got to Macon with the guys it was like night and day, so comfortable and so cool. Great weather, great friends, great music, food —the H&H— yeah it was cool. Very friendly and you know, really Southern. I was definitely soaking in it. Going down into the basement into the reverb chambers. We would crawl in and smoke a joint together. They were concrete boxes with tile on the inside for natural reverberation, microphones and such down there hooking up upstairs. So that was a good time. Then we toured and had lots of other good times, oftentimes with the Brothers, and then the New Jersey Chicks, a group of women who were our good, good friends who always met up with us when we were there and hung out and took us places and all.

We spoke earlier about the Brothers. Could you elaborate more on your feelings and relationship with the Allmans?
The Allman Brothers were just full-tilt awesome. The band flat out cooked. I really didn't know what to think. Just powerfully great music. And there was a damn wildly interesting hotel and afterhours scene in Macon. Duane was a gentleman, always. He was a really nice guy. Got right down to business too, no fooling around. He really helped push me along and gave me a few Duane stories to tell in the coming years. I am totally blessed for the time and interactions I had with him.

On the whole, the Brothers were extremely kind to us, kind of like we were their little brothers. But they also respected the music we made and the vibe and wisdom we had within us. Of course we completely loved and respected them and their music.

I remember Berry, and probably some of the others, coming up to me backstage and saying, "Pete, get into black music." They made already into it to a point, but their urging took me in a new direction. I probably had a black life or two in the past. (Laughs)

Gregg was more cool and reserved, but also still so good to us. Of course, Butchie was already our friend from way back. Dickey was always really cool and nice to us too. I didn't have too many interactions with Berry, he was like Duane, really cool, down to business, call it like it is, live fast, full and hard, and play your ass off.

One more Duane story. When we were in Muscle Shoals Studios ready to do "Please Be With Me," Duane was going to play the Dobro slide. Well, the Dobro has those little metal baffles, resonating things, whatever they are called. Duane was getting ready to play, and one of the baffles is rattling as he plays. So I look at him and pick up this thin little magazine, a real estate mag, you know, shiny paper, a little stronger. I roll it into a tight roll and shove it down one of the f-holes until it comes up against the rattling baffle. The rattling stopped, and Duane took off. That first take was so damned awesome! I really don't know if he knew how good it was. He just played it and then shot out the door and onto his bike and the next place. We all loved Duane. Still do, wherever he is. Feels like he is still around. I will let y'all figure that one out. Yep.

What are your memories of playing the Fillmore?
The whole thing was just a dream. A really fun one. I remember Jethro Tull, how Ian Anderson would run backstage in the middle of his show and just walk around and chat, run back out, wiggle his foot at the spotlight—really fun.

What are your memories of recording the second album?
On the second album, *5'll Getcha Ten*, I had a bit more influence. The songs were a bit more advanced. Still, just great fun. At times I was probably a pain in the butt because sometimes I would think I wanted to do harder rock. But in the end, I really enjoyed and benefitted from the country rock sound we had. I thought the album was just great, still do. Certainly magical things happened. Like Tommy's lead guitar on my song, "What I Want is You." Like the ending of "Looking for You," where very subtly me, Duane, and Chuck Leavell did some stuff that just blended into one thing, really, really special stuff. And Pete Carr gave me the idea to use a volume pedal and fade notes in and out during the end of "Looking for You." And there were a host of other great spots.

What were some of the highlights of your time with Cowboy?
Oh, all of it. Living together, playing together, going on the road and having a ball. Creating beautiful albums full of great music. Hanging out with the Allman Brothers and all the other incredible musicians who came through. Living out in the country was great. We had lots of friends—maybe too many (laughs)—hanging out with us. Walks in the pine forest behind the house in Macon. Fantastic! Going out in the corn field and

smashin' down a spot and then getting nekkid and laying in the sun. The Brothers actually came out one time and jammed in our front yard!

When I met you guys at Johnny Sandlin's studio last year it was just a thrill for me, and the reunion album you all recorded was sounding excellent. Now, due to whatever problems, I hear it may not be released. What are your thoughts?

I have never really had the pleasure of meeting Carl, the record company guy. But there are two ways he could go from here. He can hold back and conclude that it is not a good business venture, or he can forge forward and put some backing behind it, knowing that we are talented musicians and will definitely turn out something good, given more time. We only had about ten days. We exchanged songs and did some listening and back and forth talking before we actually came together, but still, ten days just ain't enough. And it's true, us Cowboys don't live in the same area, which would make it easier to spend time and fashion songs and reconnect. Maybe the way to go would be to not bring it out for a place and be a band again for a while. I would be willing to do that. I'm sure we would accomplish some good stuff, and it would be exciting to see. I'd like to hear what we have so far if that dadgum Scottie would send me a copy! (Laughs)

But it seems a shame to waste all the work we have put in so far. It either dies for now, or expands, enlarges and deepens, and we do more writing and recording together. I know everyone has their own projects, so that would have to all be worked out.

Actually, I am putting my project first right now, the Pete Kowalke Band. I have songs selected for the next CD and great musicians to help me do it. But still, Cowboy, yeah, I'd be willing to do it a bit down the line.

Tell me about your non-Cowboy projects, past and present.

I have one CD on Amazon called *Pete Kowalke, Glad to Be Here*. I did most of it in Florida at home and in a studio. Added a couple of songs to it out here. That was a few years ago, and I am really ready to enter into a more intense recording phase.

What's the most important thing you have learned in this lifetime?

Wow, there are a few. Have confidence in yourself first. Take your mistakes and learn from them. But don't wear them for the rest of your life. Whatever dreams you have, do them now; don't wait. Tomorrow is not guaranteed. Try to smile a lot. Be helpful and kind, but stay true to yourself. Like the Brothers would say, "Say it like it is." Definitely "let it eat, heartily!" Play what you love. Do what you love. Live it. And try to be a better man every day. As Duane said, "Pass on the knowledge you have gained and try to always learn from the knowledge that others share with you. Live in harmony with the earth, people, and all things as much as you possibly can. Take care of yourself and help others too.

Pete records these days under the name Peter Giri. In 2016, he released a new solo album called Still Want to Go.

Randall Bramblett

2008

Randall Bramblett has a hot new album out this month on New West records called *Now It's Tomorrow*, but this ain't his first rodeo. Bramblett has been playing keys and sax and singing in his smoky, near-perfect voice for nearly four decades, performing both as a solo artist and as part of a group, teaming up with Gregg Allman, Cowboy, Sea Level, Traffic, and more. He was a major team played during the glory days of Capricorn Records.

His songwriting is unparalleled. His songs have been recorded by Rock & Roll Hall of Famer Rick Nelson, roadhouse legend Delbert McClinton, and, most recently, by the incandescent Bonnie Raitt (who covered Bramblett and Davis Causey's "God Was in the Water" on the 2005 album, *Souls Alike*).

Today, the Randall Bramblett Band is a unit of ultra-talented players that can put on a show like nobody's business, opening for bands such as Widespread Panic and selling out their own gigs as well. We caught up with Bramblett between takes at the recording studio in his hometown of Athens, Georgia, for an exclusive interview.

~

We finally made it! After trying to hook up for five years.
Yep. Now here we are.

Were you born in Georgia?
Yeah, I was born in Jesup, down near Savannah.

So have you lived in Georgia all of your life?
Pretty much. I moved to New Orleans for a while, for about eight years. And I went to school in North Carolina for four years. Other than that, I've been in Georgia.

What was the first band you ever played in?
When I was in junior high, I played in a band called the Five String Alongs. (Laughs) Then I played in King David and the Slaves.

Oh, I read about that band in the *Heeey Baby Days of Beach Music* book (by Greg Haynes).
Yeah. We played a lot during high school and my college days. It was just one of those bands that played mostly soul music covers.

There were a lot of those bands around that time, I believe.
Oh yeah. A lot of them.

Who were your earliest musical influences and inspirations?
Probably people like Elvis and Ray Charles, Jerry Lee Lewis and Little Richard. People like that and James Brown. And Bob Dylan started me writing songs, really.

You were a big part of the whole Capricorn Records scene during the '70s. I know you played on Gregg Allman's *Laid Back* album and then toured with him, which is chronicled on the *On Tour '74* album.
That was the first time I ever went on a national, big tour. Before that I was playing with Cowboy and living out at Idlewild with them and doing sessions in Macon at Capricorn Studios. I think it was a blossoming of Southern music going on at that time. It was a real exciting chance for me to go out with a big tour and play some music that was really good too with Gregg. I had been recording and playing some before that in Atlanta and in Athens, but going to Macon I think really helped me get started in the music business. There was just so much going on then. Capricorn was doing real well, and Gregg's tours were doing real well. We had an orchestra and everything, it was just a real exciting time.

What can you tell me about Johnny Sandlin?
I still work with Johnny over in Decatur. We did a Bonnie Bramlett record recently and a Cowboy record. Johnny is a great producer. He's a real easy, laid back guy. He always gets those great sounds he's always gotten, you know? He's always consistent and really easy to work with.

You mentioned Cowboy. I know you have been working some with Tommy Talton lately.
Oh yes, Tommy. Our paths have been crossing a lot lately.

What are your memories of working with Boyer and Talton—Cowboy?

Well, most of us lived out at Idlewild. Tommy and Scott, David Brown and me, out on the lake there in fish camp kind of situation; it was really fun. And we just rehearsed there at the house. I did one record with them and we toured. It was a great band. It wasn't exactly what I was looking for you know, for me. Musically I was more into rhythm and blues and they were more in a country rock vein. But it was fun while it lasted, and then I moved on to Sea Level and Gregg and doing my own stuff.

I know you played on two of Bonnie Bramlett's Capricorn albums, as well as her latest record, *Beautiful*. The duet between you and her is amazing. What are your thoughts on Bonnie?

Bonnie's one of the classic great soul voices. She's got such a spirit and energy about her when she sings. She's a winner. She is a survivor. And she's got that voice that nobody else has. She's unique. I always enjoy working with her. She's a great spirit. A kindred spirit.

How did you come to join Sea Level?

Well, Chuck [Leavell[and Jimmy [Nalls] and Lamar [Williams] and Jaimoe had already formed Sea Level and had done a record as the jazz side of the Allman Brothers. Chuck and my band had been playing some dates together, and for their second album I think Chuck wanted me and Davis [Causey] to come in and help with the writing and the singing. Just expand the group a little bit. That's when I joined, right after my first solo record.

Any special memories of working with Sea Level?

Well, we rehearsed over in Chuck's basement in Macon. It was a really exciting time. We played the [Grand] Opera House in Macon, I think that was one of our first gigs. It was really fresh and new and exciting, the combination of jazz and funk and rock, or whatever we were doing; it was pretty unique. The first record we made together, *Cats On the Coast*, is a really good record. It had "That's Your Secret" on it, which I think was Sea Level's most successful song, that and "Shake a Leg," I guess. It was a lot of fun at first, but then some of us, like me, were sidetracked with other issues, like partying too much and not writing enough and squabbling inside the organization. It was just a time when there was too much indulgence going on, and we couldn't sustain what we were doing. But we made some more records, and there were some good ones. *On The Edge* was a good one. But it got less and less successful. Capricorn folded, and we—I'll speak for myself—I was doing too much of everything. But it was great playing with Chuck. And Jimmy Nalls—all of them.

How did you enjoy working with Steve Winwood?
Oh, I loved it. Steve's a great guy and has great songs. I always loved Traffic when I was in college. He's one of my favorite singers and players of all time. It was a great honor to be asked to be in his band. I played with him for about fifteen or sixteen years.

Recordings too, I imagine?
I did one album with him, and the Traffic reunion in 1994, which was recorded. He records most of his stuff himself, or with a couple of other people.

I found it interesting that you went twenty years between solo albums before you returned with *See Through Me* in 1997. Why so long?
I was working with other groups mainly. And when I moved to New Orleans, I took some time off and just didn't do anything for a while. Got into recovery and stopped doing alcohol and drugs and just focused on that for a while. I got married. Then I got the call from Steve Winwood. I played with Levon Helm on a couple of tours in the eighties, but after that I focused on recovery and sobriety. Then I got back into the music with Steve, but it was time to focus on my songwriting. People encouraged me to start recording again, and that's when we did *See Through Me* in Atlanta for Capricorn.

Tell me about Davis Causey.
Davis and I have been together since '69. He was in King David and the Slaves, Third World Band I guess it was called then. Then we broke that up and just tried to write. We worked together and lived together for many years. He's always been a close partner. He's always been in my solo bands. He's a great player. He's running the studio now; that's what he's focusing on now. He and I used to write a lot together, too, but I imagine we'll always be playing together. He's a great player. A very unique player.

Tell me about the rest of your band.
Davis and I had been doing some sessions with Jerry Hanson, the drummer. We knew he was a great drummer, and I called him up to see if he wanted to play some gigs. This was about four years ago. He eventually agreed because he's a real busy studio guy. He liked what we were doing, and I said, well, we need a bass player and another guitar player, so he knew Mike Hines and Mike Steele from doing sessions with them. I had never met them before that. So we brought them in, and after our first rehearsal we knew we had a great band. They were just kicking ass, and they knew all the material. Then we did the album *Rich Someday* at Jerry's house. Jerry's a fantastic drummer and a great producer and engineer. He's the best producer I have worked with. He is a song person—they are all song people; they pay attention to the songs. Jerry just knows how to make the best of a song. They are all just great, great guys, and I feel fortunate to have found these guys and to have them working with me.

What are your thoughts on the new album?
I think it's a bigger and more commercial sounding record than *Rich Someday*. It's more structured and more produced in a way. I wrote most of the stuff myself this time, so I had definite ideas about what I wanted to hear, But I believe its a more energetic, more commercial-sounding record, I hope. It rocks.

I understand that the CD release party in Athens was a great success.
It was great. It was totally packed. We drew on the energy of the Athens crowd. It was fantastic. We had a great audience. Fans that have been with us since the '70s. And new people too.

You are not only a great musician, but a very successful songwriter. Tell me a little about your process, how you write. Do you work from a title, or music first, or a phrase?
I write in a journal every morning, kind of free form. If I get an idea out of that or a scene or a phrase I put it in the back of the journal. Then when I'm in a writing mode, I tear out the pages and take them downstairs to the computer and grab a guitar. It's much easier for me to write if I have words to sing along. It's a lot harder to have music and try to put words to it because you are constrained so much by the melody and the music. But if I

write from lyrics first, I can just sing the thing and build the song around it. That's the way I do anyway.

Do you have any favorite songs that you have written?
Well, I'm recording one right now that I really like. It's called "The Grand Scheme of Things." It's just piano, bass, and drums. There are several songs I like on each record that I've done. On this one, "We Used to Rule the World," and "Some Mean God" are my favorites. I like "I Don't Care," and "Nobody's Problem," and "God Was In the Water." And "Get In Get Out." Those are some of my favorites.

As an aside, tell me a little about living in Athens, Georgia.
It's great. It's as laid back as you want it to be. Or you can get involved in the music every night downtown too. It's the perfect town. I don't think the job situation here is very good. There's too much over qualification. Everybody's got a doctorate. The living I think is perfect for a musician if you've got a little bit going on, or if you're a writer. It's my favorite town I've ever been in. It's a kind of liberal oasis with lots of culture and music. Just a great town.

Dru Lombar

2005

Even before Duane Allman rose to fame in Jacksonville, Florida, there were other rock and roll pioneers who made a name for themselves in the city of orange groves and beaches, one of whom was a guitar player in possession of a heart full of soul and lightning fingers on the electric six-string—a man whose voice and guitar work would front a band called Grinderswitch, one of the rockingest bands to call the South home during the peak days of Capricorn Records, the Allman Brothers Band, the Charlie Daniels Band, and the Marshall Tucker Band: Dru Lombar.

Lombar has been around the world several times, backing Bonnie Bramlett, performing with Grinderswitch, and opening shows for the Brothers, Charlie, Tucker and countless others. He's written a peach-truck full of great songs and recorded and played with the best of the best.

Today, he fronts his band of ten years, Dr. Hector and the Groove Injectors, based out of his Florida home offices. We sat down for a friendly chat with the guitar slinger just a few weeks before the tragic death of his brother of the road, Joe Dan Petty.

꙳

How did you form Grinderswitch, and who was originally in the band?

I went to Macon in December of 1972. I had heard that Joe Dan Petty, who was working with the Allman Brothers Band, was going to put together a band. So I went up there to see about that, and I hooked up with him. And with Larry Howard and Rick Burnett, [who] had come up from Aburndale; they were friends of Les Dudek. We ended up living in this house in the country, where we lived and rehearsed, and wrote and played twenty-four hours a day. We lived off of twenty-five dollar a week—Joe Dan would pay us. He was the only guy working, as a crewman for the Brothers, so he was keeping us in cigarette, beer, and food money. We did that until Paul Hornsby came along and listened to the tunes, and he got Phil Walden interested. Then we went into the studio, and off we went.

What was life like on the road during the '70s in a rock and roll band?
When you're twenty-one years old, and you're out there playing for ten or twenty thousand people a night, you know, you're just loving it, man. And people are loving it, getting off on what you do; it was just a good, high-energy, positive situation. It was work, I mean. Like when we toured with the Brothers, they might have a day in between each gig. We'd spend that day driving. Say they were in Greensboro one night, and the next night they might be in New York or Atlanta. They'd get on their plane. They had a jet they chartered, and they'd pop right up. Us, we'd get in the van and hit the road. But we didn't care, you know? We spent most of out time on the road. When we weren't playing with the Brothers, we were playing with Skynyrd, or the Tuckers, or Charlie. We did a lot of dates with Charlie Daniels and Marshall Tucker. I mean a lot of dates. And we did the stuff with Wet Willie, and the clubs, of course, where we'd get to headline our own rooms.

What was it like to work with the Allmans?
Only the best, you know? On the road, there are some bands that feel like, "You can't use this monitor," or "You can't use these lights"; you can't do this; you can't do that. But the Brothers said go out there and use whatever you want. And if we got an encore, they'd say, "Go out there and take your encore." They were real supportive guys, man.

What are your memories of the original Marshall Tucker Band?
They were a great bunch of guys. The salt of the earth. Carolina boys. Country boys. Not pretentious at all. What a unique sound. They gave a hundred percent. They hit the stage, and they'd go out and give the people their money's worth. They were great guys, man. And once again, there was a relationship there where they were very supportive of us, and you know, it was like a big family with all those bands.

Same question, Charlie Daniels.
The godfather, man. He's the one. All of his band were great guys, always supportive, talented, always in your corner, always willing to give you a shot.

Lynyrd Skynyrd?

The bad boys. (Laughs) I grew up with them guys in Jacksonville. They were the bad boys, but hard-working and committed. Ronnie Van Zant was a great talent, a great writer and singer. That's a sad situation, that whole thing. They lived maybe a little too fast.

Wet Willie?
Soulful. A band full of soul. Nice cats. Jimmy Hall, the best-kept secret in the South. That guy can sing and play, and showmanship—he should have been a big, big, big, big star. But he's a real humble, laid back guy, and not a pusher. A beautiful cat. They wrote some great songs, uplifting stuff, like, "Keep On Smilin." They were the funk side of Capricorn, I thought.

What would you say were some of the highlights from your Grinderswitch days?
Charlotte Speedway. The August Jam. We played with the Brothers and Emerson, Lake and Palmer, in front of 300,000 people. I've never seen so many people in one place at the same time. We flew in on a helicopter, and said "My God, look at this!" It looked like a sea of people. It was an incredible experience. And the Brothers shows, especially Madison Square Garden and Long Island, they were just really great shows. And doing Central Park with the Tuckers. That was real cool, man. Right in the middle of New York City, all these guys in cowboy hats. I loved it. And when we went over to Europe with the Tuckers, and we took Bonnie Bramlett with us. We were her band, as well being Grinderswitch. That was real cool, because she is the queen of soul, man. I mean, she is probably the very best white woman soul singer on earth.

I'm sure there was a lot of jamming going on at the end of those shows. Do you enjoy jamming, or do you prefer to play straight up songs?
We jammed all the time. That was always the thing, man. With Charlie or the Brothers, or the Tuckers, there was always some jamming going on. But I like it both ways. The jamming, when you play with great players like that, to me it's fun.

That had to be a fun trip.
It was great! It was crazy, you know? We were over in Europe, all these cowboys drinking that German beer in the beer garden and listening to the

oompah band, you know, and Bonnie gets up there and starts jamming with this polka band. We were just whacked, man. It was fun.

What caused Grinderswitch to break up?
Oh, man. (Laughs) Disco kind of took over the mainstream. And if you don't sell records and you don't sell tickets…you know what I'm saying?

Oh, yeah.
We began grinding down. Of course, we weren't up to the level of the Allmans. You know, down to the Brothers was a lot less down than down to Grinderswitch.

When did you finally throw in the towel?
About 1981. We did one final tour, and we went with Bonnie and did a bunch of things in Canada, and that was it. It was over. Boom! It was over.

So when did you form Dr. Hector and the Groove Injectors?
1986. After a brief break from the music industry. I'll tell you who's with me now, I can't even remember who was with me then. (Laughs) Rick Johnson, he's been with me about eight years. A great sax player and keyboard player. He was the one that was out with Lynyrd Skynyrd on their reunion tour. Then I've got Clint Carver, a Jacksonville boy, here on bass and vocals. And a guy named Gene Meledreras on drums. He's out of New England and used to be with Matt "Guitar" Murphy.

How many albums has Dr. Hector done?
Four studio records. And we're working on a fifth one. Of course we released *Cure for the Common Groove* (King Snake Records) which was a compilation. We got a little press from that one. A good bit from you, actually.

I love that album. When you play out now, do you guys do any Grinderswitch tunes?
We do "Pickin' the Blues," but that's about it. Nah man, it's like, I wrote new tunes. You know what I'm saying? But I'm always toying with the idea of redoing one or two of them.

Do you think you'd ever put Grinderswitch together and tour again?
No, but me, Joe Dan and Larry are talking about doing an album. If that is received, I wouldn't mind doing a Grinderswitch tour.

Maybe you could join Charlie's Volunteer Jam tour.
I think we could. I love those jams. For me, that's what it's all about. We could come out and do a show, but it's pretty cool when you can introduce somebody outside your circle into it, and that makes it that much more interesting. Have Charlie come out and play some fiddle with you. Like last fall, the Brothers were here and I went to the gig, and they said, hey man, you want to play? So I did a couple of tunes with them at the end of the gig, and it was like old times.

I know you stay in touch with your Grinderswitch band mates. Didn't you play on Larry Howard's gospel CD, *American Roots*?
Yeah. That was almost a Grinderswitch reunion right there. Joe Dan ended up playing on it. It was fun, man. And that's when we started talking about a new Grinderswitch album. I'd probably do some of my stuff from Dr. Hector, but do it more like Grinderswitch. I'd write some new stuff too. Maybe we'd even recut some old stuff. And I know Larry's got some tunes.

About a year later, Hittin' the Note *magazine assigned me a new interview with Dru following the untimely death of Joe Dan Petty.*

Hello Dru. Do you mind a few more questions?
Not at all. Fire away.

You have just put out a CD called *Unfinished Business*, a never-before-released Grinderswitch record, dedicated to Joe Dan. How did that come to be?
One morning in December I woke up and started thinking about going into a new century, and I was trying to think of things that should be finished before the New Years. I decided that this record should be released, even if I had to just do it on a one on one basis (I had already had it mastered). So I sent out a few emails and postcards to some long-time GS fans making them aware I was going to do this. The response was strong enough to take it up a few steps. So I came up with a name *Unfinished Business* and

sent out some more emails saying I needed a cover, and did anyone have any ideas.

I got about four or five emails with cover art, but the one that got my attention was from a long-time fan from Japan. His name is Koji Takagi, and he sent me the train track going through the clouds into the circle of light. I was knocked out by it, so we emailed each other back and forth to get the text right, and finally I had it printed. I added the dedication later. While all this was going on, I got the call from Larry Howard about Joe Dan's death. It floored me. Joe Dan was a very strong man with a lot of moral fiber. He was always honest and fair. In the rock and roll business, he was the exception to the rule. He was not only a band mate, but he was a mentor to all of us in Grinderswitch.

We all went to Macon for the service. Larry and Kirk West really put it all together. As sad as it was, it was good to see a lot of old friends who had lost touch with each other. So if anything positive came out of JD's death, it was that it brought a lot of people together and made them realize the importance of staying connected. That's what Southern Music was always about, the sense of kinship like a big family. Joe Dan was one of the most honest, moral, and committed men I've ever known. We will miss him greatly.

I suppose there's no hope for a Grinderswitch reunion now.
I don't think Grinderswitch will reunite as some of the guys are into different types of careers. I just don't know. Sometimes I'd like to go out and just play the old tunes, but it would just be me, and I'm sure it wouldn't be the same. We'll see. Presently I'm working on a new Dr. Hector CD as well as producing a fifteen-, sixteen-year-old blues-rock band from Jacksonville called Thunder and Lightning and planning a live Grinderswitch CD later this year.

Grinderswitch did indeed reunite in the form of Dru, Eddie Stone (Doc Holliday), and a cast of new players, and recorded an excellent CD Ghost Train From Georgia. *Just days after playing our first GRITZFEST in 2005, Dru suffered a major heart attack, went into a coma, and slipped away a few days later. We had lost another dear friend.*

Larry Howard

April 2001

Former Grinderswitch guitarist Larry Howard talks about his old band, his friends the Allman Brothers and Marshall Tucker Band, and his journey toward a higher calling.

☙

I wanted to find out where you were born and raised and first became interested in music.

I was born in Winterhaven, in Central Florida, in 1950. Winterhaven is close to Disney World, about twenty miles, but when I grew up there was nothing there but swamps and orange trees. I was born in Florida and went to school there; I didn't graduate from high school. I wasn't really interested in it too much. I had some cousins that were ahead of me in school, and when they would come home in the afternoons I would come home with them and do homework with them and they taught me a lot. When I started school I was probably already on the third- or fourth-grade level. I got bored with school pretty quick.

I grew up there in Central Florida, and when I was fourteen or fifteen I had an opportunity to be around my dad and his brother [who] had a bluegrass band when we were growing up, and as far back as I remember I was around musicians. Vassar Clements used to come by and sit in in my dad's band when I was a little kid. My mom has a picture of me as a kid at about eighteen months old sitting on the couch as home with the jumbo Gibson guitar and my arms wrapped around it. That's pretty young. When I was thirteen or fourteen, a man named General Van Fleet in Florida, who was a prominent general in World War II, paid for me to attend a special education school at the University of Miami for two summers where I was able to study theory and composition, which was an interesting thing. When I first got started in music, I was interested in classical music. So I went there to study theory and composition and composing.

The second year I went there, [jazz pianist] Count Bassie was on campus doing a clinic for the whole summer and had his solo chair players from the rest of his band. The rest of the people came out of the college. I went to audition and made in into his band there at the school. I was able to spend the next six weeks with Count Bassie playing every day in the summer music program at age fourteen. This culminated in a large concert at the Orange Bowl with Count Bassie. After coming home from doing that, some guy in town—and understand this was 1964 and at that time there were no local bands—this guy [who] knew that I was heavily into music came to me and wanted me to play guitar in their band. I had never played a guitar, but they convinced me to try it, and they got a guy named Carl Chambers who had written "Close Enough to Perfect" for Alabama, and "I'm a Brand New Man," and a bunch of other stuff.

He also played with the Bellamy Brothers and Ricky Skaggs, I went to him, and he physically put my hands on a guitar and then showed me how to play some songs, and in six weeks I played my first gig as a guitar player. At that time the band was called the United Sounds. That is the band I was telling you that Les Dudek joined later. Then Les and I played in another group in the '60s called Blue Truth, the first progressive all-original-material band that we did. I guess that was 1965 or '66 when Les and I played with Ricky Burnette, the drummer from Grinderswitch. We started playing and touring then. We did all original music and toured with and backed up lots of bands coming through Florida.

We had a group together in Florida, and when Duane got killed, of course we all grew up playing the same circuit in Florida—Dickey's [Betts's] band, the Jokers, and Gregg and Duane and the Allman Joys. We all played the pier in Daytona and all the same places in the mid '60s. We all knew each other and played together at times. When Duane got killed, Dickey started a band called Solo; he actually recruited the keyboard player that we had at the time, Peter Celeste—he is from Sarasota. He and a couple of other guys left Florida to come to Macon and play in Dickey's band.

Then after the band had been together for a short period of time and all these guys had moved up to Macon to play in the band, then they decided that they would continue the Allman Brothers Band. The record company and the people in the band did not want Dickey to do a solo project at the same time he was trying to keep the band going without Duane. Berry was still alive at this time, but he had brought these guys to Macon, moved these guys up there, and he did not want to just break the group up after just having moved them up there. He contacted Les, and Les came to Macon to take Dickey's place in the band Solo, and this was to go on to become its own entity. So Les took Dickey's place in Dickey's own band. That is how

Les ended up playing on *Brothers and Sisters*—because he took Dickey's place in Dickey's band. So Les was here in town with the band that Dickey put together when Duane died. Les went into the studio and played on "Ramblin' Man" and "Jessica." That's where the connection between Dickey and Les came in. During that period of time, Joe Dan Petty was a roadie for the brothers. Joe Dan had been the drummer for Dickey's band in Florida, the Jokers.

Joe Dan was up here in Macon and just working for them and not playing with anyone. He told Les that he would like to start playing again and put together a band. Les said he had just left a band in Florida and the drummer and guitar player are still down there, and Danny Roberts had taken Les's place. Danny was in a band when we left to come to Macon, and Danny went with a band called Mud Crutch. Me and Danny and Ricky were playing with a band when Les left to come up here. We kept the band together, and then Les called and said we should come up and meet with Joe Dan and jam and play with him and see what would happen.

Me and Ricky came up and met Joe Dan, and the day we got here we were out at the Brothers farm and Joe Dan fell off a horse and broke his collar bone. We were up here to play with Joe Dan, but after the accident, we couldn't play with him. So we sat down and had a long talk about what we wanted to accomplish musically and what our musical philosophies were. Then we went back home and packed all our stuff and moved to Macon and started a band called Grinderswitch without ever having played with Joe Dan. The band was formed on the basis of similar philosophies and ideals. The band Mud Crutch went with Danny and moved to Colorado and tried to get something going and began recording with Shelter. That band is where Tom Petty came from. He was the lead singer in Mud Crutch. They did some recordings and demos but could never get a deal. The band split up and the next group that formed was Tom Petty and the Heartbreakers. Tom is from Gainesville, and he was in Gainesville at the time, and this whole crew was playing together in different formations in different bands at that time.

How did Dru Lumbar end up in the band?

Here is another point of interest that is odd to me. I have been living out in the country outside of Macon, and I have been out there for about seven years, and I have just moved into a house in Macon, and then I was standing on the front porch, just in the past two weeks and realized that this house that I am in now is just two doors down from the original house that I moved into when I came to Macon back in 1972. So after thirty years, I am right back on the same street that I started on.

That house that I moved into then was Dr. John's Band—Alex Taylor's Band—that was Chuck Leavell and Lou Mullinax and all those guys were in that house. Lou Mullinax was the drummer that played with Alex Taylor and also Dr. John. But he OD'ed here, and that broke the band up and that house was available. So me, and Joe Dan, and Ricky moved into that house. Then I was at Grant's Lounge here in Macon one night and heard a guitar player and singer playing in a band called the King James Version. I liked them, and when it was over with, I went to the Carousel, a barbecue place, and here is this guy standing there from the band, and I went up to him and told him how much I liked his guitar and singing, and he asked what I was doing. I told him that me and Joe Dan and Ricky were in this band together, and I said that it was too bad he was in that band because he should come and jam with us. He told me that was his final performance with the band, and that band went separate ways, and Dru came to our house and played together for about six days, and he went home and got his stuff and came to live at our house.

That is where Grinderswitch was formed: two doors down from where I am living now. When Ricky and I decided to live in Macon and go home and get our stuff and move, we had been at the Big House hanging out for a month, and when we went home to Florida, Berry got killed. We left town to get our stuff, and when we got back Berry was gone.

Do you have special memories of Grinderswitch and the people in it? Also, elaborate on the members, Joe Dan—his passing—memories of the band.

The biggest high point of that band was the fact that all the members of the band were together for about eight years, with me in the band, and after I left, they did a couple of albums. During that period of time, Gregg would kid us about never coming home. We worked, realistically, all the time. We would go on the road with the Allman Brothers, and then we toured for several years with us, and Charlie Daniels, and Marshall Tucker Band. We would go out for forty or forty-five days at a time and come home for three or four days, and then do it again. Then we booked clubs and everything we could between that.

This is the only band I was ever in where we literally worked every night we possibly could. Through all of that, the four original members—and then later on Steve—I think the high point of that band to me, was the fact that it was really a family. We went through unbelievable good times and bad times, and everyone to this day is very respectful of each other. We are brothers and more in the real sense than blood brothers. We had incredible highs and lows together.

Ricky and I started playing in a jazz, Dixieland band together when we were about thirteen years old. We had been playing music since 1963. I had never played in a permanent, fixed band with anyone but Ricky. This was since the age of thirteen years. But the first band I played guitar in, Ricky was the drummer, and up until 1980, he was the only drummer I had ever played with. Joe Dan was an incredible person; he and I were very much alike, and very strong personalities. We butted heads over the years and were very protective of the other guys in the band over the years. You couldn't call this a love-hate relationship—it was a love relationship, just like a marriage. We fought sometimes, and everyone in the band did. I did not know any of the Southern bands that did not fight. Joe Dan and I did not ever get physical, but Dru and I did a couple of times. There were nights when we went onstage and literally fight with our guitars, literally in a battle with the guitars, and then into the dressing room continue it there. The next morning we would hit the road again. and I think the band—more so than any of the other bands we were close to—we were able to rebound from whatever our problems or differences were then. I can cite you personal things that we went through in the band that were incredible as far as some of the relationships with other people, in particular in the area of females; we went through some incredible changes, but the next morning we were on the road, and everyone was smiling.

What do you recall about the tour with Marshall Tucker and Bonnie Bramlett in Europe?

Well, I had such a great time, I hardly remember it, it was one of those tours. (Laughs) When we got into London on the first day—we had been playing at the Starlight Amphitheatre right before—actually, we had been on that tour that culminated at the end of Europe. Grinderswitch had been on the road for about 120 days straight. We had done a whole tour of the US, starting in the northeast, across the US, and all the way down through California and Texas, and through the Midwest, back down into Louisiana and Alabama, and that whole area, and then into Macon for three days of rehearsal with Bonnie and straight to Europe for one month. I do not think I had a day off for 120 days.

When we got over there, we had been at the Starlight, and some people we had known from a motorcycle group came to the Starlight to see me and Toy [Caldwell] and said, "When you get to London go to the Hard Rock Café. Someone will meet you and be there to go with you throughout Europe." When we got there, Toy and I got a taxi and went to the Hard Rock Café and had no idea who would meet us. Toy and I were in our usual form—which was pretty shaky—and we got this taxi and the driver took off like a New York taxi driver and Toy started yelling and got down in the floorboard of the taxi. (Laughs) Toy was screaming at the guy and hollering at me wanting out of the taxi. We went to the Hard Rock Café and went into the bathroom, and this guy came in and said he was supposed to meet us. Toy and I both did not know how he knew we were from America, but we were standing there with cowboy boots and hats on, and no one else looked like that. (Laughs) We were so naïve. We didn't stop to consider we looked so different from everyone else. I can tell you for sure that I know all these people, and no one is going to tell the true story of what happened between 1971 and 1980. It will never be told, no one will ever tell it.

I know for a fact from the many Southern Rockers that I have interviewed—we would be off the record talking—and they will say, "Well we might as well stop at this point and not go too far because a lot of the stories could shake the foundation of families and the legal system if it was talked about." (Laughs)

I think we were either in Paris or Scotland, and the newspapers came out the next morning after the concert that night; I think we did that live album in five different countries on that tour. We would go to a country, and there would be mobile trucks full of stuff there waiting on us. That *Straight Southern Rock* album was actually recorded in five different countries. But I remember waking up the next morning, and the headline of the paper said something about the cowboys came to France to rock, and they came onstage reeking of whiskey and hash. That sort of sums up the tour.

The tour was sponsored by Jim Beam, and when we got there, the first concert we played they brought in cases of Jim Beam whiskey, and the tour people were upset because we did not want to drink it. We were drinking other things, and they just wanted us to drink the whiskey rather than buy something else. We finally got angry and said, well, if you want us to drink this we will. That lasted about three days, and then the promoters decided to get us whatever we wanted. (Laughs)

How did you come to leave Grinderswitch? What caused you to make that decision, and what did you do after you left?

The main thing that led to that decision was that I had a severe drug problem at that time. When I came to Grinderswitch, we started in 1972, and I think that particularly myself and Joe Dan came to the table with drug habits already. This was not a thing where our association with Southern Rock thing began all that—that began years before anyone had coined Southern Rock. After a couple of years Joe Dan became completely straight. He hardly ever even had a beer. Which is amazing to me that he tolerated all of us going crazy all the time. I had gone through for a very long time and had been through a very serious drug-addiction problem, as did other people involved with that whole thing; were in the same category. The thing that was the final straw for me to finally leave the band, I had been to a couple of short-term treatment programs and on an extended tour with David Allan Coe.

I had been roaring pretty heavy on the road with David. When we got home, the guys in the band said I needed to check in someplace and get treated and straightened out. This was becoming a liability legally and otherwise with the band. I knew that what they were saying was true and that I had tried treatment programs before and it did not do anything for me. I had even gone to a psychiatrist, and he had refused to see me anymore. I was paying someone to see me, but they said they did not want to see me anymore. I wished I could blame it on the drugs, but the drugs were a symptom of what was going on inside of me. I had begun to realize that the lifestyle that I was leading was influencing the thousands of people that came to see us; they were emulating what we were doing. What had started in the '70s that had been an innocent party situation had turned into a real devastation to the people around me.

That thing made me stop and leave the band and stop and take a long look at what I was doing. Early on in the '70s, I would go out and play when we were touring with the Brothers, and we would go out onstage and everyone showed up to party and have a good time, but later on, in the latter part of the '70s, I was showing up heavily addicted, and I was seeing in the eyes of the audience that they were really in the same condition I was in. In a very real way they were emulating what we were doing. The Southern Rockers are coming to town, and we are all going to let out the stops and party until we can't move anymore. Unfortunately in the early '70s those people came and did that then they sobered up and went to their jobs. But we did it over and over every night. In the later '70s I began to realize that these people had been coming around for a long time and many of them were fighting the same things we were fighting: long-term alcohol and drug abuse. This was destroying our families and people's families. People were dying around me and in the audience. I just stopped and looked at it and said, is this what I want for my life and how is this the direction I want to lead other people in?

When I left the band in December 1979, for two or three months I just sat in the house and got high. I just boarded up the doors and played my guitar and got high around the clock. I was dealing with this whole issue of where had this whole road lead me to. I had destroyed my marriage and was working on destroying another marriage; I had seen everybody around me do the same thing. After two or three months of this, I moved back to Florida to see if I could get myself straightened out. I moved into this mansion with some very wealthy people, and instead of getting better, I got worse. Everything that I had been doing was there in abundance, and we just got into a perpetual party, and I just could not get away from it. Then on 20 August 1980, I overdosed for the third time, and this time in Florida, and I ended up in the hospital. I was in an operating room in the hospital for nine hours. Oddly enough, I knew this was where all of this was leading. During the time I was in the operating room, my family was in the waiting room and the doctors had told them that there was no way I would survive. At some time during all of this, I was out of my body watching all of this, me on the table and seeing my family and trying to talk to them, but they could not hear me. I had been going through this process for about one year, and all of this was going on inside me every night when I was hitting the stage. What am I doing and where is this leading me and other people? I realized that I had finally come to the end of the road and probably was going to die.

Having been raised in the South, I believed that there was a God, and it had not really served me in anyway. Believing that there was a God, I was not acknowledging that. In the South, when you grow up there are Christian people around, but I had never applied this to my life. The knowledge of this was not doing me any good at all. I wish I could say that I had some kind of spiritual awakening, but actually what I had was a death experience, and in the midst of this I said to God that I believed he was there somewhere, and if you are there put me back in that body and I will do whatever you want me to do. It was not really about religion; it was not about anything but me saying, God if you are there, I want to have a relationship with you. I woke up in that operating room as straight as I am now. The people in the operating room freaked out. I had fallen face first on a slate floor and busted my face open. I had been up for days freebasing cocaine and taking Quaaludes with it. When I OD'ed, I had fallen on my face and fractured my jaw and split open my chin. When I woke up on the operating table, I was still in that condition, and they had not tried to repair any of the damage because they did not feel I would live. When I woke up, I was totally awake and straight. They began to sew me up and put me together, and I have been straight ever since that day.

What did you do right after that?
I was released from the hospital the next day, and have been drug and alcohol free for twenty-one years. I am not saying that in a pious way. I am not condemning anyone for their behavior or whatever they are doing. This is what made major changes in my life. I have never been a religious person. The dictionary describes religion as man's search for God. I think that leading up to that point I was searching for some type of a true God and some type of Godliness because everywhere I looked was destruction. It was that day that my search for God ended, and I tell people that I am not into religion, and it could get you in lots of trouble. You can search down all the wrong avenues and not know God. I am not into all that stuff, but I know for sure that day I was looking at myself from out of my body and I said, "God if you are real, put me back into that body," and it was an instantaneous thing.

So you are looking at your relationship with God as more of a personal thing, more than some labeled religion. Do you feel that going to church is the only way to be a Christian?
To begin with, from the Biblical standpoint, what makes you a Christian is accepting the fact that Christ was who he was and did what he did—and you accept that by faith; that is what makes you a Christian. The Bible says that if you believe in your heart and confess with your mouth that Jesus Christ is Lord, you shall be saved. Going to church does not make you Christian. There are lots of people that go to church that are far from being

Christian. I have people ask me about church, and say that they do not want to go because of the corruption and greed and hypocrisy. If anyone tells me that they are not already involved in that in their life, there is no such thing. I go to church, but not out of obligation. I go to meet new people and have friendships with other people.

I have always felt that the majority of people I have met in church are some of the weirdest people I have ever met. On the other hand they are feeling the same about me. I am as weird as anyone can be when it comes to a traditional church atmosphere, but I have made up my mind not to let the weirdness keep us apart. So I deal with their weirdness and they deal with my weirdness. I go to an independent church; it is multicultural, and we are up to people of about thirteen different races. There are doctors, lawyers, and welfare people. This church is like the world we live in, and there are about a thousand people in our church, and we have grown to two services per Sunday. There are lots of traditional church people there, and it is still weird. At the same time, I show up there and am very involved in that church, and they feel the same way about me. They feel I am weird, but that does not stop us from having common ground in getting along.

It is all humanity. Some people are not aware of it, but I have been an ordained minister since 1987. I did not send off and get my papers through *Playboy* magazine. I take that seriously. I am able to marry people's kids from around here. I married Joe Dan's kids, and I am able to help in times when we have deaths in the community of music here in Macon. I presided over Joe Dan's funeral, and I spoke at Sam Whiteside's memorial, and I take that seriously. At the same time I am not into religion. I think that can get you into a lot of problems. I do believe that I have an ongoing and fruitful relationship with God, and I am glad that it is. The thing that burns me up most about people is that they tell me that they do not want anything to do with religion, and I say, "Good, there is hope for you," and number two is that people say they are not into this "God thing," and I say, "How can you not be into God when you do not know anything about it?" To me, it just makes me feel bad when people tell me that because I feel like they are being totally ignorant. According to world report, here is something that can potentially help you make the necessary changes in your life and give you some kind of eternal peace. They tell me that they want nothing to do with it and know absolutely nothing about it.

At the same time, 19 August 1980, I was in the same condition, sitting on the side of the bed freebasing cocaine and wondering what was wrong with me and what was wrong with the world. God draws people to him in such a way that people respond and people are drawn to that relationship. It is not anything that I can do and not anything that a church person can do. All we can do is be there and help to assist in that. It is not something that I can say that you need to quit what you are doing and go to church every time the doors are open. That is not any of my business, and what it is is your understanding and your relationship with God that will ultimately bring you to where you need to be. All I can do is be there and answer questions and let my own life and twenty-one-year experience with life be some sort of barometer for people as to whether or not this is true or of any benefit to them. I do not go preach to people. I would like people to observe what is going on in other's lives and that they know that have a relationship with God. You are going to find people that are going to claim that and there is not going to be any proof of that whatsoever.

I tell people that by faith, I cried out to the God that might do something for me in desperation, and it was not a spiritual awakening or nirvana; it was out of desperation to make a change in my life, and at that point to make a change in my death. At that point I was obviously dying. The good thing about it is that since then I do not have to accept it by faith anymore because I can go right down the line and prove to myself and anyone else that God is in my life, and my relationship with him is real, and I have proof of that. I think that people just have to accept it by faith, and I think that is how God intended it to be. But it does not remain there. God will do things in your life that are incredible, and lots of times he is doing those things in our life and we just do not recognize it and give him the credit for it. We just receive the benefit from it. I know when I was on the operating table in 1980. I have not done anything differently except try to keep a relationship with him, keeping an open mind of communication with him, and since that time, my whole life has turned around. I have my own studio, and I will not have to bow before another record company. I do not chase after a record company to release a product because I am doing it for a different reason. I do it because I think that music should be something that is helpful and helps people in some way or another. At the end of 1979, I felt like the music and lifestyle I was leading was destructive to me and my family and everybody I came into contact with on- and offstage. I do not feel that way anymore.

I feel like my music is designed and made to make people to feel better and offer people some kind of hope in their relationships and their relationships with God. I am not interested in commercially exploiting it. I am interested in whoever wants it or needs it has it. That is why I give the majority of it away. In my last project, I gave away thirty thousand pieces of product. It was in the inner cities, Indian reservations, in foreign countries, all over Russia. We are giving away twenty thousand pieces of product on the eastern border of Russia.

I have been able to work with other musicians and produced a number of albums over the years now, and especially over the past four or five years. I am producing more albums, and I have a non-profit organization. Some of the people that I said were weird at church have been able to finance me going to an Indian reservation where there is absolutely no money or hope, and because of the support of people around me, I can financially afford to go to these places and do concerts and spend time with them and go to their homes and leave music with them that is uplifting and not have to charge them. The new product that I am working on right now, when I got ready to do this, I contacted people who help me do what I do, and this whole project was paid for before I even started, and this was in two weeks time. This new CD project was totally paid for before I even walked into the studio. Everything in that studio is totally paid for. If people want proof that there is a God, just follow me around and see what he is doing.

Starting on Thursday, I am going to all the prisons in Georgia with a team of others, and I will be in there doing concerts in all these prisons, and the only way that happens is that I make my music free of charge. Now, there is nobody that I know in the Southern Rock business that could not be doing a life sentence in prison right now. I make it a point that I am going into these places and see these guys and these are some of the guys that were seeing some of the shows that we played. It is amazing to see people that are locked up in this country that were at multiple Southern Rock concerts. Now I have a chance to give something back. These people know me through all of this and go back and give something back. Some of them are locked back in cells so far back that I can't play for them, but I get back in there and spend fifteen minutes with someone who has been locked in a cell for ten years. I am fifty years old and have made a commitment to give back to others for the next twenty years if I live that long. I appreciate all the fabulous experiences I have had throughout my life. Do I wish that I had not done the things that I did throughout the whole Southern Rock thing? No, I am not sorry, I did this, and I am at the point where I do not need my ego built up and do not need the help of the music industry I am financially in a place where I can do what I do.

After all the years in the industry with Capricorn, I died on an operating table broke and busted. My brother Toy Caldwell died the same way. I can go down the list and give you names of people that went through that whole experience and ended up with nothing in the end. Do I wish I had not done it? No, it was an experience that very few people in this world will ever experience. But now at fifty I do not need another record out there to prove to people that I am talented and I can play, write songs, engineer. I need to go back to people less fortunate and spend time with them. I am not saying everyone needs to do that. I am not on a campaign saying that if you were in the music business in the '60s and '70s you should go back and do penance for it. This is just where life brought me to this. It is hard to hear the passion that I have for what I do over a computer.

I am going to Russia soon to help some musicians in Russia to produce some music and have the opportunity to make a CD. I have made a ton of them and lost count of how many I have done and I don't even know anymore, but there are some people out here that have not had an opportunity to do any, and Omega Arts is a non-profit organization that helps people to find a relationship with God and utilize the art gift that God has put in them, and there are no obligations or strings attached to them. In the music industry I am not as visible as I once was, but it does not mean that I am not as busy as I once was. There is a difference in trying to put yourself in the spotlight and trying to be busy helping other people to achieve their goals and desires in life. I have been sunburned from the spotlight and blind from all that stuff.

It does not hold an allure for me anymore. In some way, everyone who steps into the spotlight is looking for approval and acceptance. I have found approval and acceptance in my relationship with God. I don't need that, but I do not shun it. There is nothing I enjoy more than playing live, but I do not need that for acceptance or approval. One of the things that I have in my studio is what Pascal said, "All of man's miseries derive from not being able to sit in a room quietly alone." I think that is probably one of the truer statements I have seen in my life. I have reached a place in my life where I can sit quietly in a room alone and realize that I am not alone.

This has been different from so many of the interviews that I have done, and this has been really interesting to me.

You have this new CD coming out. What are your immediate future plans?

The new CD is called *Wood and Steel*. It is combination of blues and black gospel and Southern Rock mixed together. In the music, Jack is playing with a lot of brushes and plastics instead of sticks, and the majority of the album is retro as far as style, and I have a combination of acoustic leads and acoustic piano. There are several people playing on it. Bonnie [Bramlett] is singing on it, Dru [Lombar] and Chuck [Leavell] are playing on it. I have a guy that used to sing with the Imperials that sang with Elvis doing some background vocals. It is a further continuation of different styles that I do. It seems like every album has to be a different slant on the blues. I wrote all the tunes, and all the mixing, and everything in production by myself. I have never done that, and it is proving really interesting. I don't even have an assistant. It will be interesting to see how that turns out. I am producing a project in April on a guy from Missouri, Jimmy Bratcher, and the Russian event, and a festival in Memphis in June called the One Festival that deals with social awareness, and the Cornerstone Festival in Illinois that is an alternative Christian Festival, and it has about forty thousand and a five-hour blues jam. Bonnie is coming, and Dru's band, and my band, and Glen Kaiser's band, and I think Jimmy Nalls will join us, and Craig Martin if he gets free that day. Bruce Brookshire will be there as well. That night we are doing a set with all the Southern Rockers coming together for a jam. I am exploring the idea of having something like this on a regular basis with all of these Christian performers.

Doug Gray

Spring 2004

The Marshall Tucker Band has never stopped rocking since their inception in the early 1970s. There has always been a Marshall Tucker Band on the road and in the recording studio. Popular myths circulated for years that the MTB had broken up in 1984. Well, the truth is, the original lineup did indeed call it quits not long after the untimely death of bassist and band leader Tommy Caldwell back in 1980. However, Doug Gray, the band's original lead singer, has managed to keep the band's legacy alive all these years. In a band that at times included such notable musicians as original member Jerry Eubanks, guitarist Rusty Milner, bassist Tim Lawter, drummer Frankie Toler, and many other greats, keeping the love alive has not always been easy, but it has always had great rewards.

The twenty-first century finds Doug performing with guitarist Stuart Swanlund, who has been in the band for more than fifteen years; Chris Hicks, who has been in the band off and on again for seven years (Chris was also a former member of the Outlaws); B.B. Borden on drums, a former member of Mother's Finest, the Outlaws, and Molly Hatchet; bassist Tony Heatherly, who has a special connection to the band, having been a member of the Toy Caldwell Band for many years prior to Toy's death; and Dave Muse on sax, flute, and keys, a member of the Top 40 hit-making band, Firefall.

This April, the Marshall Tucker Band releases their twenty-first recording, *Beyond the Horizon*. "Number 21 for the twenty-first century," according to Gray. That, and the re-release of their classic Capricorn albums, remastered with bonus tracks by Shout! Factory, and a never-before-released live album by the original lineup called *Stompin' Room Only*, makes 2004 the "Year of Tucker."

We met with Doug Gray in the GRITZ offices for a one on one interview about all things Marshall Tucker.

☙

What motivated you and the original guys to form a band to begin with?

We wanted a place to go on Friday and Saturday night, so we figured if we formed a band we could get into all the places without having to be a member of a club or stuff like that. That was the only thing that we knew. (Laughs) We knew we liked to listen to music, so we turned it from listening into being a part of it. Showing off was basically the original reason for starting it all.

After y'all formed Marshall Tucker Band, did you have any idea that it would last for thirty years plus?
No, no idea. We didn't have a lot of real drive to do anything. All you want to do is stand on the stage and have a good time. There was not really any such thing as making money back then, so if you weren't making money, your best interest was just to get up and have a good time on stage. That is kind of why we are still doing it.

I know that when you guys went out there in the beginning, it seems like you were on the road for the biggest part of the year. How was it being away from home for such long periods of time?
For me it was probably easier because I was not married at that time. But even before the band, we knew we were going to have to go further out than where we had been playing. We were just playing around here, and you can only do that for so many weekends, right? You had to go and spread your wings so others could hear you. It started slowly from North Carolina, Virginia, Georgia, and all these different places. Then you start going on tour a year or so later with the Allman Brothers, and Wet Willie, Jimmy Hall and all these other people. At that point, you are in front of large crowds. And you just don't get up there in front of a large crowd and think you are just going to pull it off; you got to show it off. That was one of the reasons that kept us out there. It was kind of nerve-racking for us at first because we had never seen such large crowds of ten- to twelve thousand people. It was amazing to be gone and then come home to Spartanburg, and it was like you never really left.

I know you have done countless tributes to both Toy and Tommy Caldwell over the years, and I want you to give us an anecdote or a little bit of favorite memory on each of these fellows starting with Tommy Caldwell.
Well, one of the things that people are probably aware of is that Tommy had most of the drive in the band, as far as making it succeed. Toy and I

were there, but we were more about just finding a place to play, and we will get up there and do it. But Tommy was more concerned with making a step forward. He was always about directing traffic. That's the best way I can describe it.

Toy Caldwell?
Toy and I were just concerned with standing on the stage. There was no competition between any of the original six of us. Paul was the youngest of us and still in high school then. He had no idea what he was getting into at the time. (Laughs) He was thrown out there, as we all were. George was married at the time and I guess it was harder for him to go on the road. Jerry was married too, after the first year or so. His attitude was, let's just go have a good time. You didn't know what the plan was. How are you going to know what the plan was that young? We had been to war, and that screws you up. But to get onstage and see people that really enjoyed seeing your singing and play—after being gone for 280 days, you didn't really know where you were most of the time.

On this recent program on CMT called, *Country's Most Shocking: Southern Rock & Outlaw Country* (which the author appeared on), when Janine Turner introduced the Marshall Tucker Band, she said that they were not known for fighting but for generosity and brotherhood. Would you agree with that statement?
No question about it. We did a lot of stuff for others, as they did for us. It was a brotherhood, and Tommy was our protector. We knew when we went home we would hear the bad stuff, and Tommy didn't want anyone to hear any rumors about us. We were like all the other people on the road at that time, we did all the drugs and drank all the liquor, if anyone said that we didn't they are not telling the truth. We participated in every function that could possibly be except for being gay. (Laughs) It was amazing to be a part of it all. You would roll out of the bed and go get on the bus or airplane. You just got up and went to do it.

Do you think that the band out there today has that same feeling of brotherhood?
We know each other very well and each other's families. We are concerned with each other like we were years ago, and each of us will stand up for one another. Stuart has been on board now for about eighteen or nine-

teen years, and Chris has been there for six or seven years, on and off. That is hard for me to believe. We have had pretty much a plug-and-play kind of band for many years. But this band goes down the road together and makes decisions together, and in the original band we didn't always do that. We kind of grew apart because of families and different problems that we would have to face individually. We are now to the point where we make one or two calls and get together with everyone and sit in a restaurant and discuss things and share with each other. You don't want to stay in the hotel room all the time. And we are the only ones that know what happened the day before.

When out there on the road all the time do you do things to stay in shape while on the road?
I walk a lot. Cabin fever gets you if you stay in the room. Business keeps me busy a lot, and the other guys have all kinds of other side projects going on.

Having Tony Heatherly, who had played for years with Toy Caldwell's band, and Chris Hicks who has mastered a lot of Toy's licks and style, do you think these two fellows might have brought more of the Toy Caldwell flavor back into to the MTB?
Without a doubt. I would be lying to someone if I said I wouldn't love to have Toy and Tommy in the band today. But you can't go back in time. So in order to fulfill your dreams you try to come as close to it as you can. You don't settle. This is not a band that I have settled for. I am trying, instead, to create the feeling that those kind of things can still happen. And it keeps the memory of Toy and Tommy alive, which is a great thing.

How did it feel for you to have the *Stompin' Room Only* album out after all this time?
To me it was exciting. *Stompin' Room Only* was the essence of what we were doing at the time. It is grabbing hold with the old material that we did overseas, and that was a special time in our life. Most of us had never been overseas, especially to London and Paris. While we were over there, I gained at least twenty-five pounds eating and drinking warm beer at the end of the night. (Laughs) *Stompin' Room Only* is something great for all the people that never heard the original band live, and that's what it is all about. If they

got a chance to see and hear the original band live, then maybe they will remain a fan today, even though the lineup has changed.

It's interesting that you have such a wide array of fans today.
I think that is attributed to the energy that we put into it live. People tend to bring their kids back to share in the experience.

Tucker has gone through lots of personnel changes over the years. How do you feel the current band measures up to the past versions of Marshall Tucker?
This is the ultimate Marshall Tucker Band, not because we have all these CDs out but because this is what I have dreamed of for years. We are a complete band the way we are. Will it change? We never know; it could change next week. I have watched them come and go in the band, and these guys are completely happy where they are now, as I am. That is keeping it going.

This question is like the one I asked earlier. I think Chris Hicks has played a very important role in the band. As the leader of the band, how important do you feel that Chris is to the *Beyond The Horizon* album?
Very important. The songs he has written prove that Chris should be there. Chris has real talent. Lots of people have heard him and his music and not appreciated him like I think we appreciate him. We wanted him prominently on this album, not to introduce him but to re-introduce him to the public and let him know that he is a part of the Marshall Tucker Band. It will be a long-lasting relationship.

Is this his first Tucker album?
Yeah, it's hard to believe as long as he has been around. We recorded "Midnight Promises" years ago. but he never played on any records until this.

Where was the album recorded, and who produced it?
It was recorded at Southeastern Studios in Powdersville, near Easley, South Carolina. Buddy Strong was the master engineer, and I produced it, but we couldn't have done it without Buddy and Chris. They were Chris's songs, and he knew what he wanted. I tried to translate it into what was the real meat of the song while making sure that everyone was heard.

Could you share some memories with us about recording down in Macon at Capricorn Records?

When you walked into Capricorn it was an open-oor situation. That was the first time musicians were able to have an opportunity to walk into the boss's office and say, "Hey, man, what about this?" Dick Wooley was down there and was the promotions guy. The beauty of it was that everybody down there had a real say in what was going on. Their ideas were appreciated and taken into consideration. That was the biggest thing that I noticed from being an outsider. When I walked in, that was the second or third recording studio I had been in. Phil Walden had such respect. Without Phil there would not be a continuing Marshall Tucker Band. Marshall Tucker would have been just another Southern band going down the road. As good as we might have been, he knew how to take something like us, and basically we were raw and untouched, and he put us into a format that would sell.

That answers my next question. I was going to ask you about Phil Walden.

To me, he made the Marshall Tucker Band. Phil knew what he wanted, and he had the goal, not letting anything ever stand in the way for us or anyone else. He kept on going. I have nothing but great things to say about Phil.

What do you remember about Frank Fenter?

Frank was a great guy. I met his son about five years ago. I know that he has been gone for a while now. He was a guy that had the guts to open a French restaurant in Macon, Georgia. That takes a lot of guts. (Laughs) Maybe grits or barbecue, that's one thing, but French food in Macon? Brave!

Another thing that pops into my mind when I think about old recordings was Tom Dowd, do you have any memories of him?

Yeah, Tom was tough. We would go into the studio, and he would give everyone a hard time. He would tell Paul to quit trying to play so much and just simplify it. Make it easy. He gave me a hard time. He was funny because he got the work out of you. He would want us to simplify, simplify, simplify, and here we were trying to play every note that we had ever heard in every language in every world. He was respectful, and his job was to make a good record. He made everyone listen and helped you better yourself. That is what I remember about him.

There is a lot to say about your new album, *Beyond The Horizon*. I have heard it, and it is great. I think the best thing to do is to let people hear it.
I think if people listen to this, they will know everyone in the band because their personalities will shine through.

Do you have any plans to do a DVD?
Actually we are going to do one, and it will be up to Shout! Factory. There is plenty of material out there.

Tell me, just out of curiosity, of the music that is being put out now, what would you say are some of your favorite songs or artists?
Whitney Houston is a favorite of mine, but right now she is not able to hit the note. Mariah Carey's last album was not a good seller. Had we been that famous, I don't know if we could have handled our personal life any better than she has. It was hard sometimes to just decide what shirt to wear. (Laughs)

What are your future plans?
Continuous tours, and this is no different from what we always do. Most of our real dates are weekends and festival dates. We will do about 150 shows this year to promote the record.

Doug and the MTB continue to tour relentlessly with no signs of slowing down. George McCorkle, Stuart Swanlund, and Tony Heatherly have all passed away. The current lineup includes Doug, Chris Hicks, B.B. Borden, Pat Ellwood, Marcus Henderson, and Rick Willis.

George McCorkle

June 1998

There truly was "fire on the mountain and lightning in the air" on 4 June 1998 when I caught up with George McCorkle by telephone from his Nashville home. His house is located at the top of a mountain, and there were weather warnings calling for "tornadoes and dangerous lightning."

~

I spoke to Marshall Chapman the other day, and she said you guys had written a new song together.
Yeah. We did that a couple of weeks ago. It was me and her and Gary Nicholson. I was real glad to get a chance to write with both of them. They are both fine writers.

What do you do after you write a song like that? Do you place it with a publisher?
You can. But all three of us are self-published, so I just run it through my publishing company and assign it to BMI, demo it, and have my company go out and plug it, work the song.

I went up to Nashville for a while, just to check it out, and feel out the competition in the songwriting market, and it scared me half to death.
It is scary. It's very, very scary. There are so many people here, from Donna Summer to John Hiatt. Everybody lives here, and it's so competitive, it'll scare you to death. It scares me every day. But you know, I just sort of take my guitar and jump in the middle of it.

What was the first group you played in with Doug Gray?
The Toy Factory. I didn't really know him until then. I knew the name, but I didn't know him. And the next band was the Tucker Band.

Before that you were in the Rants, and Pax Parachute, right?
Yeah, that was my first band with Paul [Riddle].

Someone told me when you guys originally got your contract and began recording your first album, everybody rode down to Macon every weekend in your car. Is that true?

That's exactly right. I had a '66 Chevelle. That thing made so many damn trips to Macon! That's how we traveled. It's all we had. We were cutting a record, but we still didn't have anything.

Lots of old interviews addressed the fact that when you all were home, you spent as much time with your families as possible, but that you were always anxious to go back out on the road again.

We used to have some fun, now. Doug and Jerry and all of us were probably as tight during that time as we were with our own families. We spent more time with each other than we did with our own families. That band loved to play, now. There was one thing about us, it was hard to keep us off the bus. We really did love to play. That was the highlight in all of our lives, I think. Every show we played.

Do you think there will ever be a reunion of the surviving original members of the Marshall Tucker Band?

It seems like I heard a little something about Capricorn Records might be interested in doing something, I'm not sure. But you know, Michael, I am a very open person. My phone lines are always open, my doors are open. I don't say yes or no either way. If somebody approached me with it, I'd be more than happy to listen.

What are your thoughts on Charlie Daniels?

I hold him in high praise. He has been doing it a long time, and he is still doing it. Even living up here, I don't see Charlie that often because he's out working all the time. Me and his son see each other a lot. He is the president of Charlie's Wooley Swamp publishing company.

What is you favorite Marshall Tucker record?

I have two favorites. I love *Searchin' for a Rainbow*. I just think that was the turning point for us that opened a lot of doors. And I like *Tenth*. It was one of my favorite-sounding albums. And I love the live album. I think that Toy and Tommy and Doug did some monumental things on that record that set the pace for the future. Doug's voice, like on "Ramblin," was amazing. He delivered the songs as good as a writer would deliver his own work.

That was a big plus for us. As a writer, you have to consider that you have a singer that can deliver that song just like you hear it in your head. Tommy's bass and Toy's lead, ain't nobody else could do that.

When I was first getting interested in playing music in high school, that album scared me to death!

(Laughs) It scared me, and I was there! And I had the honor of being a part of that. Also, it was half live and half studio, which was unheard of.

Who do you listen to a lot now?

I listen to a lot of John Hiatt, and I still listen to Stevie Ray Vaughn. Eric Clapton. And I love Garth Brooks. I just like him, and what he stands for. He speaks for all of us.

I love Garth. He's a master showman. I just got his new video, and he really has one of the best shows going.

To me, he's the spokesman for all of us. Singers and writers. He's the real deal. I was just with him the other day. I'll tell him you said that. He's a very warm human being.

What advice would you give anyone wanting to get into the music business today?

Get a real job. (Laughs) No, I'd say, follow your dreams. Follow it 'til you just can't follow it no more. If you really, really want to do it, you have to jump in with both feet. You can't just put one foot in and expect it to happen. You have to totally commit. And when you totally commit, it'll happen, if your heart tells you it's going to. You have to do it all the way. You've proven that. You started out knowing what your dream was, and you've done it. We both have. We're both still chasing a dream, but we have to. I'll probably die still chasing a dream.

There's a lot of worse ways to die.

So true, buddy. *Carolina Dreams* (my first book—MBS) started out as a dream, didn't it?

I wrote it with absolutely no idea who was going to publish it, but I felt in my heart someone would, and they did. There's a big tape-trading thing

going on in the Marshall Tucker fan circles now, the same as the Deadheads. All sorts of board tapes and live tapes have surfaced.

Yeah, there are a couple of guys in the country that that's a real big deal to. It really helps keep your name out there.

George passed away 29 June 2007. The world lost a great talent, and I lost a great friend. This interview is dedicated to George's son, Justin McCorkle.

Chuck McCorkle

August 2009

On 29 June 2007, Marshall Tucker Band founding member George McCorkle died. To those of us who loved him, it was a shock we still live with to this day. Then in March 2009, George's brother Chuck died at his home in Columbia, South Carolina. I had lost another dear friend.

I had known Chuck for many years, and we met for lunch many times when he came up from his Columbia home, and we always had great conversations about music. The following story was written following an interview I conducted with Chuck in Spartanburg, S.C., back in 1996. It was supposed to run as a part of a large article on the band in *Goldmine Magazine* but didn't make the cut.

I sure do miss both of those McCorkle brothers something fierce. The fact is, I haven't met a member of the McCorkle family yet that I didn't like.

❦

"The very earliest things I remember was when mother bought us a guitar," remembers Chuck McCorkle, the older brother of Marshall Tucker's original rhythm guitarist George, today living in Columbia. "That was for two people, a single guitar. She did the best she could. We were very poor, and my father had left us. I think I was about fourteen, George was twelve, and she bought us an acoustic guitar from Montgomery Ward. If I remember correctly, it was $19.95. It came with a little instruction book that showed how to make the chords, and it came with a pitch pipe for tuning. Ironically, I was more interested in the guitar than George was."

When their mother would go to work in the morning, and George would go to school, Chuck would get that guitar out and start playing it. He was obsessed.

"Pretty soon, George would be home from school, and I would have been playing that thing all day without realizing it. I never had another obsession like that in my life, except my love for [my wife] Freeda. We lived over on the south side of town then, near Southside Baptist Church, where Jenkins Junior High used to be. Eventually, mom bought a small house over in Park Hills. It's kind of cloudy to me now how we got to know Toy and

Tommy and Franklin and those. They already lived there. We moved there when we were in junior high. We all started getting together and playing music."

On Saturdays, while other kids were playing basketball, the McCorkle boys played music. At first, they played in an old room on Spring Street, behind the old Smith Music Store. Tommy Caldwell played drums a lot during those days, and Chuck was usually the guitarist.

"The first time George and I played together was in a band called the Originals," says Chuck, " That was with Dave Haddox and Ronnie Cooksey. I met Ronnie in junior high. He was about twenty years old and in the ninth grade. His brother played too. One of the things I remember most about the Originals was that we all wore matching outfits. We had black ones and white ones. One night we were playing at some bar out here on Greenville Highway, near the old South 29 drive-in. I saw a guy get stabbed to death. Several people jumped on this guy and started stabbing him to death. We just kept on playing. The police came and hauled everybody off. Later, after we finished the gig, the guy was outside with a .45 automatic, threatening to kill us. He said he'd kill anybody who came out the door because he had been waiting for the owner all night. The owner owed us $15 each, and he wanted to pay us with this prostitute. Hell, I was only fifteen, and this was a big girl. I don't remember what happened, but I think we called the police, and they lead us out at three in the morning.

"The only other story I remember with the Originals was the time we played this party at Rainbow Lake. There was this song we played, and the people wanted to hear it again. Well, it was quitting time, but we played it again anyway. Then they told us, "Y'all aren't going anywhere. We want to hear it again. They were real drunk, and they made us stay an extra couple of hours and play, or they'd whip our butts. Then a fight broke out, and we were running and unplugging our amps and stuff. We got our stuff and got out of there."

Like David Haddox, Chuck McCorkle remembers how the band decided on the name for the Originals.

"In the ninth grade we had a teacher named Rosey," says Chuck. "Well, there was a band out called Rosey and the Originals, and they had a record out called "Angel Baby." We all had the hots for this teacher, and she was probably about Ronnie's age, come to think of it. (Laughs) We were all trying to hit on Rosey, and she always liked the attention.

"I think about the time I was in the Originals, I was always strictly rhythm, Ronnie played all the lead, and I think George played bass. Of course, David was the drummer. That was about the time I met and fell in love with Freeda. She and I were inseparable, and still are. We've been married now for twenty-eight years. I quit playing in bands, but I still played and jammed. We used to play in the Caldwell's basement, as well as Wilkie's garage. The Rants started rehearsing, and I'd jam with them and stuff. But what I remember most is that it seemed like overnight one weekend, Toy became this killer guitar player. I mean he got good, real good. We all had Silvertone guitars and amps, little cheap shit. I walked in one day and Toy had this Gibson 335 and a Fender Twin, and he was just smokin'. I said, "Toy, how do you play like that?" He said, "I don't know, that's just how I play." It was like Toy had been blessed overnight and had just transcended into a higher realm, to become the best guitar player around. Tommy was always the killer drummer and bass player. I was so busy pulling up out of the poverty we had come up in. I wanted to go to college and I did. I went to Spartanburg Junior College and Clemson University. Then we formed a band called the Puzzle, and started playing around. And there was Pax Parachute. But when Toy came out of the service, all of the band members started congregating around him. He was just so good. That's the way the Marshall Tucker Band came to be."

In 1973, Chuck started his own band, the Early Wyldes, in his home, Columbia, S.C.

"We opened shows for Marshall Tucker, and got good reviews. We played places like Syracuse. University of Pennsylvania. It was great fun. It's really a rush to play in front of 30,000 screaming bodies. When you walk onstage, and plug your guitar in and the 'thump' sounds like an explosion, and the entire crowd begins to scream. There's nothing like that."

Chuck McCorkle ended up going on the road with his brother's band on two occasions, once in the mid-seventies, and again in the early eighties.

"The first time I went out on the road with Tucker was 1975," says Chuck. "I went out as photographer for the band—that was my minor in college. I shot over a hundred rolls of film. They used my photos for the artist to go by for the *Where We All Belong* album. We stayed in the best hotels, they rode us around in limousines, and they rode us in and out of gigs in helicopters. It was great, man. It was amazing to me. I remember standing on the stage with Wolfman Jack at the August Jam in Charlotte. I worked with Marshall Tucker in 1981 and early 1982. I was guitar technician.

George always carried a shit-load of guitars on the road, some of which were mine. We still have some guitars in common that are both his and mine. But my job was to keep the guitars tuned and cleaned, and everybody was fine with that ... all except Franklin Wilkie. He wouldn't let me do his bass. He said, 'I take care of my own bass.' And he took it and put strings on it. What it was, was Frank thought it was beneath me to clean and tune his guitar. Of course, it was my job, but that was really nice of him, and I'll never forget it."

Charlie Daniels

Fall 2000

I have had the privilege of interviewing Charlie Daniels many times over the years. The following interview took place in October 2000, just as Charlie had released a new album that found his band covering classic Southern Rock songs by many of his fellow bands, including Marshall Tucker and Lynyrd Skynyrd.

≈

What inspired you to record the songs you recorded for your new album, *Tailgate Party***?**
It's something I wanted to do for a long time, to pay tribute to Southern musicians. With special emphasis on Tucker and the Brothers and Skynyrd, people we worked with. And some of the new guys, Hootie and, well, ZZ Top is not at all new. They're not usually thought of in the same genre, but they are very Southern. It was an idea I had for a long time that just happened.

You dedicated the record to Duane Allman. Was Duane an influence of yours, or a favorite player?
Duane was a favorite and an influence. I don't believe there has been a musician come along from our part of the country since that early Allman Brothers Band that hasn't been influenced by Duane in one way or another, at least by the caliber and intensity of Duane's playing. I know I have.

Early on, you had the chance to record with lots of great performers. What were some of your most memorable sessions?
Well, I had a great time recording with Bob Dylan. They were great sessions. It was real loose, and there was no pressure to do this or that or the other. He wanted everybody to play their own thing. And that's basically how his music is. He writes the song and everybody just sits around and plays whatever they feel fits. It was a lot of fun. I enjoyed playing with Leonard Cohen. A lot of the country artists were just straight-ahead sessions.

You recorded with one of the Beatles. Was it George?
Yes. It wasn't released. It was George and a drummer named Russ Kunkel and myself. And I recorded with Ringo Starr, but it was pretty much a straight-ahead country session.

You've written and recorded a lot of songs. What would you say has been your favorite?
I can't do that. It's hard for me to choose between songs. Of course the biggest song we ever had was "The Devil Went Down to Georgia," but I can't really say that's my cut-and-dried favorite song. It's just be hard to say. So many songs meant a lot to me. "Carolina I Remember You" means a lot.

Would you tell us a little about each one of the band members?
Sure I can. Taz DiGregorio [keyboards] is from Southbridge, Massachusetts. He's been working with me for about thirty-four years, other than a few years he was in the Army. Charlie Hayward [bass] has been with me for twenty-three years. He's from Holt, Alabama. Jack Gavin [drums] is from Niagara Falls, New York, and he's been with me for about thirteen years now. Bruce Brown [guitar] is from West Frankfort, Illinois, and he's been with me for almost ten years. The new kid on the block is Chris Wormer, who is in his fourth year now.

Are you currently performing any of the songs from your *Blues Hat* CD during your shows?
We're doing "Just to Satisfy You" and "Long Haired Country Boy." Of course, that's not a blues tune, but it was on the album.

What do you find to be the most rewarding aspect of being a popular entertainer?
The most rewarding thing is being able to do whatever I want to do for a living. I can't imagine doing anything else. I've enjoyed this; just being a part of the music business for all this time has been great.

When you have time to listen to music, who do you listen to?
You know who I listen to, probably more than any other artist? Stevie Ray Vaughan. I love Stevie Ray. I love the blues; obviously you do too. I listen to music a lot when I go in to exercise during the day. I ride on one of those exercise bikes for about a half hour a day. It all depends on what I pick

up off the bus. Sometimes it may be Stevie Ray, and other times it may be Beethoven, or Mozart, or a jazz album. It all depends on what kind of mood I'm in.

How did the Volunteer Jam first come to be?
Volunteer Jam was a live recording session. We were doing the *Fire on the Mountain* album, and we wanted to do two live cuts, so we figured the best place to do it was in Nashville, which was about the only place we could draw a crowd at that time. We got some recording equipment and asked some of our friends to come up and jam with us. That first year, Toy Caldwell, Jerry Eubanks, and Doug Gray from the Marshall Tucker Band, and Dickey Betts from the Allman Brothers were in town, and we invited him up. It was called Volunteer Jam, naturally, after the state of Tennessee. After the first time, we decided we needed to do this again.

Did you continue to have those jams every year after that?
We had them every year for a while, then they got to be entirely too big an undertaking to do every year. This is the first time we've taken it on the road.

What can the fans expect to see during the Volunteer Jam shows?
Just a good ol', Toy used to say, "watermelon jam." Just a good ol' Southern, down-home, fried-chicken-and-catfish-type, great, great entertaining evening. Maybe coming in not feeling too good with the traffic and stuff and leaving with a smile on your face.

As far as the Volunteer Jam tour. What are your feelings about it?
It's been special to me, working with old friends like the Marshall Tucker Band. There ain't a whole lot of the original band left, but I've made friends with the new ones. We get along great; our road crews get along great. And Molly Hatchet only has one original member, too, but hey, buddy, it's down-home week.

Do you recall the first time you encountered the Marshall Tucker Band?
I sure do. We first played a show together in 1973. We both opened for the Allman Brothers Band in Nashville, and I walked in their dressing room and said, "Somebody told me you s.o.b.'s used to go to Jenkins Junior High

School. Toy jerked around and looked at me like, "Who in the hell are you?" (Laughs) I told him I used to go there too. We just kind of hit it off. We've been doing that way ever since.

What was it like touring with the MTB during the seventies?
Playing with the MTB was great. It was a natural show. We used to end the night up with three drummers on the stage doing something everybody knew. We probably did more dates with Marshall Tucker than any other band that I know of.

I know you probably have a lot of old material from the past jams. Is Blue Hat planning on putting any of that out?
There's a problem with trying to get clearance on that stuff, Michael. It's just a total nightmare to try and get clearance. Like Stevie Ray is dead, and having to deal with his estate. Just trying to clear it with record companies; it's real tough. We have just released a Jam record from some of the Epic Records material. It's a Blue Hat Record, released through Epic. We also have a second volume of "the best of the jams."

What's happening with Blue Hat Records right now? It seems pretty exciting to have your own record company.
It can also be pretty expensive. (Laughs) We just signed a new group, two girls called Sisters Wade that are just a breath of fresh air. They do acoustic music. We had a showcase for them last night. It's just good music. One of the aims of Blue Hat Records is to release good music. We're not going to be doing fluff. This is good music.

Do you have any other projects planned for the near future?
I plan to do more recording next year, I just don't know what yet. Mostly it's the same ol', same ol', Michael. Just going out there and picking and grinning.

What do you feel are the most important things on life? What advice would you offer young people of today regarding a career in the music industry?
Salvation. I think committing your life to Jesus Christ is the most important thing you can do. If I could drive a point home to the youth of today, I would say that the single most important thing you can do is to accept

Jesus Christ as your Lord and Savior. It's the only way to true peace and success. When you have Jesus, you have everything that really counts.

As far as professionally, I would say to any young person who desires a career in the music business, to make very sure that's what you want to do, then go somewhere where there is a music business and go for it. You have to be willing to be the first one there, and the last one to leave. You have to work when everybody else is playing. To take scathing criticism in stride, and to decide that you're going to make it even if you have to work twice as hard as anybody else ever has. Be honest with yourself about the amount of talent you have. Never compare your career to anyone else's. Everybody goes at their own pace.

Charlie continues to record great albums, tour continuously, support charities and spread his faith and beliefs at every stop. Keep up with the CDB at www.charliedaniels.com

Tommy Crain

December 2001

One of the hottest guitar slingers in Southern Rock is Tommy Crain. Tommy played with the Charlie Daniels Band for fifteen years before the road took it's toll and he dropped out of sight for a bit. He is back now, playing hotter than ever.

~

Tommy, where were you born and raised?
I was born and raised in Nashville, Tennessee.

When did you first become interested in playing music?
There was a kid in the sixth grade that lived down the street. He had a guitar and he taught me how to play a four-string ukulele. We learned "Where Have All The Flowers Gone." (Laughs)

Oh yeah, long time passing. (Laughs)
Yeah, and we entered a talent contest in the school and performed it and won and at that time I knew this is what I want to do. I want to entertain.

So what was the first band that you put together.
I was in the seventh grade, and it was a school that was a private boys school called Montgomery Bell Academy here in Nashville. A very straight, upper-left kind of thing, and I got with some of my schoolmates in the neighborhood and named our group the Spartans. I believe we must have been studying ancient Greek and Roman history at that time. These guys had another guitar player that they didn't like, and then I had borrowed his guitar and amp one day and played with them, and they said he is fired and you are hired. I guess I felt kind of bad about that. (Laughs)

How quickly people come and go in this business.
I saw that early on.

What other memories can you share about some of the early groups you performed with? I don't know much about your pre-Charlie Daniels history, so what can you share about that?

Still in high school, I had made most of my living from the age of fourteen onward in music. I was a member of a fraternity, and we would play pretty much every Friday and Saturday night for the sorority and fraternity dances. The first one of these bands was called the Lemonade Charade. I was telling you yesterday, I went through a trunk-load of pictures and found some just classical shots, one of the first promo shots was me with this band in clown-like Beatle outfits, bell-bottoms and flared sleeves and very colorful. This stuff was just fun to look at.

So tell me a little bit about your brother Billy? Did y'all play together in the early years?

Here's the story on how that got started: I was playing guitar, and Billy was interested, but I didn't know he did anything. I came into my bedroom one day and my guitar was sitting up against the wall with a broken string. I went to find Billy and couldn't find him anywhere and then found him hiding up under my bed. He had taken my guitar out and played it and broke the string and was scared that I would kill him. I said, no, let's just play together. Then he got his own guitar and we started sitting together and playing without amps and learning stuff. Then we both got busted in 1970 in Nashville for marijuana, and I got out of it by going to this group therapy session thing, but Billy was under house arrest and could only go to school and come home. So every day I would come home and play with him for two or three hours after school. Then the Allman Brothers came out and it just all opened up.

This is skipping around the timeline, but tell me who Billy went on to play with later.

Billy and I had a band here in Nashville that was pretty successful locally called the Flat Creek Band. He and I both wrote some original music with this band, and after that band broke up I formed a band called Buckeye that played in the southeast region. Then when I got the offer to play with Charlie Daniel's Band in 1975, Billy took my place in Buckeye. Then Billy went on to play with Bobby Whitlock, doing the *Layla* and Eric Clapton thing for several years. Then after that, he moved to Florida and played with Henry Paul Band for about nine years, and then when Henry went back to the

Outlaws and broke that band up, he played with the Bellamy Brothers for about nine years.

He played a good bit; I wonder if he was on any of those Whitlock albums? I have all of them.
I honestly couldn't tell you because I don't have any of those records.

I have to check it out. Tell me how you came to join the Charlie Daniel's Band?
The band I mentioned called Flat Creek had a road manager named David Corlew who is Charlie's personal manager now. When the band broke up, David went on to road manage Charlie Daniel's, and in 1974 my band Buckeye opened the very first Volunteer Jam, and I actually played the first musical note of any Volunteer Jam ever because it started with a guitar riff. I have got to show you the picture of all thirty musicians that played in that first show. But I had met Charlie that night, and he told me that he was losing both his guitar player and drummer and asked me if I would be interested. Well, to be honest with him I told him that I was still playing with my brother Billy, and I didn't want to leave him. I thought it over for about one week and turned him down because of that, and in retrospect that was a stupid thing to do, but I was naïve back then and didn't know what was going on.

One year later we played at another Volunteer Jam, and at the time my band had broken up, and he asked me again and I gladly accepted. Charlie said that we would be going on tour the first of the year in 1975, so my wife and I drove down to Knoxville and saw a show, and she left me at the hotel and went home, and Charlie and went up to the hotel room, and I roomed with him for six years after that. I learned all the songs from the *Fire On The Mountain* album, and he and I just sat up in the room with just two electric guitars and no amps and just played the whole thing, and it was just magical. I had never experienced anything like it.

I can truthfully say having seen you guys together a few times that it has never been quite the same without you. There are some *great* players that have played, but there is something about you and Charlie together that just can't be duplicated.
At that time they were touring with Skynyrd. Charlie said that he wanted me to come on the road, and that the other guitar player was finish-

ing up his last two weeks, and Barry, Charlie's former guitar player left the band, and I finally got to play, and we were in Chattanooga and opening for Joe Walsh. I will never forget it. It was 28 January 1975.

Then you went on to play for about fifteen years?
Yeah, almost fifteen years.

Let me jump back for a second and ask you when you were talking about Buckeye, wasn't my friend Ray Brand in that band?
Yeah, Ray played in there after I had left. It was great to see him at the studio when I came down to play on your album because I had not seen him in years.

Yeah, he is a very nice fellow. I was fortunate to meet him, and then his band was the core band to record with my album and having you and Bonnie Bramlett on it made it even more special. About songwriting with the Charlie Daniel's band, didn't you write some of those songs?
I guess I co-wrote about sixty songs. Charlie is a super guy, and he takes very good care of his band members and treats them as front men rather than side men. When I first joined the band, like Taz said in his interview, Charlie would let us have a song on every record. Taz and I got to do one song per record, and no other artist lets you do that. As far as the writing goes, we would go out to Charlie's and put all our ideas together and start rehearsing, and this would all gel and get put together and he would give us 50 percent and he took the other 50 percent, and this was so nice of him because he wrote most of the stuff, and we all just added to it. He was super-cool to let everyone be a part of the music. That was really big of him, and there is no other man like him alive.

I believe that, I really do. Did you co-write "Devil Went Down To Georgia?"
Yeah, I did Michael. There is a little story behind that. We had cut our last track, and then Charlie's eyes got real wide and said to Taz and I, "Boys we don't have a fiddle song on this album. We have to have a fiddle song." Then he asked Taz and I to come out into the studio room, and he said that he had this idea about the Devil and this kid having a fiddling contest. I immediately came up with the beginning lick, and Taz and I and Charlie sat down, and we put the music together in about thirty minutes. We went

home that night, and overnight Charlie had written the lyrics out, and he came in and we recorded it the next day, and then won a Grammy award for it.

It's amazing. That has to be one of the most-played songs of all time. In country and rock it was so popular.
It's funny because we wrote it so quickly. You can spend hours agonizing over a song and then this one just fell together.

My buddy Scott Greene wanted me to ask you about the song "Cumberland Mountain #9." It's his favorite.
That song was written back when I was in the Flat Creek Band, I used to spend lots of time up in the Smoky Mountains, hanging around with Jerry and Mack Gayden. I would get these ideas driving around East Tennessee in the mountains like the song "Franklin Limestone." I used to go by the Franklin Limestone Company, which is right in Crab Orchard, Tennessee, and it is a mining operation. That is where I came up with that title for that one just riding by it. "Cumberland Mountain #9" is about a whiskey still, and it just kind of happened one day.

What was it like overall to work with Charlie Daniels?
Oh, well I was a front man, up there talking on the microphone, and he would have us introduce songs and things. He is a super guy to work with. You don't cross him because he is a disciplined man and has his values and issues, and he knows what he wants. He didn't get there by being stupid but by being smart. He has been through lots in his career, with managers, people that were not quite honest, but he has handled it, and he is still out there and going for it.

I can't believe how much he is doing at his age and not slowing down at all.
It is still my pleasure to be able to go out and sit in with the band every once in awhile. I sat in about for about five or six shows with them this year.

It was great seeing you down at Angelus last year, and I guess we will be repeating that again this year. Yeah, we will. I will be seeing you there. I hope to play with you again.
Oh, yeah, we will do it.

Being around during the heyday of Southern Rock, what were some of your favorite compatriots to be on the road with?

On the road, I guess it would have been Marshall Tucker Band. Toy and I were great friends, and once we got to know each other we did everything together. I just loved playing shows with them. I loved Wet Willie, but I guess I enjoyed playing with everyone. My all-time heroes are the Allman Brothers, and Duane and Greg grew up in the same part of Nashville I grew up in, but at the time I did not know them. When we finally did meet, he was really nice to me and encouraged me to play. We did some great tours with the Outlaws. They were college tours and were lots of fun and no restrictions on the concerts, and we could do whatever we wanted, and it was a blast. I used to jump off the bus and ride with the Outlaws because we were just great friends.

Were you telling me about the first time you met Toy Caldwell?

I think it might have been Tommy Caldwell, Toy's brother. David Corlew told me he had a guy that wanted to meet me named Tommy Caldwell, so I said, let's do it. He was extremely nice and welcomed me into the band and wanted to meet me and said we would all have great fun.

I have nothing but great memories of those guys.

I still miss them. Watching them play was magic.

Kind of like a freight train coming right through your living room, or right through the auditorium. One of my most fond memories was the Volunteer Jams. Do you have any thing that stands out that makes you smile when you think of it?

I played on every Volunteer Jam, even after I left the band. The first Volunteer Jam, I opened the show with my band. The second one I was with Charlie in Murfreesboro, and one of the highlights was with that guy that did "I'm Goin' Home, I'm Goin' Home," with the guy from Woodstock. When we had the Volunteer Jam in Nashville, we always had it at the Municipal Auditorium, and Charlie always got us rooms at the Hyatt House a few blocks away because we would have some beers after the show and would not have to drive home—just another way he took care of us. So after the show was over one night, I go back, and my Mom was such a great fan and she and Dad always came to the shows. Then one night I went in after the show, and there was my Mom and Dickey Betts arm-in-arm having a nice time talking. It was a sight. Doing the Volunteer Jam was always such a pleasure, and there were so many great performers that I can't even mention all of them. For the first seven or eight Volunteer Jams we would back up all the performers. We learned all their songs, and I was the bandleader at that time.

I was watching one recently, the only one I have on video, the one from 1975 that got put out in the movie theatres, too. It seemed like so much fun. Maybe it's because I am a musician, but it just seemed great fun.

We always had rehearsal on a Friday night before, and all the artists would come down, and we would meet them and we didn't actually chart the music they would just play us a song and we would learn it and go for it and know it the next night.

What would you say that out of all those years with Charlie Daniel's Band would be some of the highlights that stand head and shoulders above the rest for you personally?

We had lunch with President Carter and Rosalynn at the White House. I got to be good friends with Chip Carter, the president's son, while we were campaigning for him and playing shows, and he played a joke on me. We had lunch by the pool, and they had an oompah marine band playing in the corner, and he said, does anyone want to go for a swim? I had brought my trunks, and little Amy was playing in the pool at the time. I jumped into the pool big time and made a huge splash, and when I came back up there were four secret service men there saying, "Son, you just don't do that." Well, I got out and asked Chip where I could go change back into my clothes, and he said to go through this pink door and change. I went through the pink door, and I am standing there naked getting my clothes on, bent over, and the door opened, and it was Rosalyn's Mom standing there. I mooned the first mother-in-law. Chip was laughing his brains out when I came out of there.

(Laughs) I didn't realize what a multi-instrumentalist you are until you showed up at the studio with so many instruments. What all do you play?

Well, I play Dobro, electric slide, pedal steel, and I play banjo.

Wow. As far as guitar goes, who would you say are some of your musical influences?

Okay, when I first started playing seriously guitar, remember the old Small Stone fuzz box? I had one of those and was just making noise. I was actually grabbing a microphone and playing slide with the microphone stand. I was playing with a guy named Steve Davis that eventually went on to join barefoot Jerry. We did this concert here at Peabody Music School, and I was just making all this noise with the fuzz box, and he told me that I had to get over this and learn how to play. He told me to go out and buy a Les Paul and the supersessions album that Santana, Al Cooper, and Michael Bloomfield and some of those guys were on. So I sat down, and plugging into a Fender Twin with no effects, and started learning those licks. That kind of clued me into what I needed to do. Then Hendrix and Clapton came out, and then I learned some of that. I went up to see my sister at [the University of Tennessee] and stayed with her, and she had the Allman Brothers first record and played it for me, and my jaw hit the ground, and I decided that that was what I wanted to do.

Me and about 400,000 other people want know why you ever left the Charlie Daniels's Band?

There were many, many reasons. I was getting burned out traveling on the road. When I first joined the band, we were doing about three hundred dates per year. I was getting older, and my daughter was fixing to become a teenager, and my wife's career in endurance riding was blooming, and my brother and I had made a pact that if he had come off the road and wanted to do a band that I would do it with him. I had told Charlie years earlier that there may come a time when I would have to leave the band to play with my brother again. He said that all I had to do was let him know when that happened, so I went to him and told him how I felt, and six months later I was at home working with my brother.

What happened with that project?

Well, the band was called Big Sir, and I always hated that name, because people always misspelled it and thought we were from Big Sur, California. Then we called it the Whooping Cranes later.

(Laughs) What year did you leave Charlie?

I gave him notice in the late winter of 1989, and I had planned to stay with the band through the year and put money back to form this new band. Knowing Charlie, he is not wasting any time. He goes looking for people. About two months later, I was backstage at the Grand Ole Opry, and Mel McDaniel had just played, and he had a guitar player named Bruce Brown, and my roadie Roger came up and told me that I had been replaced by that guy standing right over there.

So you said that Jack Gavin also played with Mel McDaniel?
Yeah, Jack Gavin was originally with Mel and then joined him, and we did some auditions for drummers, and he got the job. He had told Charlie about Bruce Brown, and Charlie hired him that night after hearing him right there on the spot.

Tell me about this project with Gene Golden, the *Golden Crane* album that I personally love, and how you guys decided to do this great R&B album?
Thanks, I really appreciate that. We have known each other since high school, but not playing together. He had been on the road with Kenny Rogers for over twenty years, and then I was playing with Charlie for all that time. Then Gene had quit Kenny, and he called me one night and wanted me to come out to his studio in his house at Hermitage and just play some, and it really worked out, and we have been working together for about seven years now. We have about six- or seven-hundred songs in the can, and as you know, it is very hard to place things in Nashville—and I am not a 16th Avenue kind of guy, I stay down here in Franklin, Tennessee. away from all that stuff. The same people are there all the time and are hiring each other and tooting each other's horns. So you can't compete with them. Gene and I just decided to go other places, and we had all this material, and we decided to put something out and see what hap- pens. Gene picked out a bunch of songs that I helped him arrange.

What is the other project that you are excited about now?
Oh, this is a project that I have been working toward for thirteen years. We have Steve Grisham, formerly of the Outlaws, on guitar and vocals. We have Barry Rapp, formerly of the Henry Paul Band, on keyboards, and we have Johnny Few, formerly of the Dickey Betts Band, on bass, and Jimmy Gunn, formerly of Brooks and Dunn, on drums. All five of us are lead sing-

ers and back up singers, and we have had three rehearsals so far, and it is just coming out great, and we have great material that is all original, and it is pure Southern Rock. The band is called Gone South.

Obviously you have! Not to blow wind up your skirt, but people have been looking for Tommy Crain for awhile and all the other guys too, wow.
The person that has really pushed me along more than anyone has been my wife. When I came off the road it was to help her to become an endurance rider professionally. She does these one-hundred-mile horse races and is very successful at it. She needs me as a crew to help her do this, and I really wanted to do it. She has won medals and World Championships. For the past several years, she has said that I am not using my talents, and now I am going to do it. Just get out there and play.

What's next on your agenda.
The boys are coming up from Florida next weekend, and we have some rehearsals going, and then me and Jimmy and Johnny are going down there to stay with Steve and Barry and woodshed down there for about one week in the studio and do a couple of club dates. We got a booking agent and a representative to help get things going and want to start opening for people as early as next year.

Tommy Crain would form a band called Tommy Crain & the Crosstown Allstars that rocked the nation for several years. Sadly, my brother Tommy passed away on 13 July 2011.

Charlie Hayward

Winter 2003

Since 1975, Charlie Hayward has held down the bottom for the Charlie Daniels Band, playing bass guitar, touring, and recording with Daniels. We caught up with Hayward at his hotel in Spartanburg, South Carolina, just prior to the Easter Seals Benefit Concert for a few questions about his long and varied career.

🙚

Charlie, where were you born?
I was born outside of Hope, Alabama, in Tuscaloosa where the University of Alabama is located. I was born there in 1949 and the last of seven kids. I didn't know you were an Alabama guy. Did you come from a musical family? I can remember my mom playing St. Louis blues on the piano when I was growing up, and when she was younger she played piano in the church, and she knew all the hymns. My dad had an old Stella acoustic guitar and played, and I picked up some chords from him, and my older brother also played guitar, and I learned from him.

How old were you when you picked up your first guitar?
Probably about ten or eleven years old when I first started picking on an old Stella guitar where the strings were about an inch and a half off the fingerboard.

When did you transition to bass?
When I actually first started playing guitar was with a friend named Richard Kent, about the same time that the English movement of the Beatles and Rolling Stones was happening, about '63 or '64. Me and him would get together and play, and we would just play acoustic guitar and get together every Saturday and learn new songs, and then about '67 I changed over to bass. The first band that Richard and I had had two girl drummers—nowadays we would be hip with that. The next band was the first authentic band that we got paid to play in, me and Richard and about three other guys: a bass player, and drummer, and keyboard player. That band was called

the Hellucinations—that drummer came up with that name. I played guitar with that band, and me and Richard were having to learn the bass parts, and that was probably what got me headed in that direction, and I was starting to hear songs and learn bass. There were lots of good guitar players in Tuscaloosa at that time but not as many bass players. I just thought that might be a good thing to do.

Is that near Muscle Shoals?
Tuscaloosa is between Meridian and Birmingham.

What happened in the period of that band and the period when you ended up playing with Alex Taylor?
Remember those good guitar players I was talking about? Well, one of them was a guy named Tippie Armstrong, and he put together a band called the South Cam; and, anyway, he played guitar, and I played bass, and Lou Mullinax played drums, and my friend Richard from high school was still playing guitar and singing, and a guy named Court Pickett played keyboards.

Isn't he the guy that did the band Sailcat?
Yeah, with Johnny Wyker. When you are talking about Alabama musicians, it's all a big circle. Lou was also on "Motorcycle Mama," and he also played with Alex and I later on. Anyway, that was one band that we had and another one was me and Lou and Chuck Leavell, and a guitar player named Joe Rudd. We had a group called Care, and we played around Birmingham, and that was actually when we started getting into some recording with a black songwriter named Sam Dees—and he knew a guy with a studio. That was a great experience.

Later on, Chuck and Lou and Court all wound up going to Macon, Georgia, and they got signed with Capricorn in the early days and had a group called Sundown, and they wanted me to come over and play bass with them. They called me, and there was no hesitation at all, and we went to Macon, Georgia, and just about starved to death. It was like we didn't hardly get any gigs and nothing, and this separates people from those that want to be musicians from those that are just in it for the money. We weren't making any money at the time, but it was a great learning experience. So, anyway, when I joined them it probably didn't last but for another six months or so, and we weren't really doing anything, selling any records, and it just petered out. Then in spring of '70, we got the chance to hook up with Alex

Taylor, Chuck, Lou Mullinax, and at that time Joe Rudd was playing guitar with Alex, and he hung around for awhile, then later on we got Jimmy Nalls to play guitar with us. You know Jimmy, Sea Level? One thing about that band, it was the first real being-on-the-road band. You would actually go out and be on the road for a couple of weeks at a time. Not like these guys nowadays. We were traveling around in an old LTD station wagon and everyone packed into it, and everybody had to drive a tank of gas, and you had a van with the equipment and a couple of roadies to help with the equipment, and it was not like it is now. We had lots of fun, and I will always remember that. Alex was the first real road gig I had.

Alex is related to James Taylor.
Yeah, he is his older brother.

There is another one named Livingston?
He is more of a folk singer. There is another brother named Hugh, and he never left Martha's Vineyard, but people say he was very talented, and then there was a sister named Kate, and she was more of an R&B type singer. Alex's main style was blues and R&B.

Did you record with him?
Yeah, we did a record called *Dinnertime* with him, and Johnny Sandlin from Capricorn produced it, and that guy is one of the most fun producers I have ever worked with. He's a musician, a bass player, and a drummer. He just knows what songs need to happen.

What would you say were some of the high points that you remember from playing with Alex Taylor and Chuck Leavell and all of those guys?
We got to do quite a few shows with Duane and the Allmans, and we opened lots of shows for them. Then the next year after Duane, when Dickey kind of took over, that was before Chuck came in, just doing some of those big festivals that we played with them were great. We did some school auditoriums and clubs, and we did a show with Ike and Tina Turner and the Ikettes, and then we did a show with B.B. King back when he had just him and a left-handed bass player—Sonny Freeman. I remember just sitting out front and listening to his whole set, and he was my first inspiration in music besides my parents. I remember listening to "Rock Me Baby" when I was about ten years old. It just struck a chord in me.

Tell me your strongest musical influences in your life?
Being from the South, it is hard for me not to say that the southern influences were some of the greatest influences in the world. Those guys in Muscle Shoals like David Hood, Roger Hawkins, and then up in Memphis, you had Jack Dunn and Al Jackson. I don't know who the drummer of James Brown's original stuff was—I think the bass player's name was Bernard Oden—but man, those guys were such staunch pocket players, they just did exactly what the songs needed. Like James Jamison from Motown, some of the stuff was bubblegum, but man, if you listen to what the drums and bass were doing from a musician's standpoint, it's hard to deny that those guys were anything but just staunch bluesmen and great players and knew exactly what to do. Mostly R&B and soul and like those blues guys Jerry Germont that played on B.B. King's *Live & Well* and *Completely Well*. It would take me all day to name all those guys. The great thing was they were doing those monster grooves on just like a four-string T-base or jazz base. It's like there is so much out there now, six-string or seven-string bass and amps, and then you go back and listen to those guys, and it's different. Everything now is different, and I don't like the bass after four strings.

I got to listening to more of the authentic blues guys from down in the Delta like Elmore James and Robert Johnson and some of those guys from over in the Delta and the influence of all those styles, and they played with lots of emotions.

Did you do other things between the time that you played with Alex Taylor and the time that you joined up with Charlie?
After Alex, me and Chuck, and Jimmy Nalls and Lou, we were kind of like our whole little rhythm section, and we went to play with Dr. John for about three months. We played for Mac Rebennack. That was quite an experience.

Jimmy Nalls told me that.
We had all grown up with our own influences. We were rock, R&B, and blues-oriented guys, whereas Mac was just staunch second-line New Orleans. Talk about a weird mixture, and I think that he really wanted guys more like him in his musical style. He ended up getting the Meters when we left and doing "The Right Place at the Wrong Time." We didn't really stay with him long, maybe for about three months, and I think he really wanted

guys that were more that style. There was an album we did called *Gumbo*, and I still go back and listen to it. It was some of the best second-line groove stuff that you'll ever want to listen to. Like these guys today play many, many notes and lots of drums, but if you go back and listen to what these guys are playing, it really makes a lot of sense. It's not like musical gymnastics.

Either Jimmy Nalls or Chuck Leavell, one told me that you guys had rehearsed for that Dr. John thing and he came in there and y'all took off playing, and Dr. John just shook his head and said, I'm going to have to teach you guys how to play the second line.
That's exactly right! It is a whole different way of playing—the accent is on a different part of the beat rather than playing rock or blues. To me, it's like you grow up playing that to play it well.

When and where did you meet up with Charlie?
After that Dr. John thing we were still in Macon, and it was that fall—in October when Duane got killed—and then Chuck hooked up with the Brothers and got to be with them. Then we played up on the *Laid Back* album with Greg. Me and Chuck and Jimmy Nalls played on some of it. He had lots of different great players. We had Johnny Sandlin produce it and also played bass on a couple of tunes, and Fathead Newman played saxophone on it, and Buzzy Beatin played guitar lead on "Queen of Hearts." Tommy Talton and Scott Boyer, they were right in there, too. To this day, that was one of the most fun records that I remember playing on. The way Johnny did things, he knew just what he wanted and just went in and did it. If you listen to it with a metronome, it is up and down and all over the place. It was a great feel. He did a great job of producing and mixing it.

After that was done, I wanted to get away from Macon. Lou our drummer passed away, and I went back to Tuscaloosa and played in a band called Foxfire. We just played frat parties and stuff like that for a couple of years. Then, finally I hooked up with Charlie through Paul Hornsby, and Paul was one of those guys from Tuscaloosa that I had played with, and I had known him from years before and had been a couple of those bands I had played with. He had produced *Fire On The Mountain*, and I think that was the first album he had done on Charlie, and I think all of his musicians—drummer, guitar, and bass player—had all quit on him at the same time. Then I got a call, and he had gotten my number from Paul who had recommended me, and he basically just hired me over the phone without hearing me play a note. They played in Tuscaloosa the next night and opened for Lynyrd Skynyrd and took my bass and played a couple of songs with him in the dressing room and got on the bus and have been going ever since.

So you were not on the *Fire On The Mountain* album?

No, I came in on *Night Rider*. I have been on practically every album since. Charlie has had some great musicians come through his band. He had Billy Cox for a while, and he had Earl Grigsby and Mark Fitzgerald, and then I have been with him since March of 1975. We were doing dates with Skynyrd, Allmans, Marshall Tucker—did a lot of dates with Marshall Tucker. It was just really different in those days because of the cameraderie, all for one, but you still if you were opening you'd spark one another. Kind of push each other. Not really in a competitive way, but just give the crowd a good show.

That was my favorite part, when all the players would just come onstage and jam together, without some suit telling his band, "Now, you can't go onstage with Charlie tonight because of a clause in you contract." There was a lot of that old jamming going on at Angelus this year, and I loved it. When you joined the band, how did those first few gigs feel? Were you scared or confident?

I was totally scared to death. First off, a lot of Charlie's songs are not like just going out and learning a straight song. Songs like "No Place Left to Go," they have a lot of changes in them. Basically me and Tommy Crain and Don Murray just worked into the band while we were on the road. When those other two guys left, I came in two weeks after they left. One thing I have to say is Mark Fitzgerald, he hung around for a couple or three days until I could kind of get a handle on everything. But all of the sudden I went from this band in Tuscaloosa playing clubs to playing ten-thousand-seat halls. It was intimidating, but also kind of exciting. Learning everything off-the-cuff, so to speak.

I used to work in a grocery store in Spartanburg, South Carolina, where a lot of the Marshall Tucker Band bought their groceries, and from time to time I'd talk to Tommy Caldwell. He always spoke highly of you. Yeah, Tommy and Toy both, man, it was just so amazing to play with them because you could stand over on the side of the stage and watch them. They'd both play with their thumbs. They learned that from their dad. And they'd play so fast sometimes you couldn't hardly even see 'em. Both of those guys were great people. They were both military, too. When people would see Marshall Tucker, a lot of them would be watching Doug sing, or Jerry on the flute or Toy playing lead, but I was always watching Tommy and Paul and George. They were always in the pocket. They never relinquished the groove. It was like a stranglehold from beginning to end, you know?

Those really were the days. Tell us about Charlie Daniels. Not the public image, but the real man.
Well, let me begin by saying we were a little wild and crazy when we were younger, and Charlie would tell you the same thing. There are a lot of things we are not proud of about our past. But none the less, they are a part of who we are, and we are mighty fortunate to still be around. But Charlie, what you see is what you get, pretty much. He's a guy who believes in treating people fair. There's been times, many times over, when he could have fired a lot of us. But I think he holds to seniority, and for sticking with him through the rough times. Maybe that more than talent, sometimes. I'm not saying he hasn't had good musicians all the time. But probably there have been times in his career when he could have gotten some aged musicians, but it wouldn't have been the kind of band concept that he likes to have. He's just a solid person, very dependable too.

I've seen others in the business that get chewed up and spit out, but he just kind of grabbed the bull by the horns and rode it on out. Through the big years and through the lean years, he always maintained his focus on what he wanted to do in music. He never gave up. I think Charlie has just been a great guy to work with. I hear about all these other guys that are hired by the tour, and they come up to you and fire you at Christmas time because they don't want to pay you, or whatever. Charlie's like an abnormality in the music business, he really is. And I'd like to add that Charlie has probably been a Christian all his life, but I came to know the Lord back in 1984. And since then we have even more of a closeness because of our similar beliefs. And just having a handle on life. He is not just a music guy. Family is real important. He likes to go home and ride horses or go fishing or go to the mountains. That's the way I am too. I like to spend time with my family. You have to have some kind of balance. You can't be just all music. I don't know about cats like that. There are some guys like that, all they do is live and breathe music, but me, I've got to get away from it sometimes.

Speaking of Christianity, I have seen you guys several times lately showing up on the Billy Graham crusades.
I think they'll start being with Franklin Graham this year, I think he's taking over for his dad. But Charlie, he can reach people who might not ever go to church. Out here on the road, he gives a little bit of a testimony every night about the Lord.

I've heard a lot of comments from our readers, and the biggest part of them say that Charlie makes them feel safe at his shows, like it's okay to have the kids there. A real family environment. Okay, here come the cornball questions. (Laughs) What's your favorite CDB album that you've recorded with Charlie?
Can I say two?

(Laughs) You sure can!
Reflections and *Full Moon*. Those were a total, consummate band effort. Sometimes Charlie would have an idea of what he wanted, and sometimes we would start from scratch: "make a chord." One of us would get an idea for a groove, and we'd just bounce ideas off of each other. And Tommy and Charlie were so into writing, they would just spur each other on. Tommy's the kind of guy who has endless ideas. He'd throw three or four out there, and then he's got another dozen. And rehearsals, I'd leave and my fingers would just about be bleeding. We'd practice for a long time.

What have been a couple of the high points for you as a member of the CDB?
As a Christian, playing the Billy Graham crusades. And also we've done a lot for the military service, overseas in Korea and Germany. There's been winning a Grammy and CMA Awards, and that was okay. But the Billy Graham Crusades were the most important.

Taz DiGregorio

December 2001

After thirty-one years as a member of the Charlie Daniels Band, keyboard wizard Taz DiGregorio has released his debut solo album, *Midnight In Savannah*. I spoke with Taz a few days prior to his return to the recording studio to begin a new record.

➰

Where were you born and raised?
Well, I was born in Worcester, Massachusetts, and I lived there until about 1962, when I went on the road at that time. The first band that I played with was called Paul Chaplin and His Emeralds, and they were famous for a song called "Shortnin' Bread," and we sold about 250,000 records in 1959.

So you were on that record?
Yeah, it was one of those things when I was seventeen-years-old and did not know much about life or music and knew about eight chords, and I recorded the song and it hit. Then by 1960 to '61 the band was completely gone.

How early did you play music?
I started when I was about sixteen, and I learned a Fats Domino song called "Blue Monday." I had been listening to Fats Domino and Little Richard and Elvis, and that was what was going on at the time. I just sat down one day and played and sang the whole song. My sister was there at the time, and it just totally freaked her out, and she said, "How did you do that?" and I said, "Well, I don't know." That's how it all started.

Who would you say are your musical influences?
My biggest influence was Ray Charles, at the age of fourteen. In 1958 I hitchhiked 150 miles to see him. He had his original band with him. He had Fathead Newman, Hank Crawford, Margie Hendricks—and I think she has passed on. He had about sixteen people with him, and I was the only white

person in a sea of about five thousand black people in 1958. He was at that time the hero of all black people. I can see why; it was like being in a church. I still draw from that one experience today. This was about a two-hour show, and I was on the edge of the stage and soaked up the feeling, and I still draw from that feeling. I can still see it in my mind today just like it was yesterday, and it has been a long time.

Were you in any other bands before you hooked up with Charlie?
Well, yeah, I had bands of my own and toured with other bands and played in a house band in a place called the Golden Nugget in Worcester, Massachusetts, and backed up Fay Adams and the Drifters and did my own kind of thing. But I learned early on from the Ray Charles experience up until I worked in that black section in Massachusetts in a black club and there were only three white people: me, the club owner, and his son. I learned early on what that was to reach out and touch people from that experience.

When and how did you hook up with Charlie Daniels?
It was 1964, and I was in Orlando, Florida, staying in a place called The Palomino Motel on Orange Blossom Trail. I was working in a lounge band that did just a variety of music. I sang, and we did not use a bass player—I played bass pedals on the organ—and the sax player, Jerry Kaskie, was his name, well, he got drafted, and then we hired a guitar player, and he got drafted. Well, I was out of work for about four or five months, and finally I got a job in a place called La Flame that was out near the air force base in Orlando. I worked there with just the drums and organ, and I could do a five-piece band with drums and organ, playing bass and singing. He came into the club as the main attraction one night, and I was playing the breaks. His guitar player quit, and he was playing bass at the time. He went back to playing guitar, and the funny thing is when I met the man, he said that he was looking for someone to start all over again with a band, and he said let's have lunch. So we had lunch, and he told me that if I would cut off my long hair and beard he would hire me to be in his band. It was very funny. That was 1963 and 1964. I played for a couple of years with him in a band called the Jaguars, and I got drafted, and he went to Nashville and played with Bob Dylan. We were playing not really writing and trying to figure out how to do it. By the time I got out of the army, he had the flip side of "Kissin' Cousins" called "It Hurts Me," and he was on his way.

After you got out of the service, was that when the original Charlie Daniels Band was formed?

Yeah, basically, the original band was Charlie, Jerry Corbitt from the Youngbloods, Billy Cox from Band of Gypsys, and Jeffrey Meyer and myself. That band did not stay together but about six months, then it just dissolved. Then it was me and Charlie, and Jeffrey, and a guy named Earl Grigsby. The original Charlie Daniels Band still can be heard, if you can find it. It is a bootleg, and it is called *Corbitt and Daniels, Live at Carnegie Hall*.

We opened in 1970 for Delaney and Bonnie, and it was a showcase, and they brought Atlantic Records, and all of these companies came and basically they wanted me and Charlie and did not want anyone else. We decided we would all stay together.

How did it go from that point to recording your first album?

The first album was supposed to be called *Corbitt and Daniels*, but what had happened in Carnegie Hall, Delaney and Bonnie's sound man, whom we knew recorded our show also and after the show—I am not sure what happened, but something happened with Corbitt, and he quit the band. Charlie was really very upset, and they were supposed to go in and do an album called *Corbitt and Daniels*, the contracts had been signed, and the money had been put up, and Corbitt quit. So I took Corbitt's place on the first album. He sang half and I sang half, and from that point on we just kept working at it until we finally hit on it.

Which album was that?

Te John, Grease and the Wolfman.

I have that one with the beautiful picture of you guys on the gatefold. (Laughs)

(Laughs) That day that they took that picture, we had forgotten that they were coming. We were having the after recording party—just the four of us on Long Island about one hundred miles out of New York City. We were pretty partied out by the time they got there, and we did not even know that they were coming. The guy just looked at all of us and said, "Whatever you do, please don't look at the camera." (Laughs)

What did the title of that album actually mean?
Well, Te John was the bass player, and Wolfman was the drummer, and since I am half Italian and half French Canadian, I was Grease. It was one of those things where Charlie loves to give people nicknames. That was one of those Southern Rock cultural things. Grease never stuck but Taz did! He hit that one right one the nose.

Taz is a nickname. Is it from the Tasmanian Devil cartoon?
It came about on the bus when we had the first road manager we ever had. Jesse Craig was his name, and I had hair down past my shoulders, and one morning I was sitting up in the front of the bus about daylight, and my hair was sitting straight up, and the road manager was laughing at me saying I looked just like a Tasmanian Devil. He went back to bed. Then after a while Charlie got up and all of the guys started to kid me and laugh, and on the next record that came out, it just said "Taz," and all of a sudden I had acquired a nickname overnight.

That name has been well known now for years and years, and I remember hearing about you when "Uneasy Rider" first came out and people said that Charlie had this keyboard player named Taz. Early on in the Charlie Daniels Band you guys were opening for other people. Can you kind of give me a picture of what that was like? There was a lot of the Southern Rock and jam kind of thing happening. Give me some of the feel of that time period.
The whole Southern Rock thing was a brotherhood, a family, and we were at that time when we started out. We toured with the Allman Brothers Band, the Marshall Tucker Band, Wet Willie, Lynyrd Skynyrd, Black Oak Arkansas, and these people were gracious and loving people that allowed us to open shows and play in front of a lot of people. They allowed us and taught us. For instance, the Allman Brothers Band's Red Dog taught us about road cases. He asked where our road cases were, and we did not know what he meant. It was an education.

Marshall Tucker Band's Tommy Caldwell came to Charlie and said he knew we were broke and gave us a thousand bucks and told us to take it and pay him back when we could. What a nice gesture of brotherhood. They really took care of us. We all worked together. We toured with Skynyrd a lot and would finish the shows and all pile into one room—both bands and both crews in one hotel room, and you cannot get a better brotherhood than that. It was really something. (Laughs)

I can imagine that was a pretty crowded room. (Laughs)
You've got to hope that everyone has had their shower.... The thing about that is that you have to worry about the hotel sending the cops up there!

You were talking about Tommy Caldwell, I did want to ask you about the Caldwells—they are near and dear to my heart because I grew up in Spartanburg and was always around those guys. I just wanted to ask you about them and get a memory of those guys and of course, Charlie. If you could elaborate a little on them, I would appreciate it.
Toy and Tommy were just incredible people. They were great musicians. As far as Toy is concerned, the only other guitar player that I ever saw in my entire life that played—and I won't say the same style, but with the same technique—it is B.B. King. Toy was so close to B.B. King, and I did not understand it until he had passed away. Toy played with more of a country feel, but they played with the same intensity. Which is really something. Tommy Caldwell, I had never in my life saw a bass player like Tommy. Tommy would keep time with his feet just scoot up towards Paul Riddle, and then the whole thing would come up. They were very good to us. Let us open shows for them and they helped us out and really helped us out a lot. They were one of the premiere Southern Rock bands because they touched on all types of music, they were good people, and they were GIs in the Marines. Artimus Pyle was, I think, Toy's buddy in the Marines. They were real Americans that played real American music. I don't know anyone who plays like that anymore, not with that intensity. It just doesn't happen anymore.

Moving on to my friend Charlie, let me tell you what. No one has ever heard this story before. When I came to the Charlie Daniels Band, I had no earthly idea of what the basic fundamentals of how to write songs were, and this man came and got me in Huntsville, Alabama, in a haywagon and put my B-3 on it, and we came to Nashville, and I lived with him for a couple of years. He taught me how to write songs and about life, and this man has a heart like no other man I have ever met. This man cannot only write songs, but he is the most talented man I have ever met in my life. He does it all. In the studio, he did what they call head arrangements, and he is a totally brilliant man. This is how good of a friend he is, I believe it was 1980, not really sure of the year but I think it was, we had an album called *Full Moon*. I had a song on that album called "No Potion For the Pain." He allowed me to write, sing, and just about produce one song on every album. No other artist would ever give anyone, another writer that opportunity. The record company said, "absolutely not," and he went to New York City on a plane and said "absolutely yes," and we are going to do this whether you like it or not. He is about as much of a friend as you can have; it doesn't get any better than that. He is a very understanding man, and you cannot do anything that he hasn't already done. He understands where you are coming from because he has already been there. There have been times over thirty-one years that it is not always the best of relationships because you are always going to have some disagreements, but we have always transcended that, and the main goal has always been the band. A guy asked me the other day, what have you been waiting on to do the [solo] album? Well, I have been busy with the band—and as long as there is a Charlie Daniels Band, there will always be a Taz in the band —and that would be me!

What are some of the highest points for you personally working with Charlie?
One of the highest points was back about 1971 in a hotel in New York and playing the War Auditorium for the Vietnam war. We had done our part and were sitting in a hotel room, and the phone rang, and it was Al Kooper—and he was the guy that had produced Lynyrd Skynyrd and the Sounds of the South label and the Southern Blues Project—and he said to Charlie, "Who is that guy that is playing the B-3?" and Charlie said, "Joe," and Al said, "That is the guy you need." I had just started, and for me that was like getting a Grammy, getting a compliment from Al Kooper. There were lots of other things that have happened, and I think it is great to see a 65- year-old man get a hit record like his "This Ain't No Rag, It's a Flag." I am very proud for him.

I got an email and forwarded it to Charlie today from some people stationed in Germany, and they are getting ready to be deployed to Afghanistan. They had heard the flag song and entered the contest to win a record and the single. They wrote this thing that would bring tears to your eyes about how much the song meant to them, and I wrote back to tell them they did not have to wait to win but that I was sending them one out today. It's amazing what effect that song has had.

We had a lot of songs like that for instance, "Still in Saigon," that prompted death threats for about one year. We had "MIA," that did really hit—a lot of people liked it. We had "In America," which at the time when "In America" was done it was on the West Coast Country Music Awards, and we came out to a 60'-by-80' flag behind us and did it, but we did not have the product in the store the next day, so that was a problem.

I think that the Charlie Daniels Band has always been a people band, and we have always done songs and written songs that people feel close to because of the lyrical content. This song came along at a time when it was needed. Whenever there is any kind of military action like that, I think the entertainers should do their part to let all the people know that go into battle that they are coming out of this alive and well—and that we are praying for them. I am proud of him for coming up with this.

What compelled you to record this, and tell us anything you can about this record? I think it is a great record.

It is a very funny story. I had a call and we had done three to six albums in a couple of years. We had done the blues album, the fiddle album, the greatest hits album, and then this guy called me that I knew for twenty-five years and used to play in the band. Buddy Davis is his name, and he called and said, "Why don't you do an album?" I told him that I did not want to do that now because it takes too much time and we have to spend lots of time on it.

He insisted that I send him some stuff and he would put it out. So I sent him some stuff, and he thought it was good and that I did need to do it. He called back and said, "Are you crazy? These twelve to fifteen songs are great." I started feeling like maybe it was time to do it and got some studio time and went and did it. I had started writing a lot, and I realized that by holding on to demos, my writing would never get any better, and by holding onto those demos I would never go any further. It was time to do it.

Who plays on this album besides yourself?

There is a guy that plays guitar that played with us in 1972, and his name is Barry King, a great guitar player. He played on it, and he's from Louisville. Jack Wessell, who plays with Leon Russell, and Pat McDonald, who is an incredible drummer and now plays with the Charlie Daniels Band, and my friend Bonnie Bramlett, who said that if I ever did an album and I did not let her sing on it she would kick my butt.

And she would too…

Yes sir! And then Carolyn Corlew sang, and one of my favorite guitar players in the entire world named Tommy Crain—whom everyone remembers as a former guitarist in the CDB—played slide on "Born With the Blues" and "Standing in the Rain," and Charlie himself played on "Spirit in the Dark," and then Johnny Neal, who used to play with the Allman Brothers, who I think wrote the hit song "Good Clean Fun," he played horns on "Ya No Me Duele Mas," and Jamie Nichols who played on *Fire On The Mountain*, he played percussion—and then my friend David Dunston who played strings on "Somewhere." Also Marty O'Jeda played sax.

This album is out now, but I hear you are working on another record, is that right?

I am working on an album called *Shake Rag*. It's a collection of songs that I wrote last year in about an eight-month period. It takes in Latin and Latin Blues formats—formats that have really not been exploited, slick R&B, and it is basically about every kind of Southern Music there is. Including original jazz that came from New Orleans.

Are there some of the same guys on it or new people?

These are different musicians. Barry King is playing on it. This is a funny story, everyone on it, Barry King, the bass player is Shane, and William Ellis who is a percussionist, all of these guys studied at [the University of Tennessee] and are from Knoxville, and they all have the same kind of mindset. The record *Midnight In Savannah* would never have come out if it had not been for a lady named Anita Walls. She runs a company in Nashville called Masterworks, and she is from Memphis. She has always told me I am from the wrong city and that I needed to be living in Memphis. On the 5, 6, and 7, of December we are going into a studio, and everyone is studying the script, and we will do it one take, one time like we did *Midnight In Savannah*.

So it is live in the studio.

Yeah, it is live in the studio. *Midnight in Savannah* was live in the studio. When we finally started to roll, we did it in two days, and solos were cut, and we did it, wham, wham, and the solos were done, and the first ones are usually the best. These musicians were real professionals. Oh, yeah, and one person I need to mention is my long-time co-writer, Greg Wohlgemuth. He's from Oklahoma, and co-wrote several of the songs on both *Midnight In Savannah* and *Shake Rag*. I can be in the room with him, and the songs just come. It's magic.

Do you have any closing comments or words of wisdom to any of your fans?

If you want to be in the music business, or have any musical aspirations, the best thing I can say to anyone is do it! Don't ever quit. There is room for *everyone*, plenty of money for everyone, so get out there and do anything that you have to do. The world is a great place, and there is room for everybody, and you just have to go out there and persevere. I have been truly blessed. I have no musical education and cannot just sit there and write music, but what I hear in my mind is a blessing from God, and every day that I get up I thank God for these blessings with this thing in my head where I write lyrics and music. If you are an aspiring songwriter, and you want to write great songs, you have to clear all of the negativity out of your life and love everything in the universe. If you hate spiders you must learn to love them—love the spider. Love everything, and just sit still and it will come to you.

Tragically, Taz died in an auto accident on his way to meet the tour bus near Nashville on 12 October 2011. He is loved and missed greatly.

Elvin Bishop

March 2011

From his early days with the Paul Butterfield Blues Band, to his string of hits while at Capricorn Records, and an ongoing list of great solo blues albums, Elvin Bishop remains one of our generation's best guitar slingers. We spoke with Elvin about working with the Allman Brothers Band, his Capricorn day,s and his latest album *Red Dog Speaks*.

☙

It's good to speak with you again Elvin. Tell me a little about how you first connected with Paul Butterfield.
Well, I fell in love with blues by listening to it on the radio. I'm from Tulsa, Oklahoma, which is probably not that different from where you grew up in Spartanburg, but, anyway, I went to Chicago in 1960, and the first guy that I met in Chicago was Paul Butterfield. I was walking around the neighborhood when I got there, and he was sitting on some steps playing blues on a guitar and drinking a quart of beer. When I met him, he didn't hardly play any harp. He played guitar, but he played blues. Then he picked up the harp, and in about six months he was like a shooting star. He got about as good as he was gonna get in six months. He was just a natural genius on the harmonica.

This month, the Allman Brothers celebrate the fortieth anniversary of the recording *At Fillmore East*, which you sang on.
Yeah, wow. What a job they did on that album. The band was so poppin' at that time, just so perfect, you know? I was honored to be on there. I used to hang out with those guys whenever I got a chance. It was more of a jamming time than it is now, you know. Guys would just get together and jam and not worry so much about the other stuff. But they called me up, must have been three or four o'clock in the morning, and we jammed.

Kinda like when you were at Capricorn? Those were my favorite years. When guys would get together and jam and not worry so much about being politically correct or what some record company suit thought.

Yeah, or worrying so much about the show that they didn't want to have anybody on that hadn't rehearsed the tune. They didn't used to think about that. They'd say, oh, there's my buddy, come on up here and play.

Those were great times. And speaking of jamming, I mentioned Marshall Tucker earlier, and I wanted to ask you to share your memories of the late Toy Caldwell.
What a guy! One of my favorite guys in all history! And so funny!

Toy was hilarious.
He had those one-liners for all occasions. He wouldn't just say, "I'm hot." He'd say, "I'm hotter than a fresh fucked fox in a forest fire." (Laughs) That's him ain't it? He played with his thumb and fingers at a time when nobody else did, hardly. He had his own original sound, and he just went for it. A great songwriter. There just wasn't anything to not like about Toy.

We got known just minutes before the Tuckers did. The Capricorn thing was rolling. We had a gig in Sacramento sometime during the early seventies, and Marshall Tucker was opening for us. They got into town a day early, and Toy and George went to some club downtown, and they told them that Toy was Elvin Bishop and George was Johnny V, and they rolled out the red carpet for them, and they drank free all night long. They had a great time. (Laughs)

We went fishing the next day, me and Toy. We hit it pretty hard back then, and we had a hangover. It got to be a little past noon, and we're out in the boat. Toy kept on saying, "Boy, I'm hot. It's just too damn hot." I looked over at him, and I could tell he was doing it on purpose. He just started slowly leaning over and just fell out of the boat. He let himself fall in the water. (Laughs) He paddled around a little bit, and then got back in the boat and said, "Man I feel a lot better."

How did you end up on the Capricorn Records label back in the day?
It was because of Duane [Allman] and Dickey [Betts]. I had met those guys, and we just fell right together and made friends. I went to one of their gigs at the old Fillmore in San Francisco or Winterland, and after the show there was a party. And they grabbed Phil Walden, the president of Capricorn, and made him come in a room and listen to some of my songs. He just signed me up the next day. But it was all because of Dickey and Duane.

What was the vibe like around Capricorn and Macon, Georgia, at that time?

(Laughs) Oh man, Macon was still like a part of the old South at the time. It hadn't been modernized the least damn bit. There were guys walkin' around with pistols strapped on their sides. You'd go to the barbecue stand, and the guy in front of you would have a big ol' pistol strapped on. That cut out any urge you might have to say something smart. Once in a while they would take me out to one of these places way back out in the woods, and they would have picnic tables and sawdust on the floor and get some of that corn liquor. (Laughs) Capricorn Records was the only thing happening in town that was different from anything in a thousand other towns around the South at the time.

Who are your favorite guitar players?

My number one guy is Earl Hooker. He's my favorite slide guy. He's the guy that I kind of took after. He would never put his guitar in a special tuning like most slide players do. He played in normal tuning. If you put the slide on your little finger, it leaves three fingers to play chords and other stuff along with your slide. And if you've got three fingers, you're doing one better the Django Reinhardt. (Laughs) He tried to play like a human voice, and he did. Then there's Derek Trucks. You've got to admire him. And there are a couple of guys out here you might not be familiar with. There's a kid out here from Norway named Kit Anderson. He's played on a couple of my records. He's just a monster. He's played with [Charlie] Musselwhite before and a bunch of others. And there's another kid out here named Bob Welch that's really fantastic. I like Warren Haynes—and I like all known blues guitar players. My favorite blues players of all time are Albert Collins and Luther Tucker. And Duane and Dickey, I always thought a lot of them, and Toy. There's no shortage of great guitar players, that's for sure.

Well, you are one of the best yourself brother.

I'm working on it.

(Laughs) I really don't think you have to work on it any more. What would you consider to be the highlight of your long career—so far anyway?

I don't know, man. You remember who Flip Wilson was? He had a variety show on TV in the '60s where he did a bunch of characters. He had Geraldine and all, but my favorite character was Reverend Leroy because he was the pastor of the Church of What's Happening Now. I'm a member of the congregation. I've enjoyed every minute of my career, but I don't look back at any one time and say that was the good ol' days. I'm just enjoying the present.

Elvin remains a force in the blues-rock world, taking the album of the year award at the 2015 Blues Music Awards in Memphis.

Donnie Winters

February 2014

Donnie Winters has been playing guitar for a lot of years. Maybe that's why these days all you have to do is call out the key that the song is in and he will play right along with you. Seriously. He's one of the hottest guitar slingers in Southern Rock, but you'd never know it by talking to him. He's humble, but I have seen him with my own eyes. I have heard him hold his own beside folks like Toy Caldwell, Charlie Daniels, Tommy Crain, and Dickey Betts. Usually, he did a little more than "hold his own," to be honest.

In this exclusive interview, Donnie opens up about his music, his musical family, the Winters Brothers Band, and rocking the Volunteer Jam.

❧

Let's go all the way back to the beginning. Were you and your brother Dennis raised in middle Tennessee? Tell us about the family, your Dad and Uncle Zack, the whole family thing.

My granddad had a band in the '40s called Pop Winters and the Southern Strollers. They played mostly South Georgia and Florida. My dad sang and played with his band, and later his sister Rita also sang with the band. Zack Tucker played and sang with the band, too, and he married my dad's sister, Mary. Aunt Rita also had a career both solo and with Anita Carter and Ruby Wright, called Nita, Rita, and Ruby. I was born in Florida but spent most of my life here in middle Tennessee.

When did your father start out as a singer?

My dad started with his dad, then moved to Nashville in 1953. He recorded for RCA Victor, and Coin Records, and Columbia. You can actually find some of those on YouTube. He has a rockabilly kind of cult hit out today called "Pretty Moon," and the flip side is "Be My Baby, Baby."

Tell us about Don's career, the solo work, and of course working with the legendary Marty Robbins.

Dad had a single out on Decca Records called "Too Many Times," and on the flip side was "Shake Hands with a Loser." It was kinda booked onto shows, and Marty Robbins approached him backstage at the Opry one night, probably early '60s when dad was employed with Webb Pierce. Marty told him if he wasn't doing so well on his own, did he want to come to work with him? And dad looked at him and said, "When do I start?" And he worked with him almost twenty-three years.

At what age did you and Dennis start playing?

I started playing guitar myself when I was about thirteen years old. I'd just turned thirteen, and I'd fashioned a little something with my dad's old guitar strings, plywood, an L-bracket, and some finishing nails and just flailed on it kinda like a banjo. There wasn't any way to really tune it, and my neighbor up the street, Mr. Roger Price, felt sorry for me. He found a guitar at a flea market or yard sale, and he bought it and gave it to me. And the way I got new strings was when dad changed his and I got his old ones. Dad taught me my first six chords on the guitar, and after that he looked at me and told me I was on my own. He put me in touch and kept me around other accomplished musicians who showed me more.

Dennis started on drums probably about a year after, and he played them for about a year or so, then he switched over to guitar, too. And after that we both started writing and playing parties, you know school parties, and stuff. Nothing real professional until we got out of high school.

Give us a bit of a timeline. Did the Winters Brothers Band come first, or did you play first behind your dad?

I never really played behind my dad until much later. Now, I'd play with my dad at home, and he'd teach me stuff. We wrote a little bit together, which is where my first cut, "Do Me A Favor," came from. "Do Me A Favor" was my first song that Marty Robbins recorded. "Do Me A Favor" will be on my new CD that we're working on, but more about that later.

Speaking of firsts: my first car was a gift from Mel Tillis. It was a 1955 Ford that I commenced to drive the wheels off of. Then my dad bought me a Rambler, which I wasn't real crazy about, but it was transportation. It served as our first band vehicle. Dennis was playing drums, a close friend of ours was playing bass on an electric guitar that we had rigged into a bass, and we made an amp out of an old tape recorder that had speakers. We were a high school combo called the Open Ditch.

Talk a bit about the WBB, the original players, how you got a record deal, working with Taz. Was it recorded at Capricorn? The whole shootin' match.

When we moved out to Franklin, we lived across the road from Marty on his property. There was this old shack that Dennis and I turned into a band room. That's when Jack Pruett, son of Jack and Jeannie Pruett, played bass, and an old high school friend, Bruce Campbell, was our first drummer, and that was the first Winters Brothers Band. That was about 1974, then we got to the point where we got decent guitars and amps, and we picked up our first gig with that band in Greenville, North Carolina, in 1975. We didn't even have a contract, but it was fun. We ended up making some friends and meeting some bands. After that we got a little more serious. We played a school's-out party at Fair Park in Nashville, but since we weren't making any money, the band members changed from time to time.

We first met Charlie Daniels when dad was doing some recording with Marty and Charlie was one of the guitar players on the session. Charlie already had a couple of records out by then. And dad started talking to him and told him that we were looking to get into this new thing called Southern Rock and asked if Charlie would give us an audience, so to speak, and tell us where we needed to go for management, booking, recording, and stuff. Charlie and his wife Hazel invited us into their home one evening, and Dennis and I sat down and played him a couple of songs on acoustic guitars, and he liked what he heard. We asked him if he'd be interested in producing us since he'd produced some stuff. He said he was getting real busy working on this new album he was working on called *Fire On the Mountain* but that his keyboard player, Taz DiGregorio, might be interested. We had seen Charlie Daniels, Marshall Tucker Band, the Outlaws, and Grinderswitch live a few times, and we liked their music and thought that was the direction we'd like to go. So we thought working with Taz would be good.

Taz worked with us, getting us ready to be on stage and work with any kind of situation that might come up. He made us learn our songs backwards and forwards so that even if the lights went out we could keep on playing. That's something I credit Taz with is getting us to the point where we were a professional band.

We were never signed with Capricorn, but we did record two records there. Dick Wooley, who had a record company called Rabbit Records and was a former vice president with Capricorn, introduced us to Phil Walden and all his staff.

I have always been obsessed with the history of the Volunteer Jams. You played many. Tell us about what it was like. Please include any anecdotes or happy memories.

The first Volunteer Jam Dennis and I bought our tickets and went to the first one in 1974 at the War Memorial Auditorium in Nashville. That's when we fell in love with the live aspects of Charlie Daniels, Marshall Tucker, Allman Brothers, the Outlaws, and anybody that was doing our kind of music at that time. We had a great time, and that's when we really decided to pursue the Southern Rock thing.

By the time the second one at Middle Tennessee State University rolled around, we had started working with Taz and had backstage passes, and Charlie asked us if we wanted to come up and jam, but we didn't have our guitars, and we were just enjoying being there and meeting all these wonderful people. By the time the third one rolled around, Dennis and I had our record out, and we were invited to open the Jam. We played almost all of them after that. We ended up being on two of the Volunteer Jam albums. "Sang Her Love Songs" was on the *Volunteer Jam III & IV* album, and then we did a song called "Rich Kids" that was on the *Volunteer Jam VI* album.

What was the story with *Coast to Coast Live*?

Coast to Coast was supposed to be our second album, on the Rabbit / Atco Record label, and well, it's a long story. We went down to Miami to do it with Taz producing, and we spent about ten days down there recording, and it just wasn't happening for one reason or another, so we ditched that effort and took a break. Charlie Daniels was on the road around that Thanksgiving time 1977, and Dick Wooley got us some time at Capricorn, and we got in with producer Paul Hornsby. And we went in and did the songs we wanted to do. We came out with what we thought was a really good product, but Atlantic record representatives came down and listened to the final mix and said they just didn't hear any singles. Dick tried really hard, but he just couldn't find any labels that wanted to pick it up. So it just sat on the shelf until my wife, Paula, contacted Paul Hornsby, and he said he had masters of the final mix. We got copies and had some pressed up just to sell at shows and stuff under the name *The Lost Album*, aka *Coast to Coast*. There are two live cuts on the album. We recorded them at Rose's Cantina in Atlanta.

We opened shows for a lot of famous acts; a lot of them were due to our work with Marshall Tucker and Charlie Daniels Band. We got to work with Levon Helm, after the Band; we opened shows for the Allman Brothers, and we did several shows with Lynyrd Skynyrd. We were supposed to go back out with them again when their plane crashed.

Did you know Waylon? He's one of my old heroes, and I just wondered.
I knew Waylon, but not as well as Dennis did. Dennis worked for Waylon driving his truck and then bus, and I was fortunate enough. Dennis asked me if I wanted to do a coast-to-coast relief driver thing with him one time and got to spend some time with them.

You actually worked with Marty Robbins too, right?
That was early on, before the Winters Brothers Band. I was hanging out at Marty's office one day after his first heart attack in 1969, and he asked me to start learning the licks to "El Paso," and I was kinda curious as to why. He told me he wanted me to start playing guitar for him on the Grand Ole Opry. When he had his heart attack, he'd let his band go except my dad and Bobby Sykes. They'd do shows using just the house band at places. So I worked with him on just the Opry alone from about February of 1970 to February of 1971. And it was a great experience. I got to meet a lot of the staff musicians who I'm still friends with today. I got to stand on that Grand Ole Opry stage at the Ryman and I'll cherish that forever.

I know you've been playing a lot of music over the past few years, I'm sure you never really let up. What are some of the projects you have been involved in?
Local, basically all local. I did some recording on my friend George Harper's album, but mostly people will call me and ask me if I'll come play that weekend. I'm pretty good with cover tunes. If I've heard it on the radio several times, I can make my way through it.

Which leads us up to now. Do the WBB play anymore?
Dennis actually has the Winters Brothers Band now.

I would be remiss if I didn't ask a Southern man about family. We all know your wife, Paula Underwood Winters, is a photographer and writer and does all sorts of stuff. Is she doing something with TV?

Paula works for Larry Black at Gabriel Communications. They produce the *Country's Family Reunion* and *Larry's Country Diner TV* shows on RFD-TV, and she puts together their country music newspaper, the *CFR News*. They give the older, more traditional, country music artists a place to sing now, and they've also been bringing together the kids of those artists for shows too, calling them "Second Generations." I played a show with them at Mickey Roos a while back. There was George Hamilton V (and his dad), Robyn Young, Melissa Luman-Phillips, Jett Williams, Seldina Reed, Dean Smith, Hawkshaw Hawkins, Jr., and a bunch more. It was great!

Does she have other projects stewing?

We're turning our family farm into an event venue. I hope to have some concerts there this coming summer. Earl Scruggs recorded a segment for his special called *Earl Scruggs: His Family and Friends* there with the Byrds back in 1968, Hank Jr. recorded part of "All My Rowdy Friends Are Coming Over Tonight" out in their field, and they've had weddings for family and friends there, so she decided to jump into it and try to make a business out of it. You can see more on that project at www.mtairyeventfarm.com.

They say that behind every great man there's a woman, and I believe that. How do you feel about it?

I love my wife. We've been married going on thirty-four years, and we were together five years on and off before that. She's my life partner.

Most of us are aware of the tragedy that you guys endured last year when you lost your son, Ryan. All of our hearts were with you. Please share your happiest memory of your son.

We used to go downtown on Broadway, and he would take his banjo and I'd take my guitar and we'd hang on the corner of Third and Broad. He was a gifted musician. We just loved to do things together, Ryan and me and my younger boy, Derek.

And your happiest memory of your dad, Papa Don?

They're all happy. I can't pick just one, other than the fact that I got to play with him on the Grand Ole Opry. Getting to play with him on the Volunteer Jam was great. There's clips of that on YouTube. Anytime he'd get to go out and play shows with us, those would be my greatest memories.

Donnie, sum up if you would, your overall feelings regarding the Winters Brothers Band.
Those were some of the best years of my life, and I enjoyed every minute of it.

Who are your favorite guitar players ever? Singers?
I'll have to start with my all-time favorite, Carlos Santana. He inspired me from the first time I ever heard him on the radio. Grady Martin who plays on Marty's early recordings; my uncle, Ray Edenton who was a Nashville session player for over 40 years; Jimmy Capps who's being inducted into the Musicians Hall of Fame this month. All of the Grand Ole Opry staff musicians who I could call by name, who influenced me when I was there. Some of the finest twin guitar playing I ever heard was on the stage of the Opry: Jimmy Capps and Leon Rhodes, Jimmy "Spider" Wilson, Joe Edwards.

As far as vocalists, number one, I'd have to say Marty Robbins 'cause he influenced me so much. Then my dad would be right there with him. Not a second, but right there beside him. My dad taught me how to sing (and to yodel). Other ones, I'd have to stay with the country vein, Ray Price influenced me at an early age, and Roy Acuff. As far as rock singers goes, I like so many of them. Crosby, Stills and Nash, they influenced me as far as harmonies go. Emmylou Harris has been a big influence. I love her music. Today's artists, I love Brad Paisley, his vocals as well as his guitar playing. Josh Turner, George Strait, of course, Gene Watson (the singer—Gene Watson our old bass player is one of my favorite bass players)

What are you working on now? Are you recording the long-awaited solo record? I am really looking forward to that one!
I mix sound and host the Tuesday Writer's Night at Douglas Corner in Nashville. I also play around town with friends or at Debbie Champion's writers nights at the Commodore Lounge and with Scott Rath at Mickey Roos in Franklin occasionally.

I'm also working on a new CD, which is mostly traditional country music. It's going to be made up of songs that dad wrote, and I wrote either with Dennis or others or myself. It will have "Do Me A Favor" that Marty recorded, as well as other songs that Marty recorded. I hope to have a Kickstarter campaign up before long to help raise the money to get it finished. I've been working on it for about a year now with my friends Tim and Danny Carter [the Carter Brothers] at their studio up in Ridgetop, Tennessee, called the Treehouse.

What's the best place for folks to find you on the internet?
The best place is on Facebook or my website www.donniewintersmusic.com, which I promise to try to update more often.

The old desert island discs question. You are on a desert island with an endless supply of batteries and a CD player but only ten CDs. What would they be?
Allman Brothers, *At Fillmore East*, would be my first choice. I'd probably have to go with Carlos Santana's *Greatest Hits* because I couldn't take all of his albums. Marty Robbins, *Gunfighter Ballads*; Ray Price's *Greatest Hits*; Charlie Daniels, *Fire On The Mountain*; Marshall Tucker, *Where We All Belong*; Steely Dan, *Decades (Greatest Hits)*; Hank Williams, *Greatest Hits*; Buddy Miller, *Midnight and Lonesome*; Sam Bush, *Glamour & Grits*.

Dave Cantonwine

2009

Eric Quincy Tate was one of the greatest Southern Rock bands of all time—they just never got the recognition they so richly deserved. The Texas-based band was compared by many to fellow Capricorn Records artists the Allman Brothers Band, due mostly to their extreme talent and ability to take the music to another level in concert, playing extended jams and brilliantly executed rock songs. Two of the band's founding members died during the past year or so, leaving behind a musical legacy of great importance to those who heard them live or on record, because once you heard the band, you were hooked for life.

We spoke with bassist David Cantonwine about the band, his friends, and the whole Macon scene during the Southern Rock era.

It's been a rough few months on EQT fans, and I am sure on the band and family. First off, give me your thoughts on the late Donnie McCormick, his music and his art.

Donnie McCormick was a true friend and mentor. He taught me how to be a real musician. I guess I can say that about all the guys in the band. We spent a lot of time together, touring and playing club dates. Donnie was a one of a kind. He didn't act like, sing like, or talk like anyone else. And he was great at making you watch him while he was singing or playing the drums. Hell, I used to have a blast watching Donnie perform—and I was in the band! Best seat in the house.

Same question, Wayne "Bear" Sauls.

Wayne Sauls was another true friend who would do anything for you. We were playing down at Grants Lounge one weekend, I think it was Saturday. We all got up and wandered around Macon and found this fresh meat market, and Bear said, "I bet they got pigs feet in there." So we go in, and Bear told the lady that he wanted four pigs feet. She said, "Honey are these all for you?" Bear said, "Yeah." She says, "Okay, I'll give you four pigs feet. You gonna eat them all at one time?" Bear said, "Just four pigs feet please,

%#$*&!!" The lady hollered out, "Junior! Give the man sixteen of them pig feet!" I guess you had to be there but we all laughed our asses off. But yeah, Bear was a friend and damn good guitar player—sorry, great guitar player.

Back to the beginning. How did the band come to be formed? What was you guys "battle plan" when you first got together, and what year was that?

In 1967, I was having the time of my life, It was like—wow! Joe Rogers and I played together in a band named the American Way. We were still in high school at that time. Dyke McCarty, our drummer, had this brother Allen who was the host of an American Bandstand-type TV dance show on Saturday mornings called *Teen Time*. We were on TV every other week. Our manager owned the biggest rock venue in town, the Stardust Rollercadel, so we played there every other week. I was seventeen and in high school. The band, the girls, sex in the parking lot during lunch—we were local rock stars.

I really can't remember why our band broke up, but Joe and I parted after that and played with other bands. Somehow I wound up in Austin, Texas, jamming with all those acid freaks—remember this was still '67. Anyway, I got a record deal with International Artists out of Houston—more acid. (In funny voice) IthinkthatwasonaFri-Fri-Fri- Da - Da - Da -Day. (Laughs) I was suppose to start recording an album on Monday, so I decided to go down to see my parents that weekend, who lived in Corpus Christi. Long story short, while I was there, I went out to a club called the Muddy Turtle, and that's where the birth of Eric Quincy Tate took place. What a mess—gooey shit everywhere. (Laughs)

How did Tony Joe White figure into your success?

The first time I met Tony Joe White was at our local music store. I remember asking him why his guitar was so dirty. He told me that it gave it soul. Gators got your granny…

Donnie and Tony Joe were good friends and had grew up with the same influences. Donnie had put out a couple of 45s and had a local hit with "LCB" (Liquor Control Board), then Tony got this record deal and had the national hit "Polk Salad Annie." Tony went on to the big time, and on the way got us this record deal with Atco records, which led to Capricorn, starring Phil Walden and Frank Fenter.

Did you guys do a lot of shows with the Allmans? What was that like? Did you know Duane?

We did quite a few dates with the Brothers and everyone else in between. Doing dates with them was always party 'til dawn, sleep all day, next gig. Knowing Duane back in those days was no big deal. We saw him and Gregg a lot in Macon, when we were recording. Duane did some session stuff with us, and Gregg and Donnie used to bullshit a lot. Back then the Brothers weren't that big yet, and I still couldn't believe I was making a record in the same studio that Otis Redding recorded in. That was the biggest thing to me. All the Macon acts used to hang out at Grants Lounge 'til closing time, then go up the street to Hodges Hot Chicken Restaurant. The chicken was so hot your nose hairs would burn off before you could get it to your mouth. The other Capricorn bands, we all new each other on a "Hey how are ya" kind of thing. We all did gigs together all over the country so we would run into each other all the time, party 'til we puked and hit the road again. Those were the days.

What do you recall about working with Paul Hornsby?

Again, I was at that stage in my life where I could not believe I was in a band that had a record deal with the company that recorded Otis Redding. But recording with Paul Hornsby was a big learning experience for me. As I remember, he was very patient with us and brought out the best in everybody. We still stay in touch a little on the digital highway.

Where in the world did you guys get your band name?

It came from Eric, for Clapton, Quincy for Quincy Jones and Tate as in potato.

Do you feel at all slighted by the powers that be? Many have said you should have been as big as the Allmans. Your thoughts?

We should have been bigger than Led Zeppelin. All the money was on the Brothers at that time. So what are ya gonna do.

Tell us about some of the real high points in the career of EQT.

Meeting all the famous people was a real high point. Once we opened up for B.B. King in Central Park. I was sitting outside smoking a cig before the show, and this big black guy walks up to me and says, "Hello, I'm BB

King," and shook my hand. I about shit in my pants. I shook B.B.-fucking-King's hand.

Here's one for ya. Back in '69 when the band first got together we were playing this club in Austin, Texas. When we took a break, the manager walked up to us and asked if we minded if some guys got up and jammed on our equipment. We said great, y'all play as long as you want. We went outside for a smoke, and I said, "You know who that is? That's Jimmy Page. I think he was in the Yardbirds. Zeppelin was playing in Austin that night with Spirit. Remember Spirit?

Sure. Randy California. Great band.

They were on there first US tour. Okay, one more. I met Little Richard. EQT and his people were staying at the same hotel in Hollywood. We had just played at the Whiskey-A-Go Go—that's a whole 'nother story. Anyway, I asked Little Richard if that was his real hair. He grabs hold of his hair and yanks it off his head and says "Hell yeah, that's my hair! I bought it!" That son of a bitch sold me an ounce of pot that turned out to be pipe tobacco.

What do you remember about that twenty-year reunion show?

I was scared shitless. My face was flour white. We hadn't played together for a while, except for rehearsing, and I had quit playing altogether. Tried to do the family thing for few years.

Who are your favorite bass players?

Jack Bruce is number one. Then there was Jack Casady, throw in Paul McCartney for some silly pop, and I think that's about it. I'm sure there's more, but those were my biggest influences.

Tell me about your other musical projects, past, present, and future?

I bought a bread route here in North Augusta, South Carolina, a few years back and that keeps me pretty busy. I still write music and record demos in a mini-studio I have in my house. Check out You Tube and search Damned Ole Dave. I've got a couple of things on there. Keeps me off the streets and out of the bars.

David keeps the memory of EQT alive with the release of rare archival recordings, as well as his own solo material.

Appendix

Phil Walden Memorial

May 2006

Phil Walden, 66, the Capricorn Records founder who launched the careers of Otis Redding and the Allman Brothers Band, died on Sunday, 23 April 2006 after a long battle with cancer. Walden died at his home in Atlanta.

Founded in 1969, Phil Walden's Capricorn Records was the premier American music label that helped put Macon, Georgia, on the map as a major Southern Rock hub. It was home to such renowned artists as the Allman Brothers Band, Wet Willie, Elvin Bishop, the Marshall Tucker Band, the Dixie Dregs, Delbert McClinton, Captain Beyond, and many others. At both Capricorn Records and his earlier endeavor, Phil Walden Artists and Promotions, Walden signed artists based on what he heard and felt, not on corporate research or popular trends. Over the last forty years, Walden had a hand in shaping not only Georgia music history, but popular music history as a whole.

Walden's two most famous artists, Otis Redding and guitarist Duane Allman, both died tragically: Redding in a plane crash in 1967 at twenty-six, and Allman in a motorcycle accident in 1971 at age twenty-four.

The Allman Brothers Band, the quintessential Southern Rock band that the guitarist founded with brother Gregg and others, continued after Duane Allman's death.

"They weren't trendy," Walden said in a 1996 interview with the *Atlanta Journal-Constitution*. "You had all these British groups dressed up in Edwardian finery," Walden continued. "But there was never any attempt by the Allmans to be a show band. They played music. On occasions, when they were allowed to, for hours."

Duane Allman and his brother Gregg would soon become the stars of the Capricorn label. The Allman Brothers Band's third album, *At Fillmore East*, was hailed by critics as one of the best live rock albums ever produced. This live double album was dubbed "the finest live rock performance ever committed to vinyl," by *Rolling Stone* magazine. "Phil was a visionary," said Chuck Leavell, who joined the Allman Brothers on keyboards in 1972 and now plays with the Rolling Stones. "He just had a great vision and a true, deep passion for the music."

In 1979, the label dissolved under the distribution company PolyGram Records, forcing Walden to file for bankruptcy in 1980. Walden then steered his career in a different direction, returning to artist management. In the '80s, Walden represented Jim Varney, best known for his role as Ernest P. Worrell, and the then little-known actor and director Billy Bob Thornton.

The Capricorn label made a strong comeback in the 1990 in Nashville, Tennessee, and within the next year released its first album by Athens band Widespread Panic. With Capricorn's resurrection came a new line up of fresh, new, young acts including 311 and Cake. Walden moved Capricorn to Atlanta, Georgia, in 1996 and sold half to the company to PolyGram/Mercury. This venture allowed the reissuing of many of Capricorn's earlier recordings since PolyGram/Mercury owned many master tapes. The label was sold in 1999, but Phil was not ready to put his love for music in the past. In 2001, Phil and his children Philip and Amantha began Velocette Records in Atlanta.

During the 1970s, Walden was an early backer of then-Georgia governor Jimmy Carter. He helped with Carter's bid for the presidency financially, as did the Allmans, Marshall Tucker, and other Capricorn groups, who played benefit shows.

Carter said in a statement at the time of Phil's passing that he and wife Rosalynn were sad to hear of Walden's death. "Phil was one of the preeminent producers of great music in America," Carter said. "His many performing partners, including Otis Redding and the Allman Brothers, helped to put Macon and Georgia on the musical map of the world."

"In the late '60s I was just getting into the t-shirt screening business," says Jerry W. Henry. "Phil believed in me and what I was doing. He gave me one of my first orders. I was in need of money, and his orders helped keep me in business. The music business would not have been the same without him."

Walden was born in Greenville, South Carolina, 11 January 1940 but grew up in Macon, Georgia. As an undergrad at Macon's Mercer University, Walden began his venture into the music industry by booking bands for local high school and college events, eventually opening his own office and expanding his agency in the southeast. Phil introduced his younger brother Alan Walden to the music business, making him a full-time partner in Phil

Walden Artists and Promotions. Together, Phil and Alan represented Otis Redding, Sam and Dave, Clarence Carter, and Percy Sledge. Alan went on to work with both Lynyrd Skynyrd and the Outlaws.

As a young R&B lover, there was no better place for Phil Walden to be in the late '50s than his hometown of Macon, Georgia. The black music scene was thriving with homegrown talent such as Little Richard and the Pinetoppers. And Walden, still in high school, was determined to be a part of it. Beginning his career by managing a local group named the Heartbreakers, as president of his high school fraternity Walden started booking R&B acts. His break came when a guitarist he was managing, Johnny Jenkins, introduced Walden to a young singer named Otis Redding. The two became fast friends and, opening an office in downtown Macon, Walden dedicated himself to making Otis Redding a star.

Redding and Walden's close friendship made them outcasts in the segregated South, Redding's widow, Zelma Redding, recalled in 1997. She said Walden's passion for black music made him "the little white boy who everybody was wanting to beat up on."

Remembering Capricorn's Frank Fenter

The Push to Get Him into the Georgia Music Hall of Fame

Frank Fenter (25 February 1936–21 July 1983) is truly an unsung hero of the music world, especially in the world of Southern Rock. Today, there is a movement afoot set into motion by Fenter's stepson Robin to get Fenter into the Georgia Music Hall of Fame. His work with Atlantic Records and subsequent move to the new Southern label Capricorn at the request of the Ertegun Brothers make him a prime candidate for induction.

Frank was born and raised in Johannesburg, South Africa, before moving to London, England in 1958 with aspirations of becoming a professional actor.

In 1966, Frank Fenter was chosen by Atlantic Records's Nesuhi Ertegun to head Atlantic Records in the United Kingdom. During his time at Atlantic, Fenter discovered such artists as Yes, King Crimson, and Led Zeppelin. He was also instrumental for breaking R&B music in Europe, bringing the Stax tour to Europe in 1967.

In 1969, Fenter and Phil and Alan Walden co-founded Capricorn Records after securing a distribution deal from Atlantic Records that Fenter secured and negotiated with his mentor, Ahmet Ertegun.

"We were completely supportive of the idea of Phil and Frank creating a label together that we would be involved in and that we would distribute," said Ertegun in an interview. "Together, Frank and Phil formed a great team."

Frank became executive vice president of Capricorn Records, signing many of the artists to the label roster with his business partner, Phil Walden. The history of Capricorn Records is forever tied to the history of Southern Rock. From the signing of the Allman Brothers Band in 1969, to the great bands that followed such as Marshall Tucker Wet Willie, and Grinderswitch, Fenter was a major part of the label. A quiet man who worked more behind the scenes, there is no question of how Fenter contributed to Southern Rock and to Georgia Music. Here are just a few of the many collected comments from Frank's friends, peers and artists he worked with:

"Frank Fenter, when I think of him I see a smile. He was always the one that seemed to smooth out any of the many problems arising in the ever changing world of rock and roll. Where some might get a little excited and lose focus, Frank remained relatively calm, and could see the line of least resistance or whether or not a little turmoil was worth the fight. Mostly, Frank loved to celebrate life, and it came through in his smile. A fine man that helped further the cause of music and musicians."
—Tommy Talton, Cowboy

"Frank was a great friend of mine. Throughout all the turmoil that always surrounded us, Frank was always there for me. He was a first class guy!"
—Dickey Betts, former Allman Brothers Band member

"No one was like Frank Fenter. He deserves a lot of recognition that he never got. One of the smartest men I have ever met. He was always a gentle man. Lots of class, always."
—Colonel Bruce Hampton

"He absolutely should be in there, in my opinion. He was a huge part of Capricorn Records. He made a huge impact." (quote taken from *Macon Telegraph* article, 14 December 2009)
—Chuck Leavell, former Allman Brothers Band, Sea Level, and Rolling Stones band member.

"Frank was a special person who played an integral role, not only in bringing Capricorn and its artists to the world, but also many legendary artists during his tenure at Atlantic."
—Philip Walden, Jr.

"Frank Fenter's contribution to the state's music history has been somewhat overlooked. It would be wonderful for his contributions to be recognized by membership into the GMHF."
—Willie Perkins, former ABB road manager

"Frank was the wheels that made the operation run. He was a mover and shaker with integrity. He understood the creative process, but he also knew how to make things happen on the business front."
—Bobby Whitlock, former member of Eric Clapton's Derek and the Dominos and Capricorn Recording artist.

"It is Frank Fenter who taught myself and artist manager Phil Walden the executive side of the record business in those historic years when we introduced Southern Rock to the world. Frank Fenter had one of the best ears in the music business. He had the record business knowledge, and he was a power behind the scenes at Capricorn, and everyone in the record company recognized that."
—Dick Wooley, former Capricorn Executive

"He was instrumental in bringing Capricorn Records to Macon, Georgia. We have a special interest in seeing Frank nominated, as I was his personal assistant from 1970 until 1973. Because of Frank, I met and married Chuck. He also was instrumental in getting Chuck the funding for his first Hammond B3 Organ."
—Rose Lane White Leavell, former Capricorn employee

"I am in full support of Frank getting into the Georgia Rock and Roll Hall of Fame. Frank helped further Eric Quincy Tate's career in the music biz, and helped produce one of the best records to come out of Capricorn, *Drinking Man's Friend*.
—David Cantonwine, EQT

"After we played two songs, Frank said, "Delightful. Come in Monday morning and we will sign the papers." Total gentleman is the operative word for Frank. He was kind and had a warm, sincere demeanor. He always made you feel important. He was "the elegant Captain of the ship."
—Rick Hirsch, co-founder of Wet Willie, former Capricorn artist.

"Frank loved the music business, and he was a fearless promoter of the Southern music that he loved! He was also a great man. The music business needs more cats like Frank Fenter today!"
—John D. Wyker, former session musician at Capricorn and founder of the band Sailcat

"I considered Frank and his wife, Kiki Fenter, as the center of the social hub of the Macon music phenomena during the early '70s. In particular, they were the primary hosts of parties and dinners for the Allman Brothers and other musicians of the era. If walls could talk, a book could be written on the real story of Macon, Georgia, at the height of its music history. Many stories were told by Frank and the musicians that felt at home there. While Frank provided inspiration of other musical greats, Kiki provided an opportunity for musicians to talk about their influences, and with her encouragement, those thoughts eventually made many records. Inspiration to learn and for a safe place to be who these people were, were very, very, important.

Dickey and I were invited on a regular basis to enjoy the dinners that Frank fixed and Kiki hosted. Whenever invited, Dickey and I attended without hesitation and with pure excitement. Frank provided his collection of music that was phenomenal, and Kiki was the warmest human being that helped navigate us through many a troubling time that most people in the music industry experience. They both had this experience. One of the greatest gifts was Frank's broad collection of albums that lined a whole wall from top to bottom in their huge estate home, and, if it wasn't there, he would dig into the closets that held a mass of albums. On one occasion, Dickey and Frank got into a discussion on jazz and the relationship to the fiddle. Dickey's father was a fiddle player, and this was his first musical influence as a child. Frank went into his closet and had the complete Django Rheinhart collection on the Hot Club of France. He played an album, and that was it! Dickey loved it. He talked to Frank about setting up a recording session with Django, which Frank followed up on. Unfortunately, it wasn't possible at the time. What Dickey did do was orchestrate a recording session and tour with Vassar Clements, an American country icon from Kissimmee, Florida. The album was called *Highway Call*, and the tour included Nashville and Muscle Shoals musicians, Spooner Oldham, backup singers for Elvis Presley, Pepper Watkins, etcetera. One of the tunes was called the 'Kissimmee Kid,' an instrumental featuring Dickey and Vassar.

Frank was truly an inspiration and expert in every genre of music. This is only one example of the incredible influence he had on the Macon/Capricorn artists."

—Sandy Wabegijig (Blue Sky)

Frank Fenter was inducted into the Georgia Music Hall of Fame on 11 October 2014.

***

In loving memory of Phil Walden, Frank Fenter, Phillip Walden, Duane Allman, Berry Oakley, Lamar Williams, Joe Dan Petty, Toy Caldwell, Tommy Caldwell, George McCorkle, Chuck McCorkle, Tommy Crain, Taz DiGregorio, Tom Dowd, George Clark, Wayne "Bear" Sauls, Donnie McCormick, Dru Lombar, and Steve Miller.

Special thanks to the following people for help and/or inspiration: Willie Perkins for the foreword; Billy Bob Thornton; The Boxmasters; Alan Walden; Robin Duner Fenter; Colleen Knights and April Knights for proofreading; Rob Schneck and then gang at The Big House Museum; Greg Loescher; Hilda Morrow; Dave Shuping; the Gang at Mercer University Press; Dr. Hunter S. Thompson; Lester Bangs; Cameron Crowe; Mama Louise Hudson & The H&H; Ed Grant and Grant's Lounge; and huge thanks to all of my interview subjects!

Index

Allman Brothers Band, The 1-3, 7, 8, 10, 11, 13, 14, 19, 21, 23, 24, 27–30, 36, 46, 49, 57, 60, 61, 63, 69, 74, 76, 79, 80, 89, 105, 107, 108, 118, 120, 125, 132, 135, 137, 140. 142, 160, 161, 169, 175, 176, 171, 174, 180, 184, 185, 186, 187, 193, 205, 219, 221, 239, 245, 251, 262, 263, 265, 267, 270, 271, 273
Allman, Devon 76
Allman, Duane 10, 12, 13, 18, 19, 20, 21, 29, 57, 58, 60–62, 65, 66, 76, 78, 79, 88, 91, 92, 99, 101, 104, 139, 141, 142, 144, 149, 151, 160–162, 169, 170, 174, 175, 177, 184, 191, 192, 219, 238, 252, 265, 267
Allman, Galadrielle 76–86
Allman, Gregg 3, 9, 11, 14-18, 21, 33, 61, 66, 76, 89, 91–93, 95, 99, 140, 143, 149, 153, 170, 178, 179, 191, 193, 265, 267
Allman Joys 100, 101
Almost Famous movie 8
At Fillmore East album 8, 49, 57, 79, 251, 262, 267
Beautiful album 80
Bennett, Rick 184
Betts, Dickey 1-13, 17, 20, 21, 22, 28–30, 36, 37, 46, 58, 59, 61, 65, 66, 94, 95, 109, 110, 140, 151, 152, 161, 174, 191, 192, 230, 252, 255, 271, 272, 273
Betts, Duane 2, 13
Betts, Hall, Leavell & Trucks (BHLT) 134
Bishop, Elvin 251–254, 267
Boyer, Scott 19, 33, 97, 139–146, 147, 150, 154, 157, 158, 162, 169, 172, 173, 180, 238,
Bramlett, Bekka 84
Bramlett, Bonnie 1, 9, 19, 29, 80–85, 92, 149, 179, 180, 186, 227, 248

Bramlett, Delaney 80
Bramblett, Randall 30, 35, 83, 178–183
Brothers & Sisters album 8, 27, 95, 192
Burbridge, Oteil 14, 16, 94
Burnette, Rickey 191, 192, 194
Cake 268
Caldwell, Tommy 31, 69, 204–206, 212, 216, 239, 245, 246
Caldwell, Toy 16, 31, 36, 69, 94, 107, 110, 195, 202, 204–207, 212, 216, 221, 229, 246, 252, 255
Campbell, Red Dog 245
Cantonwine, David 263–266
Captain Beyond 267
Carolina Dreams album 108
Carolina Dreams book 213
Capricorn Rhythm Section 146, 147, 156
Carr, Pete 104, 105, 175
Carter, Jimmy 130, 268
Causey, Davis 30, 178, 182, 181
Cats On the Coast album 180
Charlie Daniels Band 108, 135, 184, 185, 224, 231, 241, 242, 243, 245–47, 255, 257–259
Clapton, Eric 60, 61, 63, 65, 79, 80, 88, 144
Clark, George 141, 150, 154, 172, 158, 163, 173
Clements, Vassar 273
Cowboy 44, 94, 97, 140, 142, 143, 146, 147, 150, 152, 154–158, 160, 162, 164, 167, 169, 170, 172, 174, 177, 178–180, 271
Crain, Billy 225
Crain, Tommy 224–233, 255
Crowe, Cameron 8, 9
Daniels, Charlie 43, 80, 108, 109. 112, 136, 188, 193, 212, 219–223, 225–228. 230, 234, 237 - 241
Delaney & Bonnie 78, 79, 92, 244
Derek & The Dominos 79

DiGregorio, Taz 220, 227, 242–250, 257
Dixie Dreggs 267
Don Kirshner's Rock Concert 133
Doucette, Thom 69
Dowd, Tom 13, 21, 49–75, 89, 90, 156
Dreams: Allman Brothers boxed set 134
Drinking Man's Friend album 106
Drippin' Wet Live 134
Duane Allman Anthology album 104
Duane & Gregg Allman: The Early Years album 139
Dudek, Les 2, 4, 191
Eat a Peach album 59
Eric Quincy Tate 106, 263 - 265
Ertegun, Ahmet 60, 129, 270
Ertegun, Neshuhi 270
Eubanks, Jerry 212
Fenter, Frank 89, 125–131, 209, 264, 270–274
Fenter, Kiki 273
Fenter, Robin Duner 125–131, 270
Fire On the Mountain album 108, 109, 238. 239, 249, 257
5'll Get You Ten album 143, 154, 160, 175
Forever Young album 110, 152
Galkin, Joe 115
Goldflies, David "Rook" 134
Gov't Mule 66, 67
Graham, Bill 102, 103, 143, 162
Grant's Lounge 106, 124
Gray, Doug 135, 204–210, 211, 112
Gregg Allman Tour '74 album 15, 153, 179
Grinderswitch 29, 184, 186–189. 191, 193, 196, 257, 270
H & H Restaurant 123
Haddox, David 216
Hall, Donna 133
Hall, Jimmy 17, 21, 89, 132–138, 167, 186
Hampton, Col. Bruce 93, 271
Happy to Be Alive album 98, 152

Haynes, Warren 2, 14, 16, 22, 24, 37, 66
Hayward, Charlie 43, 97, 104, 142, 234–241
Herring, Jimmy 94
Hicks, Chris 112, 124
Highway Call album 1, 7, 36, 94, 273
Hinton, Eddie 92, 100, 101, 145, 146
Hirsch, Rick 272
Hornsby, Paul 43, 94, 99–113, 144, 238, 258, 265
Hour Glass 88, 101, 102
Hudson, Mama Louise 123
Howard, Larry 187, 189, 189–203
Idlewild South album 14, 59, 89
Jenkins, Johnnie 115
Johanson, Jaimoe 3, 20, 21, 46, 61, 107, 161, 180
Johnson, Jimmy 72
Kid Rock 73
Kight, E.G. 113
Kowalke, Pete 141, 164, 169–177
Laid Back album 95, 153, 179, 238
Layla and Other Assorted Love Songs album 57, 59, 63, 64
Leavell, Chuck 21, 24, 41, 43, 46, 94, 103, 104, 111, 142, 151, 160, 180, 193, 231, 236–238, 267, 271
Leavell, Rose Lane 271, 272
Left Coast Live album 110
Lombar, Dru 184–189, 192
Lynyrd Skynyrd 59, 68, 74, 109, 114, 122–124, 140, 185, 286, 289, 245, 269
Marshall Tucker Band 22, 31, 69, 94, 99, 106, 111, 112, 113, 124, 125, 134, 135, 184, 185, 186, 204–209, 212, 214, 215, 217, 219, 222, 229, 239, 245, 252, 257, 259, 267, 268, 270
McClinton, Delbert 267
McCorkle, Chuck 214–218
McCorkle, George 211–215, 217, 218
McCormick, Donnie 263 - 265
McKinney, Mabron 101, 102

Medlocke, Rickey 136
Molly Hatchet 68
Mullinax, Lou 106, 193
Muscle Shoals, Alabama 14, 19
Nalls, Jimmy 28, 41–48, 111, 180, 237, 238
Oakley, Berry 10, 11, 20, 21, 66, 90, 104, 134, 140, 161, 174, 191
Oldham, Spooner 273
On the Edge album 181
One More from the Road album 59
Outlaws 114, 115, 120, 122, 123, 226, 232, 257
Parnell, Lee Roy 29, 35
Paul, Henry 225
Pearson, Jack 2, 4, 16
Perkins, Willie 271
Petty, Joe Dan 29, 110, 184, 187–189, 191, 193, 194, 199
Pickett, Court 106
Pilmore, Bill 140, 146, 150, 158, 164, 169, 172
Price, Topper 145
Pronounced album 118
Redding, Otis 30, 111, 114–116, 123, 125, 267, 269
Redding, Zelma 269
Riddle, Paul T. 22, 246
Rock Your Socks Off album 46, 114
Sailcat 235, 272
Sam & Davd 269
Sandlin, Johnny 27, 33, 86–98, 100, 104, 105, 106, 110, 141, 143–145, 151, 152, 162–164, 176, 179, 236
Saturday Night in Macon, Georgia 133
Sauls, Wayne "Bear" 263
Sea Level 28, 30, 41, 45, 46, 178, 180. 271
Searching for a Rainbow album 212
Second Helping album 118
See Through Me album 181
Scott, Yonrico 16
Skydog: The Duane Allman Retrospective album 76, 77
Sledge, Percy 269

Snyder, Bud 12
Stewart, Bill 33, 104, 152, 167
Street Survivors album 67
Stompin' Room Only album 207
Sundown 106
Talton, Tommy 14, 44, 97, 140 –142, 146, 146, 147–156, 157, 158, 167, 172, 173, 175, 179, 180, 238, 271
Tate, Eric Quincy 271
Taylor, Alex 29, 41, 43, 46, 104, 193, 236
Taylor, Livingston 104
Tenth album 212
The Marshall Tucker Band album 107
The One Percent 140
The Second Coming 146
The Wetter, The Better album 110
38 Special 67
Thornton, Billy Bob 152, 153, 268
Toler, Dan 1, 3
Toy Factory 211,
Trucks, Butch 3, 19-23, 46, 139, 140, 169
Trucks, Derek 2, 4, 16, 22, 38, 94, 171
Vaughan, Stevie Ray 82
Van Zant, Donnie 67
Van Zant, Ronnie 67, 68, 118, 121, 122
Varney, Jim 268
Volunteer Jam 134, 135, 188, 221, 226, 229, 258
Volunteer Jam III & IV album 258
Wabegijig, Sandy "Blue Sky" 273
Walden, Alan 114–124, 130, 270
Walden, Amantha 268
Walden, Phil 11, 29, 33, 43, 89, 94, 96, 104, 106, 114, 115, 117, 125, 128–131, 141, 143, 151, 152, 159, 209, 264, 267– 270, 276
Walden, Phillip Jr. 125, 128, 268, 271
Watkins Glen Summer Jam 27
Wells, Kitty 110, 152
West, Kirk 30

Wet Willie 106, 125, 132, 134, 135, 137, 167, 186, 229, 245, 267, 270, 272
Wexler, Jerry 57, 60, 89, 104, 129
Where We All Belong album 109, 259
Widespread Panic 268
Whitlock, Bobby 10, 31, 41, 46, 60, 61, 63, 64, 111, 225, 226, 272
Williams, Hank Jr. 132, 136
Williams, Lamar 46, 180
Winters Brothers Band 255, 257, 259
Winters, Dennis 256, 258
Winters, Donnie 255 - 262
Wooley, Dick 209, 211, 258, 272
Woody, Allen 14, 16, 37
Wyatt, Rudy "Blue Shoes" 34
Wyker, John D. 235, 272
Wynans, Reese 140
Wynn, Tom 141, 150, 154, 157–168, 172